The Heath Basic Writer

The Heath Basic Writer

Proofreading and Revision

Blanche Skurnick

City College, City University of New York

D. C. Heath and Company   •   Lexington, Massachusetts   Toronto

For my parents,
Olivia Hébert Jordan and George Whitte Jordan;

for my dear husband,
Eugene;

and for our children,
David, Elizabeth, and Miriam

Acknowledgements

Page 58—Excerpt from ''The Second Choice'' from *Free and Other Stories* by Theodore Dreiser. Copyright © 1918 renewed 1946 by G.P. Putnam's Sons.

Page 62—Excerpt from ''The Egg'' from *The Short Story: Twenty-five Masterpieces* by Sherwood Anderson. (New York: Harold Ober Associates, Inc., 1979.)

Pages 73–74—Excerpt from *The Hidden Persuaders* by Vance Packard. (New York: Pocket Books, a division of Simon & Schuster, 1967.)

Pages 87, 162—Excerpts from *Baby and Child Care* by Benjamin Spock. Copyright 1945, 1946, 1957, 1968, 1976 by Benjamin Spock, M.D. Reprinted by permission of Pocket Books, a Simon & Schuster division of Gulf & Western Corporation.

Pages 90, 165—Excerpts from *McTeague* by Frank Norris. (New York: New American Library of World Literature, 1964.)

Pages 91–92—Excerpt from *The Jungle* by Upton Sinclair. (New York: New American Library of World Literature, 1961.)

Page 113—Excerpt from ''Indian Festival of Lights,'' by Rosemary Black in *The Record*, Hackensack, NJ. Reprinted by permission.

Pages 141–142—Excerpts from *So Human an Animal* by Rene Dubos. Copyright © 1968 by Rene Dubos. (New York: Charles Scribner's Sons, 1968.) Reprinted with the permission of Charles Scribner's Sons.

Page 143—Excerpt from *Uncle Vanya*, in *Anton Chekhov's Plays* by Anton Chekhov. Eugene K. Bristow, editor and translator. (New York: W.W. Norton and Co., Inc., 1977.)

Page 144—Excerpt from *The Tenants* by Bernard Malamud. Reprinted by permission of Farrar, Straus and Giroux, Inc. Copyright © 1971 by Bernard Malamud.

Page 144—Excerpt from *Black Boy* by Richard Wright. (New York: Harper & Row Publishers, Inc., 1966.)

Page 161—Excerpt from *Childhood and Society* by Erik Erikson. (New York: W.W. Norton and Co., Inc., 1963.)

Page 181—Excerpt from *The Ascent of Man.* © 1973 by Jacob Bronowski. By permission of Little, Brown and Co.

Page 181—Excerpt from *The Outline of History* by H.G. Wells. (New York: Macmillan, 1920–21.) Reprinted by permission of A.P. Watt, Ltd., London.

Page 187—Excerpt from ''The Youth of Alexander the Great,'' from *Medieval Romances*. Roger Sherman Loomis and Laura Hibbard Loomis, editors. (New York: Modern Library © 1957.)

Pages 189, 331—Excerpt from *Beyond Freedom and Dignity* by B.F. Skinner. (New York: Bantam/Vintage © 1972.)

Page 194—Excerpt from *The First Nine Months of Life* by Geraldine Lux Flanagan. Copyright 1962 by Geraldine Lux Flanagan. Reprinted by permission of Simon & Schuster, a division of Gulf & Western Corporation.

Page 197—Excerpt from *Understanding Media* by Marshall McLuhan. (New York: New American Library © 1964.)

Page 201—Excerpt from ''The Nature of the Artist'' by Catherine Drinker Bowen. *The Atlantic Monthly,* November, 1961. Copyright © 1961 by Catherine Drinker Bowen. Reprinted by permission of Harold Ober Associates Inc.

Page 225—Excerpt from *Salammbo* by Gustave Flaubert. (New York: The Berkeley Publishing Corp., © 1961.)

Page 226—Excerpt from ''Felix Krull'' by Thomas Mann in *Stories of Three Decades*, translated by H. T. Lowe-Porter. (New York: Alfred A. Knopf, Inc. © 1946.)

Page 249—Excerpt from *A General Introduction to Psychoanalysis* by Sigmund Freud, translated by Joan Riviere. (New York: Pocket Books, a Simon & Schuster Division of Gulf & Western Corporation. © May, 1971.)

Pages 277, 318, 328—Excerpts from ''Death in the Open,'' ''Natural Science,'' ''The World's Biggest Membrane'' by Lewis Thomas. Copyright © 1973 by the Massachusetts Medical Society. Originally published in the *New England Journal of Medicine*. From *Lives of a Cell: Notes of a Biology Watcher.* Copyright © 1974 by Lewis Thomas. Reprinted by permission of Viking Penguin Inc.

Page 292—Excerpt from ''Prophets in Their Own Country'' by Arthur Guiterman from *Song and Laughter*. (New York: Dutton © 1929.)

Page 298—Excerpt from ''Discovery of a Father,'' by Sherwood Anderson from *The Conscious Reader*, edited by

Shrodes, Finestone and Shugrue. (New York: Macmillan. © 1978.)

Page 298—Excerpt from ''Calculating Machine,'' from *The Second Tree From the Corner* by E.B. White. Copyright © 1951 by E.B. White. (Harper and Brothers, Publishers)

Page 299—Excerpt from *The Hidden Injuries of Class* by Richard Sennett and Jonathan Cobb. (New York: Vintage. © 1973.)

Page 308—Excerpt from *The Random House Dictionary, Concise Edition*. Copyright © 1980, 1978 by Random House, Inc. Reprinted by permission.

Page 310—Excerpt from ''To Sleep, Perchance to Steam'' from *The Most of S.J. Perelman* by S. J. Perelman. (New York: Simon & Schuster © 1958.)

Page 311—Excerpt from *Invitation to Sociology* by Peter L. Berger. Copyright © 1963 by Peter L. Berger. Reprinted by permission of Doubleday & Company, Inc.

Pages 312–313—Excerpts by permission from *Websters New Collegiate Dictionary* © 1981 by G. & C. Merriam Co., Publishers of the Merriam-Webster® Dictionaries.

Pages 313–314—Excerpt from ''The Aesthetics of Eating,'' by Andre Simon from *119 Years of the Atlantic*, edited by Louise Sesaulniers. Boston: The Atlantic Company © 1977. Copyright 1938, 1966 by Andre L. Simon.

Page 315—Excerpt from ''The Man That Corrupted Hadleyburg,'' by Samuel L. Clemens from *The American Tradition in Literature*, edited by Sculley Bradley, et al. Vol. 2. (New York: W.W. Norton & Company © 1974.)

Page 316—Excerpt from ''Erec et Enide,'' by Chrétien de Troyes from *Arthurian Romances*, translated by W.W. Comfort. (London: J.M. Dent, Everyman's Library, 1967.)

Page 325—Excerpt from ''Lexicography,'' by Yakov Malkiel from *The Learning of Language*, edited by Carroll E. Reed. (New York: Appleton-Century-Crofts. © 1971.)

Page 327—Excerpt from ''The Prince of Creation,'' by Suzanne K. Langer from *The Borzoi College Reader*, edited by Muscatine and Griffith. (New York: Knopf. © 1971.)

To the Instructor

The general aim of this text is to help students who are having difficulty learning to write well enough to satisfy the requirements of their college coursework. More specifically, it is designed to achieve the following goals:

1. To teach standard English grammar logically and fully
2. To explain prevalent errors in grammar
3. To teach proofreading procedures for finding and correcting these errors
4. To teach a simple composing process, useful for all writing tasks
5. To show how grammar can be used to improve writing style

In this text, grammar is presented as a tool for understanding and for making oneself understood. The proofreading techniques in this book show how to apply the rules of grammar to correct errors. Step by step, students will learn how to find the words and structures in which errors usually occur, how to tell whether particular words and structures are correct, and how to correct them if they are not. The exercises help students to recognize various grammatical structures, and they demonstrate how these structures behave, providing practice in using the structures correctly and deliberately. Many teachers have observed that exercises often make students proficient at doing exercises but still leave them unable to correct their own writing. I have tried to devise exercises to insure that students understand the steps they follow in writing and revising, exercises that show students what teachers see when we make corrections and recommend changes.

In addition to the grammar and the exercises, the book calls for a great deal of writing, mostly in the form of short essays. All of these assignments require the student to proofread for the particular error studied in the chapter and to make specific revisions for style. Repeated throughout the semester, the combination of a writing assignment with specific instructions for finding errors and improving expression yields dramatic changes by the end of the semester. The number and kinds of student errors decline appreciably, and the organization and wording of papers markedly improve.

The writing assignments, the proofreading techniques, and the exercises call for concentration and hard work. They will raise some questions, but they will also resolve many, as they present challenging and comprehensive concepts. I have tried throughout the book to present grammar as an elegant, sensible system rather than as a series of disconnected principles and rules. Like the student's own sentences, the examples range from simple to sophisticated. The purpose is to show how the same principles govern both simple and complex constructions.

A further note: there is more material here than you will need. The many exercises reflect a range of difficulty. For those who want structure, the book offers a firm sequence that can be followed throughout the semester. For instructors who wish to use the book more flexibly, capsule previews of the grammar chapters and a grammar summary chapter are provided.

After Mina Shaughnessy established the basic writing sequence at CCNY, she observed that many students were learning grammar formally but were not learning how to control error in their writing. This book began with her idea that, to solve this problem, our basic grammar and composition course should also be a proofreading course. To Mina I also owe the time she freed for a small group of basic writing teachers at CCNY to study and experiment with ideas for teaching writing more effectively. I hope that this book reflects her splendid influence as well as my gratitude to her.

I also owe thanks to a remarkable group of colleagues at CCNY. Kathy Roe read the manuscript and mixed her suggestions with compliments and support; James Hatch read the manuscript and gave me professional assistance for which I am immensely grateful; Marilyn Maiz read the manuscript, proposed several intelligent, creative ideas for it, and invented enticing titles for it over dinners at a fine Italian restaurant; Barbara Gray and Sarah D'Eloia Fortune, members of Mina's group, taught me to see the sentence anew. Barbara Gray also reviewed the manuscript and renewed my confidence it it.

I had the good fortune to share a number of techniques from the book with members of the faculty of the College of New Rochelle: Barbara McManus, Martha Nochimson, Catherine Giles, Katherine Henderson, and Leslie Oster. Their insightful responses helped me to improve a number of sections.

Many creative suggestions also came from those who were kind enough to review the manuscript: Douglas Butturff of the University of Central Arkansas, Linda Woodson of Texas Tech University, Rita Sturm of the University of Albuquerque, Roberta Gates of Southern Technical Institute, Virginia Reedy of Tarrant County Junior College, Dale A. Myers of the University of Tennessee, Katharine Stone of Georgia State University, Ondee Ravan of Georgia Southwestern College, Robert Terry Hoyle of Western Carolina University, and Janice N. Hays of the University of Colorado.

I cannot name all of the students who led me to develop techniques to make grammar useful to them, but this book could never have been written without their curiosity and their will to learn.

To those at D. C. Heath and Company who are responsible for producing this book I am indeed thankful. Gordon Lester-Massman has been swift, calm, straightforward, accessible, and immensely encouraging. Jackie Unch, who shares those qualities, has devoted to this project a degree of patience, intelligence, and good taste from which every reader will benefit, and for which this author happily records her thanks.

And to my family, who have borne with me, eaten out, and played quietly by themselves, thank you.

Blanche J. Skurnick

To the Student

You are about to take a comprehensive and challenging course in grammar, a course which professional educators, your teachers, have determined that you should have to improve your writing.

Grammar instruction will improve your writing in two ways: it will teach you first, how to write correct sentences and, second, how to make them clear, precise, and interesting. It will teach you how sentence parts work together, and it will show you how to find and correct errors you may be making. Knowing what is grammatically correct will help you to make your writing more readable. Whatever the subject may be, grammatically correct writing is a minimum requirement for anyone preparing for further education, the professions, or business. It is a requirement for formal communication of all kinds. Ungrammatical writing must be avoided because it carries disturbing messages about the writer: readers are likely to feel that if a writer can't write standard English, then he or she might not have mastered other important matters either.

Beyond making your writing more readable, a knowledge of grammar can also make your writing distinctive. When you recognize the parts of your sentences and know how they are tied together, you can arrange these parts to create the emphasis that best carries your meaning. You can add or move a detail that makes the rest of the sentence clear, or break a pattern that monotonously repeats one kind of subject, one kind of verb, or one kind of sentence. If you know how your sentences work, you will know what alternatives you can substitute for the words that came first to mind, in order to make your writing smooth and rhythmic. Knowing the rules of grammar, in other words, can greatly increase your *fluency*, your ability to write what you mean in the most effective way.

Once you've completed this course, you will not need to worry whether you've put a period or a comma in the right place, whether a verb should end in *-ed* or *-s*, whether a possessive should end in *s'* or *'s,* whether you should use *he* or *it* or *they*, or whether you've used the right verb tense: you will *know*. And as you finish each chapter on the various grammatical concepts, you will be able to correct errors related to each concept rather than waiting, as in the past, for your teacher to correct them for you. This means that as you go through this text, you will improve your writing in ways that *you* can identify, and from one paper to the next you will see your improvement. You will enjoy the knowledge that you can construct your sentences—and revise them—with confidence.

Contents

From Topic to Specific Idea

1

1. Introduction

Throughout your college years you are asked to write. Sometimes a great deal of discussion and reading goes on beforehand. You get ideas and enough information to define, present, and support them in writing. At other times, you have to write when you don't have any ideas about the topic assigned. You want time to think about and read up on the topic, and time to figure out what to say, but you have to begin.

Of course writing is easiest when you feel prepared. But teachers expect you to write whether you're sure you're ready or not—and you can.

The bulk of this book deals with the *forms* ideas take on the page rather than with the ideas themselves. It explains some of the more troublesome grammar of standard English, ties it to rules you may have learned long ago but may not have understood, and teaches you how to proofread your writing and apply the rules of grammar to eliminate errors. But before you can proofread, you have to write. This chapter tells you how to move from a topic to a subject to a specific idea.

2. A Topic Can Be Anything

Whether spontaneous or assigned, whether it goes quickly or slowly, writing begins with a topic, a thing to write about. A topic can be anything: horse racing, music, freedom, bravery, the space program.

In the fourth or fifth grade, when you were just forming ideas about what certain words mean, writing a short essay on ''bravery'' was a cinch. You wrote down what the word meant to you and felt satisfied that you'd done the job. But as you grew up, you continued to learn new meanings, and you see now how hard it is to pin down an idea. You know that bravery means different things to different people, and you may not be quite sure exactly what it means to you.

So you, and every other thinking person, would quite properly hesitate today to write a short essay on bravery. It would be like trying to put a cloud into a bottle. The problem isn't that you don't know what the word means; it's that the word has so *much* meaning.

Suppose, even, that you were asked to write an essay about yourself. You could begin with a physical description of yourself. But once you did that, you'd be in the same bewildering position you'd be in if you tried to write about any other broad topic. The possibilities would be endless: do you tell where you came from, who you are (how do you tell *who* you are!), what you do, what you like, what you are (how do you tell *what* you are!)?

It should be clear that you can't handle any broad topic without breaking it into smaller units. Even if you wrote a book about yourself, you would divide it into *parts*, looking first at one *subject* under the topic "yourself," and then another.

3. A Subject Is Something You Can Talk About

Subjects are narrower than topics. Subjects, for example, might include what you dreamed last night, what you ate for dinner, what the best bait for trout fishing is, what walking to the nearest corner is like, what the space program means to your aging grandfather, why strollers are better than carriages, who turns you on, who turns you off, why the sun rises, why the price of hamburger rises, why bread rises, how you are going to spend the next ten minutes if your brother doesn't change that station.

You can't talk about *every*thing; you have to talk about *one* thing. Take a look at these sets of ideas:

giving	gifts	the gift I gave myself
ceremonies	weddings	the marriage vow that counts
travel	traveling through Brooklyn	destination: Flatbush
crime	shoplifting	the case of the missing donut
inflation	yesterday's dollar	your hamburger, then and now
beauty	Evelyn	Evelyn's face

What could you say about the topics in the first column? "Giving should be . . .," "Ceremonies are . . .," "Travel is . . .," "Crime is . . ."; you would start to drown before you got into the water.

But you could start writing and keep writing on one of the items from the third column. They are also the ones you'd be willing to go on reading about. All of those items are *subjects* taken from the *topics* in the first column, and all promise some interesting directions. Almost automatically, you visualize a gift you gave yourself, pick the marriage vow you know is the clincher, or remember the donut that disappeared into a customer's pocket as he pointed to the napoleons on the back shelf.

If you take pictures, you know about the trade-off between getting good definition and getting the entire scene. If you want a snapshot of Evelyn with the sun hitting her hair *and* her patent leather shoes, then you are not going to get good definition of the dimples in her smile. If you want the dimples, then you won't get her patent leather shoes. When you sit down with a topic, you're faced with the same kind of trade-off, only you can be sure that you'll be better off shooting for the dimples.

4. Focusing on a Subject

The second column lists topics that are narrower than those in the first column but still only midway to your best material. The topics in the second column deal with what you know, what you feel, what you remember, what you can safely say. They do not include *every*thing that the word *giving* means, nor the whole story of inflation. But they aren't narrow enough either. These middle topics are about *any*thing: any gifts, any weddings, anything about yesterday's dollar, and so forth. And you can get just as stuck trying to talk about *any*thing as you can trying to talk about *every*thing.

You need to pinpoint the *one* thing that you can talk about easily and with assurance: the thing you can describe, find examples of, give your impressions of, tell a story about, draw conclusions about. To find a subject in a topic, ask yourself

1. What do I know about this topic?
2. What have I read about this topic?
3. How do I feel about this topic?
4. When did I first encounter something having to do with this topic?
5. What does this topic suggest?
6. What is interesting about this topic?
7. What instances or cases do I know of involving this topic?
8. What questions does this topic raise?
9. What have I observed about this topic?

The test of whether you've gotten from a topic to a subject is the detail of the picture it summons to mind. When the focus is right, you can see the dimples forming.

5. Moving from Topic to Thesis

Whatever your subject calls to mind is what you want your reader to see. Suppose the gift you gave yourself was dance lessons. You can see a series of mental pictures: you sitting at a table in your local disco trying to take everything in, your eyes following a golden couple who are the center of attention; you standing undecided before the glass front of the dance studio, when suddenly the door opens and the disco beat inside escapes into the street; you taking your first lesson, studying the steps painted on the glossy studio floor; and then at last, you out on the floor of the disco, in satin vest and studded leather jeans, dancing into the spotlight as it pulsates to the music.

Once you have put the pictures in words, you can say something about them.

My dance lessons brought me into a world I had only been able to watch before.

That's your idea, your *thesis*. Your thesis is what you're going to write about. You got to it by describing to yourself what your subject brought to mind. The thesis repeats the subject, "my dance lessons," and then says something about it. That part of the statement is called the *predicate*. So your idea has two parts: a *subject* and a *predicate*.

Subject	*Predicate*
My dance lessons	brought me into a world I had only been able to watch before.

To get from a topic to a thesis, take these steps:

1. Find a subject in the topic. Focus on something about the topic that you can form a picture of, tell a story about, give an example of, or compare to something else. This part of the topic that you can see for yourself and feel comfortable talking about is your *subject*.
2. Make your reader see your subject as you do. Tell a story about it, or describe it; cite instances of it; tell what it is to you, how you first came in contact with it, how it makes you feel, what it reminds you of, what it makes you think, and so forth.
3. Then, after you've put your subject before your reader, make a statement about it. Give your reader your thesis about your subject.

Above all, **don't leap** from the general topic to a statement about the topic. You might see nowhere to go from there. The *topic* is not your *subject*. A topic is just something; a subject is something *you* can talk about.

Each of the grammar chapters to follow opens with a writing assignment. The assignment gives you a topic and a subject, and asks you to present that subject and a thesis about it in writing. At the end of each chapter, after completing the exercises, you will proofread what you wrote when you began the chapter. Proofreading demonstrations using samples of student writing will help you. So that you will have enough writing to work with, try to set down between fifty and one hundred words for each assignment. You should be able to do this easily if you consciously try to "see" what you're going to write about before you begin.

Exercises

1. For each of the following topics, jot down five images:

   a. baking bread
   b. running track; playing football, basketball, or baseball
   c. having a baby
   d. renting an apartment
   e. changing an automobile tire

2. Select two of the topics above, and write a page about each. Use all of the following headings, and then keep going:

   a. how you feel about it
   b. when you first encountered it
   c. what it suggests
   d. why it bores (or excites) you
   e. cases involving it: bizarre ones if the topic suggests any
   f. questions surrounding it
   g. reminiscences about it
   h. what you've thought about it
   i. what has happened to you concerning it
   j. what you've done concerning it

   Wind up by telling yourself what possible subjects you can draw from these topics.

3. Briefly sketch out one experience you've had with each of the topics listed below and then tell what your point of view would probably be if you were to write on that topic. On the topic "baking bread," for example, you might write,

   Experience: I have never baked bread, but have sometimes bought and often eaten it. Twice in my life I have tried to bake bread. Both times I failed to get the dough to rise.

   Probable point of view: On the topic of baking bread I would probably speak as an appreciative consumer.

   a. baking bread
   b. running track
   c. having a baby
   d. renting an apartment
   e. changing an automobile tire

Basic Sentence Facts

2

CAPSULE PREVIEW This chapter explains that a sentence has two essential parts, a *subject* and a *verb*, and that it may have other parts: *objects, complements,* and *modifiers.* A group of words that contains a subject and a verb and that makes sense is a sentence.

Strings of words that do not contain a subject and a verb are sometimes written as sentences. These are not sentences, but sentence parts, called *sentence fragments.*

> The heat inside the capsule can melt metals in a matter of minutes. And change some of them to gases.

The second "sentence" is a sentence fragment because, although it contains a verb, it contains no subject. And without a subject it does not make sense. The subject, *the heat,* lies in the first sentence. So does the rest of the verb, which is *can change,* not *change.* The sentence should be written this way:

> The heat inside the capsule can melt metals in a matter of minutes and change some of them to gases.

Proofreading Techniques

To find a sentence fragment, you must

1. know that every sentence contains a subject and a verb;
2. find the subject and verb in every sentence you write.

If there is no subject-verb pair in the sentence, then the "sentence" is a sentence fragment.

To correct a sentence fragment, you must rewrite it within the sentence it logically belongs to. See Chapter 3 and Chapter 4 for more about sentence fragments.

Error: Sentence Fragment

Writers sometimes break off part of a sentence and write the part as if it were a sentence on its own. These parts written as sentences are *sentence fragments*.

```
        V                               S   ┌── part ──┐
There roamed about the city a poor man. Father of eleven.
```

```
                                S    V              ┌──────── part ────────┐
Last Thanksgiving twenty-three people ate dinner at our house. Not counting my brother,

┌──────────────────────┐
my sister, me, and my parents.
```

```
┌────────── part ──────────┐  S    V
Now in her third year of medical school. Nora sees operations every day.
```

```
   S         V                               ┌──────── part ────────┐
Sherwin finally found an apartment big enough for all his junk. And too small for company.
```

```
     S     V                          ┌───────────── part ─────────────┐
A teacher may play different roles at times. For example a parent or a brother or sister.
```

RULE   **A sentence must contain at least a subject and a verb. Don't write a sentence part as if it were a sentence on its own.**

Revision

```
       V                     S
There roamed about the city a poor man, father of eleven.
```

```
                  S    V
Last Thanksgiving twenty-three people ate dinner at our house, not counting my brother,

my sister, me, and my parents.
```

```
                             S    V
Now in her third year of medical school, Nora sees operations every day.
```

```
   S         V
Sherwin finally found an apartment big enough for all his junk and too small for company.
```

```
     S     V
A teacher may play different roles at times: for example a parent or a brother or sister.
```

Writing Assignment: First Draft

Topic: Energy

Subject: The energy that could have been saved

Recall your own experiences and write from them. Remember that it is easier to write the story of the bulb you saw burning all night than to discuss the electricity Americans waste. First present your subject so that the reader can see it as you do. Then write your idea about it.

---

1. Breaking the Sentence into Parts

How do we understand written words? Why does the word *go* make sense standing alone, while the word *on* usually requires other words to make sense? The answer is that *go* and *on* are different *kinds* of words. Most words, in fact, fall into one of three large classes upon which sentences are built—*nouns, verbs,* and *modifiers.*

DEFINITIONS **A noun is a word or group of words (a *phrase*) that names people, places, things, and actions.**

A verb is a word or phrase that states action or information.

A modifier is a word or phrase that defines, describes, designates, explains, or otherwise points to other words.

Look at these words:

> angry always wrist Kansas men paid exist boldly their me fees the
> a   an   loving

Wrist, Kansas, men, me, fees, and *loving* name people, places, things, and actions; *paid* and *exist* state action and information; and *angry, always, boldly, their, the, a, an,* and *loving* describe other words.

What has word class got to do with sentences? Here is a sentence using some of those words:

> The angry men paid the unfair fees.

Men did something and *paid* tells us what they did; *angry* describes *men,* and *unfair* describes *fees; the* makes *men* particular men and *fees* particular fees. *Men* did the paying; *paid* states the action of paying; and *fees* are what was paid. Each word has some relation to another word in the sentence. And we now know that the words in this sentence do *not* all belong to the same word class. In fact, in order to make the sentence, we had to choose words from different classes, and the sentence sets up relations between the words.

```
                    verb
         noun        |            noun
┌modifiers┐  |     ┌modifiers┐  |
The angry  men  paid  the unfair  fees.
```

The fact that there are different classes of words allows us to determine meaning. We do not find meaning in a string of words that only describe: *angry unfair;* or in a string of words that only name people, places, things, or actions: *men fees.* But we find meaning when we take one word from each class: *angry men, unfair fees.*

Now the question is, do we need words from all three classes—nouns, verbs, and modifiers—to make a sentence? We can take out the word *the:*

Angry men paid unfair fees.

We lose the sense that a particular set of angry men paid fees and that a particular set of unfair fees were paid, but we still have a sentence. We can take out the other modifiers:

Men paid fees.

Without these, we lose still more particular information about *men* and *fees.* We now do not know which group of men out of all mankind the sentence tells us about, and we do not know what kind of fees were paid, but we still have a sentence. We can even remove one of the nouns:

Men paid.

Obviously, this sentence is very different from *The angry men paid the unfair fees,* but it is still a sentence.

Men paid, however, cannot be reduced. Losing either word, the remaining word would not make a sentence. And without these two words, the original sentence would not be a sentence:

The angry the unfair fees.

Whatever a sentence is, the noun and the verb are essential. If we take the noun and the verb out of the sentence, then the other words make no statement and make no sense— we don't have a sentence. But, if we take the other words out of the sentence, the noun and verb alone *do* make a statement, *do* make sense, and *do* make a sentence. We can define this connection of noun to verb in the following way:

DEFINITION   **When a noun and a verb form a sentence core, we call the noun the subject of the verb.**

2. The Subject and the Verb

You will find this essential pairing in whatever is a sentence. There is always at least one word, a noun, that is the *performer* of the action, as *men* is the performer of *paid,* and as *plants, grandmother,* and *students* are performers in the following sentences:

>   S   V
> Green <u>plants</u> make chlorophyll.

>   S   V
> My <u>grandmother</u> walks in her sleep.

>   S   V
> Biology <u>students</u> dissect bullfrogs.

And there is always at least one word, a verb, that states an action, as *paid* does, or that states information, as *seem* and *looks* do in the following sentences:

>   S   V
> The men <u>seem</u> angry.

Seem isn't an action. Instead, *seem* tells something about the men.

>   S   V
> The hall <u>looks</u> empty.

Here the verb *looks* isn't an action. Instead, *looks* tells something about the hall.
Verbs that state action have the performers of the action as subjects. Verbs that state information have the words they tell about as subjects.

>   **S—performer**   V
> Sergeant Gunther <u>located</u> the murder suspect.

> **S—word that the verb**
> **tells something about**
> Sergeant Gunther <u>was</u>

>   <u>seemed to be</u>

>   <u>became</u>

<u>appeared to be</u>

<u>sounded like</u>

<u>was declared</u>   the murder suspect.

Was, seemed to be, became, appeared to be, sounded like aren't actions. These verbs *tell something about* Sergeant Gunther. And though *was declared* is an action, Sergeant Gunther isn't doing the declaring; someone else is. This verb too is *telling about* Sergeant Gunther.

Both the performer and the word a verb tells something about are called *the subject of the verb*.

Subject	*Verb*
performer	states action
word that the verb tells something about	states information[1]

Every sentence has a subject and verb, and the pair occurs in a lively variety of arrangements, as these examples illustrate:

- Subject and verb may be together, beginning the sentence:

    S   V

<u>Martin</u> <u>disobeyed</u> the babysitter.

        S   V

The <u>broom</u> <u>belongs</u> in the closet.

- The subject may be separated from the verb:

     S   V

My <u>car</u>, smelling of smoke, <u>stalled</u> in the center lane.

     S   V

The <u>fire</u>, fanned by high winds and fed by the dry timber of the forest, <u>leapt</u> over the highway.

- Subject and verb may fall at the end of the sentence:

Not counting my brother, my sister, me, and my parents, last Thanksgiving twenty-three

    S   V

<u>people</u> <u>ate</u> dinner at our house.

---

[1]Verbs that state information are also called *linking* verbs, because they link the subject to words that tell about the subject, or *state of being* verbs, because they tell how the subject is, or seems, or feels.

At last, with everybody starving for some cake and ice cream and waiting for her to blow

out her candles, my little <u>cousin</u> [S] <u>made</u> [V] her wish.

Once upon a time, many years ago, across the great western plains, huge <u>herds</u> [S] of bison

<u>thundered</u> [V].

- The subject may follow the verb:

There <u>were</u> [V] no <u>tickets</u> [S] for us at the box office.

There <u>have been</u> [V] some <u>mice</u> [S] in this room.

It <u>is</u> [V] true <u>that I drank your soda</u> [S].

There <u>roamed</u> [V] about the city a poor <u>man</u> [S], the father of eleven.

- The verb may be more than one word:

<u>Eve</u> [S] <u>would have known</u> [V] where to find the apple orchards.

The <u>steamboat</u> [S] from Cairo <u>is supposed to arrive</u> [V] at noon.

<u>Sharks</u> [S] <u>have been found</u> [V] in freshwater rivers.

- The subject may be more than one word:

<u>Running three miles a day</u> [S] <u>takes</u> [V] energy.

It <u>is</u> [V] expensive <u>to travel to school by car</u> [S].

It <u>seems</u> [V] unsafe <u>for you to go alone</u> [S].

- There may be more than one subject-verb pair:

$$
\begin{array}{cccc}
& \text{S} & \text{V} & \text{S} \quad \text{V}
\end{array}
$$

      S   V   S   V
The watch won't run unless you wind it.

     S   V   S V
My cat eats whatever I put in her bowl.

       S   S   V   V
The note Tess slipped under the door went under the carpet too.

   S   V   S V
Angel loved Tess, but he was too proud to stay with her.

 S V   S   V   S   V
I waited an hour, and it rained all the while, and you never came.

- There may be only the subject-verb pair:

  S   V
Bites itch.

    S   V
Questions arose.

   S   V
Times change.

     S   V
Connoisseurs discriminate.

  S   V
Cells divide.

- The subject *you* may be implied:

 V
Put your head on my shoulder.

 V
Get me some too.

  V
Forget it.

*Exercises 1–2
```
              V
             Go.
```

3. Other Sentence Parts

In addition to the subject-verb pair, a sentence may contain other words, words that function as *objects* of the verb, as *complements* of the verb, and as *modifiers*.

DEFINITION **An object is a word or phrase that the verb acts upon, that receives the action of the verb.**

```
        S    V    O
       Men paid taxes.
```

Taxes are what men paid. The word *taxes* is the object of the verb *paid*.

```
              S        V            O
       Tonight's legislation will change the course of history.
```

The course of history is what will be changed. *The course of history* is the object of *will change*.

DEFINITION **A complement is a word or phrase that tells about or identifies the subject of a verb. Complements complete information given by the verb.**

```
        S      V    C
       Hang-gliding is foolhardy.
```

Foolhardy tells about or modifies *hang-gliding*. *Foolhardy* is a complement because it tells about the subject of the verb *is*. In the following example, the word *suspicious* is a complement because it tells about the subject, Sergeant Gunther.

```
           S         V
       Sergeant Gunther was
                    seemed to be
                    became
                    appeared to be
                    sounded            C
                    was declared   suspicious.
```

---

*Exercises related to this section.

In the next example, *the murder suspect* identifies Sergeant Gunther:

```
     S          V
Sergeant Gunther was
                  seemed to be
                  became
                  appeared to be
                  sounded like              C
                  was declared   the murder suspect.
```

The murder suspect is a complement of Sergeant Gunther. In the following sentence the word *exercise* identifies *swimming:*

```
     S      V      C
Swimming is good exercise.
```

The word *exercise* is a complement of this subject.

Objects and complements both answer the question *who?* or *what?* after the verb:

Men paid *what?*

Tonight's legislation will change *what?*

Hang-gliding is *what?*

```
Sergeant Gunther was
                  seemed to be
                  became
                  appeared to be
                  sounded like
                  was declared    what?
```

Objects follow verbs that state action. Objects are the things or people acted upon. Objects are nouns. Complements follow verbs that state information. Complements tell what the subject is—identifying or describing the subject. Complements that *identify* the subject are nouns, like the subject. Complements that *describe* the subject are modifiers.

```
subject + action verb ——————→ object

subject + information verb ——→ complement ⎰noun—identifies S
                                           ⎱modifier—describes S
```

DEFINITION **Modifiers are words or phrases that describe, explain, or otherwise tell about other words.**

```
          S         M           V
```
The fire, <u>hot and deadly</u>, leapt the highway.

```
          S           M              V
```
The fire, <u>fanned by high winds</u>, leapt the highway.

The phrases *hot and deadly* and *fanned by high winds* modify the fire.
We can now define the sentence.

DEFINITION | **A sentence is a group of words that contains at least a subject and a verb and that makes sense by itself. In addition, a sentence may contain *objects* of the verb, *complements* of the verb, and *modifiers*.**

Any sentence that you write *must have* at least a subject and a verb. And any sentence may contain objects, complements, and modifiers.

Here are some of the sentences in the examples above, broken down into their sentence parts: subject, verb, object, complement, and modifier:

Subject	Verb	Object	Complement	Modifier
The broom	belongs			in the closet.
Martin	disobeyed	the babysitter.		
My grandmother	walks			in her sleep
(You)	put	your head		on my shoulder.
A poor man	roamed			about the city, the father of eleven.
Sergeant Gunther	became		suspicious.	
That I drank your soda	is		true.	

Subject	Verb	Object	Complement	Modifier
To travel to school by car	is		expensive.	

Subject	Verb	Object	Complement	Modifier
Sharks	have been found			in freshwater rivers.

Exercises 3–6

4. Using Grammar for Style

A careful look at the subjects and verbs in your sentences can help you to write better sentences. Follow these guidelines:

Avoid broad, general words as subjects.   These give statements the dreamy blur of yearbook captions:

    S V
Life is a series of ups and downs.

       S   V
The world believes it knows the truth.

     S   V
People know they can't trust each other.

or the insincere ring of words set down to fill the page:

     S   V
Things have a way of disappearing from the classrooms.

     S   V
College is a broadening experience.

    S   V
Religion comforts mankind.

Writing assignments themselves often lure students to these too-large words, for example:

Discuss your experiences at college.

Write an essay on the role of religion in your life.

Write an essay on drugs.

The wording of the assignment looks official and safe. Can you go wrong if you stick to the teacher's own words? The answer is yes. If you parrot the language of the assignment, your strongest message is likely to be one of uncertainty or indifference, not what you actually say. Your thoughts will seem superficial or not genuinely your own, which they are likely not to be. Instead, make your subjects words that the topic *suggests,* words you actually do use and think about. Turn the topic ''experiences at college'' into ''math anxiety at Grand Island University.'' Translate ''role of religion'' into ''two (or however many) questions religion can (or can't) answer.'' Make the essay on drugs an essay on ''aspirin, caffeine, and nicotine: the effects of three soft drugs on the mother of a college freshman.''

Vary your subjects.   Sometimes, in the effort to stick to a point, a writer uses the same subject over and over. This is particularly true of narrative writing, especially when the author is telling a story about himself or herself.

> I arrived in Washington at three o'clock in the afternoon. I checked my bags at the station, since I didn't have a room yet. Then I went to the information desk where I asked them to find me a room. I had to wait only ten minutes. I was lucky.

Seven out of the seven subjects in this passage are *I.* The repetition may keep the writer on track, but it is likely to bore the reader. The passage reads as if the writer saw himself or herself very well, but no one and nothing else. A similar one-subject hum dulls the following passage from a plot summary of *Tess of the D'Urbervilles:*

> *Tess of the D'Urbervilles,* a novel by Thomas Hardy, is the story of the short, unhappy life of Tess Durbeyfield. Tess finds out at the beginning of the book that she comes from a family that was once noble, the D'Urbervilles. Tess is not impressed. She wants to live like the rest of the girls in her village. But Tess is not lucky. Tess falls asleep one night while she is driving the family wagon to another town. She has an accident that kills the horse. Tess feels very guilty because she is responsible for the horse's death. Tess makes up for it by going to visit a rich branch of the old noble family to ask for money. At that point, Tess begins her downfall.

Tess does this, Tess does that, Tess, Tess, Tess! You can avoid this kind of monotony in your writing by checking through the subjects to see that there are enough different subjects to keep your writing lively. These revisions say the same things using different subjects.

>   S   V
> **Original:** Tess is not impressed.

>   S   V
> **Revision:** Family history doesn't impress Tess.

                  S V
Original: But Tess is not lucky.

               S   V
Revision: But luck isn't with her.

             S   V
Original: She has an accident that kills the horse.

              S   V
Revision: An accident kills the horse.

                  S   V
Original: At that point, Tess begins her downfall.

                      S   V
Revision: At that point, the downfall of the unhappy young woman begins.

Make your verbs action words. Breathe life into your verbs. The most common verbs— *is, are, was, have, has, do, does*—lack color. But you will be surprised to find how often you use them. These verbs frequently make up over half of the total number of verbs in a paper, barely pulling the words along. Count the verbs in the passage you wrote at the beginning of this chapter. Then count the number of common ones, the ones you scarcely see on the page. If you've written well, you've used these verbs only when you had no other choice, and the count reveals an imaginative selection. In the Tess passage, there are fifteen verbs. Among these, the common verbs tally this way: *is*—5; *was*—1; *has*—1. Seven of the fifteen verbs, nearly half, barely carry a message at all. This means the passage can be improved. Look at these revisions:

                      S   V
Original: *Tess of the D'Urbervilles,* a novel by Thomas Hardy, is the story of the short, unhappy life of Tess Durbeyfield.

                      S   V
Revision: *Tess of the D'Urbervilles,* a novel by Thomas Hardy, tells the story of the short, unhappy life of Tess Durbeyfield.

             S V   S V   S
Original: Tess finds out at the beginning of the book that she comes from a family that

              V
was once noble, the D'Urbervilles.

             S V   S V
Revision: Tess finds out at the beginning of the book that she comes from a once-noble family, the D'Urbervilles.

              S   V   S V

Original: Tess falls asleep one night while she is driving the family wagon to another

town.

              S   V

Revision: Tess falls asleep one night while driving the family wagon to another town.

Revisions like these are not hard to make. More precise verbs come readily to mind, and, as the last three revisions show, sometimes *is* or *was* can be cut altogether without loss of meaning. The key to this kind of revision is to discover, in the first place, that you are using too many colorless verbs. Now that you are learning to find verbs in your sentences, you can check to see that you're using verbs that drive your meaning across.

Vary the position of subject and verb. Like repeated subjects and lackluster verbs, patterns too can be monotonous. The typical pattern puts the subject at the head of the sentence, closely followed by the verb. But as we have seen, many variations are possible. Moving the subject and verb around in the sentence lends interest and emphasis to the statement. Compare these sentences:

     S   V

You can be jealous without knowing it.

                 S   V

Without knowing it, you can be jealous.

The second sentence delays the main idea until it has been tantalizingly modified; the first lets the cat out of the bag right away, and is flat by comparison.

     S   V

A stream of raw sewage runs right through the center of the glorious Catano River.

                          V   S

Through the center of the glorious Catano River runs a stream of raw sewage.

Exercises 7–8

In-class writing
1–3

The first sentence uses the rather weak word *right* for emphasis. The second sentence eliminates the weak word by postponing the subject and verb and then presenting the verb first. The inverted order puts the most important word last—an emphatic position.

Exercises

1. Two sets of words in each sentence below have been underlined. Circle the set that contains either the verb or its subject.

   Example: (The reappearance) of the Hudson River bass astonished naturalists.

   a. With their tape decks and stereo systems, new cars (take you) out of the doldrums and out of town.

   b. On their application forms, (students in the liberal arts program) were given different instructions.

   c. For his scoring record over the last two years, Bubba Sampson (won a trophy.)

   d. (The painting on the easel near the window) has better color balance than the other paintings in the room.

   e. True to form, your husband (has already eaten the leftover steak.)

   f. Standing on the sidelines after her victory, Madeleine, for the first time in her life, (heard her name) on a loudspeaker.

   g. That sad-looking waitress always stares at the floor, (thinking of her troubles.)

   h. Yesterday she (found a five-dollar bill) tucked under the pepper shaker.

   i. Somebody used to hard luck but rich now (must have seen her red eyes.)

   j. People with a lot on their minds don't usually have time (to pay attention to a droopy waitress.)

   k. Wrestling with their own problems, (they ignore other unhappy people.)

   l. To find their own solutions, they (cut themselves off) from the face at the counter and the face in the cab.

   m. But yesterday one of them woke up, (like a prince or a knight or just a good person.)

2. Write the essential verb and subject beneath each of the following sentences:

   a. Those underpaid men paid unusually high taxes.

   MEN, PAID

   b. Sleeping children make no noise.

   CHILDREN, MAKE

   c. Captured weapons told the tale.

   WEAPONS, TOLD

d. Worried sick, Yolanda paced.

    YOLANDA, PACED

e. Broken and unwanted, the chair caught my eye.

    CHAIR, CAUGHT

f. To surpass their own achievements is the goal of athletes.

    ATHLETES, IS

g. The chair, broken and unwanted, caught my eye.

    CHAIR, CAUGHT

h. Yolanda paced, worried sick.

    YOLANDA, PACED

i. Her sewing done, Sarah donned her bonnet.

    SARAH, DONNED

j. To tell the truth, the ice cream melted.

    ICE CREAM, MELTED

k. Rochester left Thornfield, a blinded but not broken man.

    MAN, BLINDED

l. The ice cream melted, to tell the truth.

    ICE CREAM, MELTED

m. To have achieved so much proved worthless.

    WORTHLESS, PROVED

n. Our calling for help brought no response.

    RESPONSE, BROUGHT

o. Rusted blades cut skin, not hair.

    BLADES, CUT

3. In the items below, the essential subject-verb pair is provided. Add to the sentences as indicated. Punctuation will be discussed in Chapter 6, but for now, try to sense the words you might use with the comma and words you might use without it.

Chapter 2 • Basic Sentence Facts

a. Insert words after the subject and verb.

Alice ran _ON THE TRACK TEAM IN HIGH SCHOOL._ .

Alice ran, _WITHOUT REGARDS TO HER INJURY._ .

b. Insert words between the subject and verb.

Alice, _CRIPPLED WITH PAIN_ , ran.

c. Insert words before the subject and verb.

IN THE DEAD OF NIGHT , Alice ran.

d. Insert words that might invert the subject-verb pair.

VERY QUICKLY ran Alice.

4. Using your own subject-verb pairs,

a. write a sentence in which words follow the subject-verb pair;

THE DAY WAS DARK AND DREARY.

b. write a sentence in which the subject is separated from the verb by other words;

AN EXAMPLE OF MANKIND, DESTROYING MANKIND.

c. write a sentence in which the subject and verb are delayed until the end of the sentence;

EVEN WITH THE DOCTOR ON HAND THE MAN DIED.

d. write a sentence in which the verb precedes the subject.

SKIPPING ROPE IS GREAT PHYSICAL EXERCISE.

5. The expressions below are only clusters of words. Convert the clusters to sentences by adding subject-verb pairs.

a. Early in the morning, long before sunrise, in the grass glittering with dew, _THE COW_ _GRAZED IN THE MEADOW_ .

b. _THE DOCTORS WORKING FRANTICLY,_ ticking ceaselessly through the long hours of their vigil, unable to speed its pace to hasten the end, or to slow it to lengthen the life of the dying man.

c. On the verge of leaving and about to slam the door, _I TURNED AND BLEW A KISS._

d. _SHE ENJOYS_ cracking the eggs, whipping them up, and slapping them onto the buttered griddle.

e. _I LAY_____ very much alert that night, on the lookout for any hint of trouble in the area.

f. To be informed of the time set for take-off, _He SAT THE ALARM ON HIS WATCH._

g. _THEY WERE AFRAID_____ climbing cautiously up the creaking staircase.

h. _THE STUDENTS BECAME UNEASY_, having broached the uncomfortable subject, _PERTAINING TO ABORTIONS_____.

i. Before us today, and more important than any past problem, _IS HUMAN ANILLATION_.

j. Situated high in the mountains above the sea, remote from the fishing villages along the coast, and isolated from the glittering cities far off to the east, _SAT OUR COTTAGE_____.

6. Read this passage, find the subjects, and list them as indicated in the column below.

The street looked empty. A car was parked near the end of the first block, but like the crushed cans and the bits of broken glass and the flattened wads of wrappers scattered along the curb, the car looked like refuse, like a piece of rubbish someone had put out onto the curb for collection. The car had once been a shade of green, probably a bright turquoise, but now appeared a lusterless grey-green, paler and greyer on its roof than on the rest of its body, and rusty where it had been dented. Its tires bulged beneath it and seemed to sigh. Its windows dulled the light that struck them. Its doors met unevenly with their frames. On the windshield, under the only wiper, two tickets summoned the owner to court.

The column below lists the verbs in the passage. In the space provided, write in the word or word group that you think is the subject of each verb.

Subject (the performer of the action or the word the verb makes a statement about)	Verb
STREET	looked
CAR	was parked
CAR	looked
SOMEONE	had put
CAR	had been
CAR	appeared
CAR	had been dented
TIRES	bulged
TIRES	seemed to sigh
WINDOWS	dulled

LIGHT	struck
DOORS	met
TICKETS	summoned

7. Sometimes writers break off sentence parts for emphasis. Advertisements are often written in this style. But in standard English, sentence parts written as sentences are sentence fragments—errors.

   In the passage below, subjects are underlined once, verbs twice. Recalling the definition below, read the passage and locate sentence fragments.

DEFINITION   **A sentence is a group of words that contains at least a subject and a verb and that makes sense by itself.**

A Frightening Journey

I used to think of air travel as dangerous. Even before my first flight. It doesn't seem possible for such a big machine to lift off the ground. And stay in the air. But last year I took the Boston to New York shuttle four times. And then one longer flight to Puerto Rico. After those trips, I lost my fear. But last summer I found it again. I took a plane to Arizona. For a visit to my brother. On the return flight, when I got to my seat and looked out the window to wave goodbye, I noticed that the rubber around my window was loose. So I told the stewardess. She told me to change my seat to one across the aisle. We took off. I started talking to a soldier sitting next to me. While we were flying over Ohio, the soldier's voice began to sound thin. And farther away. A few seconds later my own voice started to sound far away. Even to me. My ears started to hurt. A baby started to cry. Then all of a sudden the stewardess yelled for us to fasten our seat belts. And wait for the oxygen masks to drop! Even before she finished, the masks popped out of the shelves over our heads. I put mine on. Then I realized that the plane was going down. My ears hurt badly, and I was breaking into a sweat. I looked at the soldier, hoping he wasn't terrified. He was. But when he saw me looking at him with such a scared look, he took my hand. And held it. He made me feel better. In spite of my terror. Slowly the plane leveled off. Then the pilot got on the loudspeaker to tell us that the cabin had lost pressure suddenly. He had been forced to fly the plane down to 19,000 feet, where there was more oxygen. We finally landed, safely, at Kennedy Airport. In all the commotion I lost the brave soldier. But my old fear of airplanes had found me again. And is with me to this day.

On the lines below, write out the fragments you found, and following each, tell why it is a fragment, for example:

it does not contain a subject
it does not contain a verb

it does not contain a subject-verb pair

it does not make sense

a. _____

b. _____

c. _____

d. _____

e. _____

f. _____

g. _____

h. _____

i. _____

j. _____

The chart below shows what sentence parts the fragments are, and shows the sentences the fragments belong to:

Subject	Verb	Object	Complement	Modifier
I	used to think			of air travel as dangerous, <u>even</u> <u>before my first flight</u>
for such a big machine to lift off the ground <u>and stay in the air</u>	doesn't seem		possible	
				Last year
I	took	the Boston to New York shuttle		four times <u>and then</u>
		one longer <u>flight</u>		to Puerto Rico.
				While we were flying over Ohio
the soldier's voice	began to sound		thin <u>and</u> further <u>away</u>	

Subject	Verb	Object	Complement	Modifier
				A few seconds later
my own voice	started to sound		far away	even to me
the stewardess	yelled	for us to fasten our seatbelts and wait for the oxygen masks to drop		Then all of a sudden
				When he saw me looking at him with such a scared look
he	took and held	my hand it.		
He	made	me feel better		in spite of my terror
My old fear of airplanes	had found	me		again
	and is			with me to this day

You can see from this chart that the fragments are not sentences, but parts of sentences. None of these parts has both subject and verb, and none makes sense by itself. None of these sentence parts fits the full definition of a sentence. Sentence parts written as sentences are misleading. Readers expect sentences to have subjects and verbs, and they expect them to make sense.

Reread the passage and cross out the periods that separate the sentence fragments from the sentences they are actually parts of. Use the chart to make sure that you have joined the fragment to the right sentence.

8. Many students have been taught to put a comma or a period wherever there would be a pause in their words. Although this method works sometimes, it may also result in sentence fragments. The passage below was written according to this unreliable ''rule'':

The First Time Out

I <u>got</u> my driver's license when I <u>was</u> eighteen. Just before my graduation from high school. I <u>got</u> the license without taking my school's required driving course, since I <u>transferred</u> to this school from another state just six months before graduation. But I <u>felt</u> pretty confident when I <u>took</u> the test for the license. Because of driving lessons with my brother. He <u>was learning</u> to drive a truck at the time. And <u>had</u> a lot of experience driving cars. When <u>my license</u> finally <u>came</u>, <u>I</u> <u>had been driving</u> with my brother in the car. Giving hints and watching traffic with me for about two months. <u>I</u> <u>was</u> glad to get it, but <u>I</u> <u>didn't go</u> out to drive right away. In fact <u>I</u> <u>wasn't driving</u> at all. Except with my brother. Then one day when <u>I</u> <u>was taking</u> the bus to my morning classes, as usual. <u>I</u> <u>was</u> late. <u>I</u> <u>got</u> around the corner just in time to see the bus pulling away from the curb. <u>I</u> <u>was going</u> to wait for the next bus, but then <u>I</u> <u>remembered</u> that <u>I</u> <u>was</u> already late. With my own transportation parked right in front of my house. <u>I</u> <u>went</u> back to the car. <u>My heart</u> <u>was booming</u>, and <u>my hands</u> <u>were trembling</u>. <u>I</u> <u>was trying</u> to remember everything to do. But <u>I</u> <u>felt</u> good because <u>I</u> <u>remembered</u> to put my foot on the brake before <u>I</u> <u>put</u> the car into gear. And because <u>I</u> <u>wasn't</u> in traffic. <u>My plan</u> <u>was</u> to stay along the curb until <u>I</u> <u>got</u> to the corner. Thus avoiding getting into traffic. There <u>were</u> <u>no cars</u> parked in front of me. <u>I</u> <u>got</u> to the corner all right, but just as <u>I</u> <u>was</u> about to signal, <u>another car</u> <u>shaved</u> across my front bumper. An accident my first time out. <u>We</u> both <u>thought</u> <u>it</u> <u>was</u> his fault. For not seeing me on his right. <u>My brother</u> <u>said</u> <u>it</u> <u>was</u> my fault. For not knowing <u>I</u> <u>was</u> in traffic in the first place.

Now study the passage, applying the rule that you have learned in this chapter: a sentence must contain a subject and a whole verb and must make sense by itself.

Subjects are underlined once, verbs twice. Are there any sentences without subject-verb pairs? These are fragments, sentence parts broken off from the sentences they belong to. Take out the incorrect periods and, on the lines below, rewrite these fragments within the sentences they belong to.

a. _____

b. _____

c. _____

d. _____

e. _____

f. _____

g. _____

h. _____

i. _____

In addition to these, there are three ''sentences'' that *do* contain subject-verb pairs, but don't make sense. They also seem to be broken off from the statements they belong to.

$$\text{S} \qquad \text{V}$$
Then one day when <u>I</u> <u>was taking</u> the bus to my morning classes, as usual.

                S   V
And because I wasn't in traffic.

                    S   V
For not knowing I was in traffic in the first place.

Rewrite these fragments within the sentences they belong to. You will learn in Chapter 4 why even a group of words containing a subject and a verb can sometimes be a fragment.

j. _____

k. _____

l. _____

Many of the fragments you found in this passage contained words that look like verbs. But we can see that the "sentences" they form are fragments because they don't fit the definition—they don't make sense:

Wrong: Giving hints and watching traffic with me for about two months.

Wrong: With my own transportation parked right in front of my house.

Wrong: Thus avoiding getting into traffic.

Wrong: For not seeing me on his right.

Wrong: For not knowing I was in traffic in the first place.

In the next chapter we'll learn that, because these verblike words are not whole verbs, they cannot make sentences.

In-Class Writing

1. Recall the last time you gave something to someone younger than you are. Write a passage describing the incident and tell why you did it.

   Proofreading techniques:

   Underline verbs twice, subjects once. Draw an overline ⌐_____⌐ between them. Check to see that each sentence has at least one subject-verb pair.

   For style:

   Count the number of times you use *I*. Reword some of these sentences to give them different subjects.

2. Write a passage describing an event or a scene you watched with interest during the last week—a touchdown, an argument, or an excavation, for example.

Proofreading techniques:

Underline verbs twice, subjects once. Draw an overline between them. Check to see that each sentence has at least one subject-verb pair.

For style:

Count the common verbs—*is, am, are, have, has,* etc. If more than half of your verbs are common ones, rewrite some of your sentences, using more vigorous verbs or taking the common verbs out.

3. Write a detailed description of an object you would like to lose because of the trouble it causes you.

Proofreading techniques:

Underline subjects once, verbs twice. Draw an overline between them. Check to see that each sentence has at least one subject–verb pair.

For style:

Count the number of sentences that begin with subject and verb. Rewrite as many sentences as you can to postpone the subject and verb or to put the verb before the subject for a useful emphasis.

Exercises for Style

1. The passage below is a first draft. Subjects have been underlined once, verbs twice.

The Energy That Could Have Been Saved

America has become concerned with the energy it wastes, and for a very good reason: Americans waste energy all the time. Anyone who looks for energy waste can find it. For this assignment, I spent the morning taking notes about energy I personally saw wasted. There was a lot of waste to see. Here is my report.

As soon as my mother woke up, the TV was on. She says she wants to watch the news, but over breakfast she reads the morning paper, where she also gets the news. If she wanted to hear someone tell it to her, she could have used the radio, which takes far less energy than our color television set. While she was busy wasting energy listening to the President's speech in living color, my father woke up and went into the bathroom and began his morning buzzes. The first buzz was the electric toothbrush, a waste of money as well as energy, in my opinion. The only thing it does well is raise the electric bill.

The next buzz was his electric razor, which does not do as good a job as a hand-held razor, as everybody knows. People pay barbers to shave them with razors, not Ronsons. I did not personally observe this, but I happen to know that he also turned on my mother's lighted cosmetic mirror to look for his ingrown beard hairs. He also got into the tub and turned on the Jacuzzi, our water swirler. But I'm not sure that could be counted as wasted energy, since I can't think of any nonenergy or low-energy substitute except a pounding surf. While my father was taking his bath, my mother went down to the kitchen to prepare an all-electric breakfast for the family. She toasted bread in the toaster. She made coffee in the electric percolator. She fried bacon and eggs in the electric frypan. She could have used some low or nonenergy substitutes such as cereal and milk or fruit and cheese and juice. My father came down, had his high-energy breakfast, jumped into his four-thousand-pound car, and, using twenty thousand volts of electricity, turned it on to drive to work. He could have taken public transportation. As I was leaving for school, my mother turned on the dishwasher. She was on her way to the closet for the vacuum cleaner after that.

My mother and my father are a threat to this nation.

This is a very good passage, but it can be made even better.

a. Find and rewrite two sentences whose subjects are too broad.

_____

_____

b. Rewrite these sentences to change or take out the common verbs:

There was a lot of waste to see.

_____

As soon as my mother woke up, the TV was on.

_____

The only thing it does well is raise the electric bill.

_____

She was on her way to the closet for the vacuum cleaner after that.

_____

My mother and my father are a threat to this nation.

_____

2. The following sentences begin with their subjects and verbs. Move the subject or the verb, or both subject and verb and whatever words must be moved with them, to create emphasis.

a. The rat couldn't find its way out of the maze after swallowing two doses of alcohol.

_____

_____

b. Edna left the performance early, bothered by all the noise in the audience.

_____

_____

_____

c. The blast would have destroyed them if they had opened the door.

_____

_____

d. Our store stands two blocks south of Broadway, facing Independence Square.

_____

_____

The Verb and the Subject

3

CAPSULE PREVIEW   This chapter explains the differences between whole verbs and other verb forms. Whole verbs *make* sentences. Other verb forms only *suggest* sentences.

Mistaking other verb forms for whole verbs may cause you to write sentence fragments like the one underlined below:

> <u>By choosing my clothing carefully and waiting for sales.</u> I have built up a good wardrobe for school and work.

Proofreading Techniques

To find and correct this kind of fragment, you must decide which words in your sentences are whole verbs, and which are other verb forms—verbals. Label all verb forms as either whole verbs or verbals so that you can tell where you have a sentence and where you haven't.

verbal   verbal
By choosing my clothing carefully and waiting for sales.

I have built up a good wardrobe for school and work.

The first "sentence" contains two *verbals* but no whole verb. You can see now that it isn't a sentence; it's a sentence fragment.

DEFINITIONS **A whole verb is a form of the verb that makes sentences.**

A verbal is a form of the verb that does not make sentences unless it has an auxiliary or helping verb.

An infinitive is the "to" form of the verb, a verbal.

A present participle is a verbal ending in *-ing*.

A past participle is a verbal ending in *-en, -ed, -d,* or *-t*.

Auxiliaries are a small set of verbs that turn verbals into whole verbs. Auxiliaries are also called *helping verbs.*

Error: Sentence Fragment

Some verb forms are not whole verbs. Sometimes a fragment looks like a sentence because it has a subject and a word that looks like a whole verb:

┌──────────────── fragment ───────────────────────

The boys had a game. Jumping off buses at the height of the rush hour in heavy midtown

┌─────────┐

traffic.

┌────── fragment ──────────┐ ┌─ fragment ─

The viewers all want better programs. Shows written especially for children. Serials based

┌──────────────────┐

on real-life dilemmas.

RULE **A sentence must contain a subject and a whole verb.**

Revision

The fragment can be joined to a sentence:

The boys had a game: jumping off buses at the height of the rush hour in heavy midtown traffic.

The viewers all want better programs: shows written especially for children, serials based on real-life dilemmas.

The fragment can also be converted to a sentence:

The boys had a game. They jumped off buses at the height of the rush hour in heavy midtown traffic.

The viewers all want better programs. Shows must be written especially for children. Serials should be based on real-life dilemmas.

Writing Assignment: First Draft

Topic: Making money

Subject: Underpayment for a service

Everyone is underpaid sometimes. But don't write about everyone. Tell how *someone* was underpaid for a certain job at a certain time. Then make a statement about underpayment. (50–100 words)

---

1. The Verb Has Different Forms

A verb has several different spellings, or forms. Take the verb *speak*. *Speak* has *speak, speaks, spoke, speaking, spoken,* and *to speak*. The first three forms are *whole verbs*. Whole verbs make sentences. The last three, called *verbals*, are not whole verbs, and cannot make sentences. An easy demonstration bears this out. Take the sentence

> Brazilians speak Portuguese.

Now substitute verbals for the verb *speak:*

> Brazilians speaking Portuguese
>
> Brazilians spoken Portuguese
>
> Brazilians to speak Portuguese

None of these verbal forms alone can make a sentence, because these forms are not specific.

> Brazilians speaking Portuguese

The example above might mean any of the following:

> Brazilians are
> were
> will be
> had been
> should be
> may be
> etc.   speaking Portuguese.

Similarly, the example below might have any of the meanings that follow it:

Brazilians <u>spoken</u> Portuguese

Brazilians have
        had
        should have
        may have
        might have
        must have
        etc.   spoken Portuguese.

And the same is true for the next example:

Brazilians <u>to speak</u> Portuguese

Brazilians want
        seem
        try
        have
        etc.   to speak Portuguese.

There are three verbal forms: *infinitives*, *present participles*, and *past participles*.

The infinitive is the "to" form of the verb: *to praise, to break, to hear, to think*.

The present participle ends in *-ing: praising, breaking, hearing, thinking*.

The past participle ends in *-ed, -en, -d,* or *-t: praised, broken, heard, thought*.

Any verb has both whole verb forms and verbal forms.

Whole verb forms	*Verbal forms*	
speak	to speak	(infinitive)
speaks	speaking	(present participle)
spoke	spoken	(past participle)
is	to be	(infinitive)
am	being	(present participle)
are	been	(past participle)
was		
were		
sigh	to sigh	(infinitive)
sighs	sighing	(present participle)
sighed	sighed	(past participle)
call	to call	(infinitive)
calls	calling	(present participle)
called	called	(past participle)

2. Auxiliaries

The words we added to the verbals in the ''Brazilians speaking Portuguese'' example are *auxiliaries*. These are sometimes called *helping verbs*. Auxiliaries turn verbals into whole verbs.

                                    verbal
Fragment: The ring <u>found</u> in the lab.

                                aux. verbal
Sentence: The ring <u>was found</u> in the lab.

                                  verbal
Fragment: The man <u>working</u> in the basement.

                             aux.   verbal
Sentence: The man <u>has been working</u> in the basement.

The following list of auxiliaries should be memorized. Being able to recognize auxiliaries will help you to find the verbs in your sentences.

	Common Auxiliaries		
have	is	do	may
has	am	did	might
had	was	does	must
having	were		can
	are		could
	been		will
	being		would
			shall
			should
			ought to
			used to

Auxiliaries also appear with the base or unchanged form of the verb.

   I <u>drink</u> strong tea. (base form of *drink*)

  I do
    did
    may
    must
    can
    etc.   <u>drink</u> strong tea. (base form of *drink* with auxiliaries)

When a whole verb isn't just a single word, but instead contains auxiliaries, it is called a *verb phrase.* Verb phrases are often broken up by other words in the sentence. You frequently see and write sentences like these:

These halls have often been the scene of informal debates.

The team may, given time and good coaching, recover its former standing in the league.

Carlos should never have bought that car.

Ernest should never have been eating without his bib.

3. The *-ed* Verb Form Is a Problem

As you know, the verb *speak,* apart from its infinitive, has five forms: *speak, speaks, spoke, speaking,* and *spoken.* But most English verbs, apart from their infinitive forms, have only four, like the verb *study.* Its forms are *study, studies, studying,* and *studied.* Now look at these two sentences:

Ernestine spoke the language spoken by the merchant class.

Ernestine studied[1] the language studied[2] by the merchant class.

In the first sentence it is clear that *spoken* is a verbal without an auxiliary. So we know immediately that *spoken* is not a whole verb. But *studied[2]* in the second sentence looks exactly like *studied[1].* Is it a whole verb? No, "the language studied by the merchant class" is not a sentence. *Studied[2],* like *spoken,* is a verbal, not a whole verb. So it doesn't make a sentence. The *-ed* verb form is sometimes a whole verb, sometimes a verbal. But since you must have a whole verb in order to have a sentence, you must be able to tell the difference between an *-ed* form that is a whole verb and an *-ed* form that is only a verbal.

Study the examples below to get a feel for the difference:

Fragment: The expected rainfall

Sentence: The expected rainfall ended the drought.

                               verbal

Fragment: Residents <u>stranded</u> by the storm

                        verb   **verbal**

Sentence: Rescuers <u>moved</u> residents <u>stranded</u> by the storm to higher ground.

                            verbal

Fragment: The wires <u>connected</u> to the light switch

                         verbal   **verb**

Sentence: The wires <u>connected</u> to the light switch <u>sparked</u>.

                    verbal

Fragment: Seven <u>vaccinated</u> collies

                    verbal   **verb**

Sentence: Seven <u>vaccinated</u> collies <u>survived</u>.

                verbal

Fragment: A lie <u>told</u> under oath

                        verb   **verbal**

Sentence: The prosecutor <u>accused</u> the witness of a lie <u>told</u> under oath.

                      verbal

Fragment: Two clearings <u>separated</u> by a mile of rough terrain

                      verb   **verbal**

Sentence: Aerial photos <u>revealed</u> two clearings <u>separated</u> by a mile of rough terrain.

                verbal

Fragment: The <u>corrected</u> papers

                  verb   **verbal**

Sentence: You now <u>have</u> the <u>corrected</u> papers.

              verbal

Fragment: <u>Confined</u> to their quarters

              verbal   **verb**

Sentence: <u>Confined</u> to their quarters, the crewmen <u>became</u> sullen.

              verbal

Fragment: <u>Defeated</u> by their own strategy

	verbal	**verb**

Sentence: <u>Defeated</u> by their own strategy, the former football heroes <u>refused</u> to talk to the press.[1]

	verbal

Fragment: <u>Buried</u> in the icy waters

	verbal	**verb**

Sentence: <u>Buried</u> in the icy waters, two miles deep, the *Titanic* <u>tempted</u> Rawson's research team.

Exercises 1–3   Verbals make sentence *parts;* whole verbs make sentences.

4. The Past Participle Modifies

If participles aren't whole verbs, what are they? Look at these sentences again:

Ernestine spoke the language spoken by the merchant class.
Ernestine studied the language studied by the merchant class.

Spoken by the merchant class and *studied by the merchant class* are both describers, or *modifiers* of the word *language*. When it isn't a whole verb, the *-ed* form modifies.

He picked up the child <u>overcome</u> by smoke and put him into the arms of his <u>relieved</u> mother.

Overcome modifies *child; relieved* modifies *mother*.

5. The Present Participle Modifies or Names

Like the past participle, the present participle can modify:

This is the <u>touching</u> story of underpaid workers <u>striking</u> for better pay.

Touching modifies *story; striking* modifies *workers*.

The present participle can also *name action*. When it does, it means "the act of . . .":

I leave <u>washing</u> and <u>cleaning</u> the car to my wife.

Exercises 4–7   *Washing* and *cleaning* mean "the act of washing" and "the act of cleaning."

---

[1]An infinitive that follows a verb as an object, complement, or modifier may be considered either as a verbal or as a part of the verb. See page 215.

6. Verbals Suggest Sentences

Verbals strongly resemble whole verbs for a reason: a verbal is in fact a sentence reduced to a sentence part. Look at this sentence:

First the bandleader came up and bowed to his audience, then to the musicians, sitting and waiting for his cue.

It suggests two other sentences:

The musicians were sitting.

The musicians were waiting for his cue.

The sentence

Apples rot in the orchards, abandoned by the fleeing farmers.

suggests the sentences

The farmers abandoned the apples.

The farmers were fleeing.

Infinitives, too, suggest sentences with whole verbs:

To be or not to be: that is the question.

From this sentence we understand

Should I be, or should I not be.

The following examples are similar:

To err is human, to forgive divine.

This suggests

Humans err; the gods forgive.

The next example

To learn how to drive a standard shift was easy.

suggests

They learned how to drive a standard shift.

We can easily visualize the sentence that a verbal suggests. And in that sentence it is a whole verb. Whole verbs *make* sentences; verbals *suggest* sentences. Make sure that each of your sentences contains at least one *whole verb*.

Differences Between Whole Verbs and Verbals

Whole Verbs	*Verbals*
state action and information	state action and information
have subjects	————
can have objects	can have objects
can have complements	can have complements
have performers	have performers
end in -s	————
-ed	end in -ed
-en	-en
-d	-d
-t	-t
-ing	-ing
	may begin with *to* (infinitives)
————	————
function as *verb* in sentences: SVOCM	
————	function as subjects, objects, complements, and modifiers in sentences: SVOCM
have fixed tense: verbs change form if sentence time is changed	don't have fixed tense: verbals remain the same if sentence time is changed

Exercises 8–10

7. The Subject

To identify both of the essential parts of the sentence, the subject and the verb, you must know how to find the subject of the verb. The method is simple. Ask who? or what? before the verb. For example, in the sentence

    Raoul can speak French and Italian fluently,

the verb is *can speak*. Who can speak? *Raoul*. *Raoul* is the subject of *can speak*. In the sentence

    Evelyn seems equal to any task,

who or what seems? *Evelyn*. *Evelyn* is the subject of *seems*. In the sentence

    Giving compliments makes some people happy,

the verb is *makes*. Who or what makes? *Giving compliments*. Now take a more difficult sentence:

    Whatever you say may be questioned.

There are two verbs in this sentence. A sentence may have any number of verbs. The procedure for finding the subject-verb pairs remains the same: find each verb. Then ask who? or what? before each one. Who says? The subject of *say* is *you*. Who or what may be questioned? The answer is *whatever you sa*·

There are two instances where the question may not work so easily. But you will quickly learn to recognize these sentences and find the subjects. One instance is a sentence in which the word *it* or *there* precedes the verb, in the place usually held by the subject.

> There must be a key under the mat.

There is not what *must be*. The thing that must be is *a key*. Put *a key* in front of the verb in the usual subject slot:

> A key must be under the mat.

A key is the subject of *must be*. *It* frequently functions in the same way:

> It was a surprise to see him.

What was a surprise? The phrase *to see him:*

> To see him was a surprise.

>   **V**   **S**
> There have been no new tenants in the building for twelve years.

>   **V**   **S**
> Once there was a law against gambling in this state.

>   **V**   **S**
> It was risky to build the expressway.

>   **V**   **S**
> It is difficult for young children to remove the bottlecap.

>   **V**   **S**
> It was thoughtful of the toymaker to enclose the directions.

Some of these sentences would sound awkward if their subjects came first:

> A law against gambling was once in this state.

> To build the expressway was risky.

> For young children to remove the bottlecap is difficult.

To enclose the directions was thoughtful of the toymaker.

In the other kind of sentence for which the subject question may not work so easily, a noun that is not the subject happens to fall right in front of the verb.

The air after a thunderstorm seems charged with moisture.

Who or what *seems charged? Thunderstorm* looks like the subject because it is right in front of the verb. But the thing that seems charged is not *thunderstorm,* but *air. Air* is the subject of *seems charged.*

The air seems charged with moisture after a thunderstorm.

In the revised sentence, the subject is placed where you expect to find it. We can even take out the expression containing *thunderstorm* and still maintain the sentence. *The air seems charged with moisture. Thunderstorm* can't be the subject of *seems* because it isn't essential to the sentence. Here is another example:

The money for this party came from the students.

Who or what came? If we don't cautiously ask the subject question, we might assume that *this party* is the subject of *came.* The result would make sense:

This party came from the students.

But the sentence does not tell us that *this party* came; we can strike *this party* from the original sentence:

The money came from the students.

Exercises 11–22
In-class writing
1–2

What came? *Money. Money* is the subject of *came. After a thunderstorm* and *for this party* are modifiers, not subjects.[2] Finally, find the subject in this last sentence:

The fallout from the bomb lasted for days.

8. Proofreading Techniques

To proofread for verbs and their subjects:

1. Distinguish whole verbs from verb forms: label infinitives ''verbal''; label past participles without auxiliaries ''verbal''; label present participles without auxiliaries ''verbal.'' Underline whole verbs twice.

---

[2]See Chapter 7 for a fuller discussion of this kind of modifier, a *prepositional phrase.*

2. After you've found a whole verb, ask who or what performs the action of the verb, or who or what the verb states information about. Underline this subject once.
3. Draw an overline ⌐‾‾‾‾‾¬ between subject and verb.

Here is a sample of student writing already proofread:

Topic: Heroes

Subject: Two acts of heroism

On two separate nights last week there were stories of heroism. One told of a plane crash

verbal
near a highway full of cars rushing their commuters home to Long Island. The highway

verbal
passes right next to LaGuardia Airport. A small plane taking off from the airport crashed

just after takeoff. Three people were aboard, the pilot and two passengers. When it crashed,

a number of motorists pulled off the road. Two of them, one a cabdriver and another a

verbal   verbal
workman, ran over to the burning plane and tried to get the screaming people out. In

spite of the flames and the chance that the plane might explode and kill them too, the

verbal   verbal
two men were able to save one of the passengers by pulling him out. In the other incident,

verbal
a young boy in grade school, who had the job of crossing guard for his school, saw one

verbal   verbal
child run out into the street in the path of a speeding car. The young crossing guard ran

after him and pulled him out of the way. Witnesses said the boy would have been hit if

the young crossing guard had not pulled him out of the way. Both of these incidents

made me wonder what goes through the minds of people who suddenly find others in

verbal
danger of losing their lives. If they help, they might be killed too. Do they think about that

and make a conscious decision, or do they just act?

9. Using Grammar for Style

With the information in this chapter, you can change your writing dramatically. That may sound a bit like an advertising claim, but it's a fact. Knowing a little about the verb suddenly gives you much of the flexibility and control that marks the best professional writing.

Use verbals to add information. You learned earlier in this chapter that the past and present participles can be used as modifiers. That means you can use participles to sharpen the picture for your reader.

> **Original:** When the day for my brother's physical came, I was surprised at how nervous he was. He went downstairs, and my mother brought him some eggs and coffee, but he was too nervous to eat. Then he remembered that he wasn't supposed to eat anyway. So he went back upstairs and put his clothes on. When he came back down, he wanted to leave right away. He couldn't stand the tension.

> **Revised:** When the day *scheduled by his draft board* for my brother's physical came, I was surprised at how nervous he was. He went downstairs, *looking around him but not seeing much.* My mother brought him some eggs and coffee, but he was too nervous to eat. Then, *pushing away the plate,* he remembered that he wasn't supposed to eat anyway. So, *needing something to do,* he went back upstairs and got dressed. When he came back down, *wearing his turtleneck and a corduroy jacket,* he wanted to leave right away. He couldn't stand the tension.

Scheduled, looking, seeing, pushing, needing, and *wearing* add details to the bare facts. They add mood and gesture to this picture, *showing* us the anxiety that the writer *tells* us is there.

That passage was personal writing, but verbals sharpen any kind of writing.

> **Original:** The American pioneer spirit still exists. Even though there is no more wild territory beyond a frontier, for every American there is still much of this country that he or she doesn't know, and the urge to move on or move away seems to be in all of us. Population shifts in the last ten years bear this out. The cities in the Northeast are losing people, while the cities in the Southeast and in the West are growing. The small towns all over this country that are not suburbs of big cities are dying.

This is not bad writing at all. These are straight facts clearly written. But there is nothing for readers to ''see,'' not much to help them remember the facts. When there is a great deal of information to get across, verbals can help to imprint that information by setting the facts in pictures.

Revised: The American pioneer spirit still exists. Even though there is no more wild territory beyond a *sparsely settled* frontier, *bracing* itself against high snow in winter and *blinding* sun in summer, for every American there is still much of this country that he or she doesn't know, and the urge to move on or move away seems to be in all of us. Population shifts in the last ten years bear this out. The *industry-choked* cities in the Northeast are losing people *looking* for cleaner air, more space, and better jobs, while the *awakening* cities in the Southeast and West are growing, *restoring rotten* waterfronts, *designing* opera houses, *paving* new runways. The small *aging* towns all over this country that are not suburbs of big cities are dying.

Move verbals around in your sentences, to vary sentence patterns and to emphasize telling words.   Verbals can move. Instead of plodding along in the old subject-verb first rut, change the rhythm and emphasis in a sentence by opening with a verbal:

Original: Snakes can be found all over New York State, *coiled* under rock ledges, *hidden* among hollow roots, even *sliding* along dry roadbeds.

Revised: *Coiled* under rock ledges, *hidden* among hollow roots, even *sliding* along dry roadbeds, snakes can be found all over New York State.

The opening verbals sketch in the snake, so that when the word finally comes, your reader's suspicions are confirmed. The sleuth that lurks in the hearts of all avid readers loves the chance to read clues.

Closing verbals have the opposite effect:

Original: Near the center of the photograph stands a *frightened* little boy in a peaked cap, with large, dark eyes.

Revised: Near the center of the photograph stands a little boy in a peaked cap, with large, dark eyes, *frightened.*

The single verbal at the end of the sentence fixes your reader's attention, slowing the pace as your reader stops to think.

Both of these patterns have a polished, literary look, probably because we seldom begin or end our spoken sentences with verbals. These are conscious, planned arrangements, not words put down as they come to mind.

Change a verbal to a sentence, and elaborate.   Verbals suggest sentences, as this chapter showed. When you have ''writer's block''—the feeling that you've said all you have to say and it isn't enough—finding some verbals in what you've managed to write and turning them into the sentences they suggest may get you started again. Look at this first draft:

In the sixties, boys let their hair grow, and girls wore shorter and shorter skirts or overalls and workboots, thinking that they would annoy their parents. At the same time, their parents were buying bigger and bigger cars, hoping to look successful. Parents were trying to impress children with the benefits of being like them, and children were trying to convince parents of the same thing, with both generations barricaded into their positions. Now things have changed. Boys cut their hair. Girls wear high heels. Their parents drive Toyotas. Children aren't as different from their parents as they were in the sixties. Nowadays, with prices rising and everyone trying to find jobs, the generations have no time to get on each other's nerves.

This writer has a 250-word assignment, but gets stuck here. She's gotten her point across, and she doesn't have any more ideas. When you reach this point, if you know that verbals are boiled-down versions of sentences, you may see that you have enough ideas to unfold into very meaty passages. The verbals *thinking, hoping, barricaded, rising,* and *trying* can be converted to sentences, which when explained or illustrated will enrich and lengthen the passage considerably.

Original: *thinking* that they would annoy their parents

Revised: They thought they would annoy their parents.

Explanation:

It was their way of showing they were grown up enough to make their own decisions.

Original: *hoping* to look successful

Revised: They hoped they would look successful.

Explanation:

If they were financially successful, then that meant that they had lived the right way. Success meant they were good people who had worked hard all their lives.

Original: with both generations *barricaded* into their positions

Revised: Both generations were barricaded into their positions.

Illustration:

School administrators (the parent side) expelled boys who wouldn't cut their hair and girls who wore pants or miniskirts to class. The flower children set up communes, smoked strange cigarettes, and vowed never to trust anyone over thirty.

Original: with prices *rising* and everyone *trying* to find jobs

Revised: Nowadays everyone is trying to find a job. The parents are retired, but their incomes don't cover their expenses. The children have to work if they want to go to college. Prices are rising, and there is no end in sight.

Illustration:

Costs of gas, housing, food, and so forth.

In-class writing
3–5

To eliminate weak sentences, turn whole verbs to verbals, and put them into other sentences. You may ward off writer's block by writing page after page of whatever comes to mind. This works, but don't hand in your first thoughts. Use them as a first draft. Many of the sentences in the passage below are weak:

> Florence Nightingale had a lot to do with the beginning of nursing as a profession.[1] You might say she founded it.[2] Over the years, the profession has tended to be joined mainly by women.[3] Today the number of men who become nurses is increasing rapidly.[4] They have realized that there is nothing either masculine or feminine about nursing.[5] And now nurses are demanding the better pay they deserve, and salaries are improving.[6] There are also different kinds of nursing.[7] Like doctors, nurses are becoming specialists.[8] They work in the operating room, in the delivery room, in the rehabilitation rooms, on the various medical services, in public health clinics, and even in the home.[9]

If you had to read through several pages of this kind of writing, you'd have a sense that you'd seen a train of boxcars, some without much freight. By turning the verbs in some of the less important sentences into verbals, you can put the information they carry into other sentences. By combining sentences, you'll have fewer, but the meaning will be carried more efficiently:

> *Founded* by Florence Nightingale, the nursing profession over the years has been joined mainly by women.[1-2-3] But today, *realizing* that there is nothing either masculine or feminine about nursing, men have been joining the profession in increasing numbers.[4-5] And now nurses are demanding the better pay they deserve, and salaries are improving.[6] There are also different kinds of nursing.[7] *Working* in the operating room, in the delivery room, in the rehabilitation rooms, on the various medical services, in public health clinics, and even in the home, nurses, like doctors, are becoming specialists.[8-9]

This is a tighter, stronger passage, which reads like professional writing. Even the last word is a meaningful one.

The trick is to know *when* to make these changes. Your own writing is likely to look pretty good to you whenever you finish it, even the first time. Why change it? Read it aloud. What you don't see you may hear. Then read it again, sentence by sentence, and ask, "Does this sentence say enough?" If it doesn't, add a verbal modifier, move a verbal for emphasis, change a verbal to a verb and elaborate, or turn the verb into a verbal and move it to another sentence. These changes can improve every draft you write. To make them work for you, remember that verbs *make* sentences; verbals *suggest* sentences.

Chapter 3 • The Verb and the Subject

Exercises

1. Write out as many forms of these verbs as you can:

   a. walk _____

   b. dance _____

   c. wish _____

   d. buy _____

   e. seek _____

   f. think _____

   g. tell _____

   h. sell _____

   i. hear _____

   j. break _____

   k. fall _____

   l. blow _____

2. Now insert the correct forms of *walk, buy, tell,* and *break* for each of these subjects:

   I _____.

   He _____.

   We _____.

   In the left-hand column below, write those forms of *walk, buy, tell,* and *break* that make clear statements with either *I* or *he* or *we* as subject. Write those forms that do *not* make clear statements with any of these subjects in the right-hand column.

	Whole verbs	**Verbals**
walk	_____	_____
	_____	_____
buy	_____	_____
	_____	_____
tell	_____	_____
	_____	_____
break	_____	_____
	_____	_____

3. Find the verb phrases in the following passage, and write them out below.

The air outside has remained below freezing for eighteen days now.[1] Though little snow has fallen, frost covers most of the windowpanes in the house and outlines every shape outside in white.[2] Though inside we have heat, we too seem to be slowly freezing: we move sluggishly, stiffening ourselves as if we could hold our heat by growing rigid.[3]

Sentence 1: _____

_____

Sentence 2: _____

_____

Sentence 3: _____

_____

4. In the following sentences, underline all verb forms ending in -ed, -en, -d, and -t. Then reread each sentence and decide which of these underlined verb forms are whole verbs or parts of whole verb phrases and which are participles, used to describe. Underline each whole verb and whole verb phrase twice.

a. The books stacked on the shelves had been collected by three generations of well-read Joneses.

b. Never before had so many insects infested the little garden growing at the back of the house.

c. Tired of her diet of cottage cheese and tuna fish for lunch, but still afraid to eat bread, Margaret stole a few of her mother's Swedish rye crackers.

d. The ferry rode deep in the river, weighted down by four school buses in addition to its normal cargo of bullion smuggled from Nova Scotia.

e. In her troubled sleep she dreamt that she was smashing windows and calling for help.

f. She awoke full of apprehension and terrified of shutting her eyes again.

g. He schemed to get her into his country and plotted to keep her there.

h. The overfed cow walked into the barn, swayed uncertainly, and collapsed onto the hay, exhausted by her long walk and the yet unrelieved burden of her milk.

i. The newspaper arrived on time but had been tossed behind the shrubs; and there it lay, unseen, growing gradually soggy and gray.

5. Cross out any of the underlined expressions below that can be dropped without destroying the sentence.

a. The books stacked on the shelves had been collected by three generations of well-read Joneses.

b. Never before had so many insects infested the little garden growing at the back of the house.

   c. Tired of her diet of cottage cheese and tuna fish for lunch, but still afraid to eat bread, Margaret stole a few of her mother's Swedish rye crackers.

   d. The ferry rode deep in the river, weighted down by four school buses in addition to its normal cargo of bullion smuggled from Nova Scotia.

   e. In her troubled sleep she dreamt that she was smashing windows and calling for help.

   f. She awoke full of apprehension and terrified of shutting her eyes again.

   g. He schemed to get her into his country and plotted to keep her there.

   h. The overfed cow walked into the barn, swayed uncertainly, and collapsed onto the hay, exhausted by her long walk and the yet unrelieved burden of her milk.

   i. The newspaper arrived on time but had been tossed behind the shrubs; and there it lay, unseen, growing gradually soggy and gray.

6. Read the following sentences and compare them to the expressions you crossed out in the exercise above. The *whole verbs* in the sentences below are forms of the *participles* in the expressions you should have crossed out above. Underline the *whole verbs* below twice.

   a. The books were stacked on the shelves.

      The Joneses were well-read.

   b. The garden was growing at the back of the house.

   c. Margaret was tired of her diet of cottage cheese and tuna fish for lunch.

      She was still afraid to eat bread.

   d. The ferry was weighted down by four school buses in addition to its normal cargo of bullion.

      The bullion was smuggled from Nova Scotia.

   e. Her sleep was troubled.

   f. She was terrified of shutting her eyes again.

   g. The cow was overfed.

      The cow was exhausted by her long walk.

      The burden of her milk was yet unrelieved.

   h. The newspaper was unseen.

      The newspaper was growing gradually soggy and gray.

7. Next to each of the participles below, write the word or words that the participle describes in the *original* sentence in exercise 5.

   a. stacked: _____

     well-read: _____

b. growing: _____

c. tired: _____

    afraid: _____

d. weighted: _____

    smuggled: _____

e. troubled: _____

f. terrified: _____

g. overfed: _____

    exhausted: _____

    unrelieved: _____

h. unseen: _____

Compare the *subjects* of the short sentences in exercise 6 and the *words you wrote out in a-h above.*
What do you find?

_____

_____

8. In the sentences below, underline all whole verbs and whole verb phrases twice; put a wavy line under all past participles. Next, on the lines provided, add auxiliaries to the participles and write out the short sentence suggested by the participle in the original sentence. Finally, list the participles and the words they modify on the lines provided.

Example :

Sentence:

The clotted blood blocked a vein already weakened by calcium deposits.

Whole verb and participle underlined:

The clotted blood blocked a vein already weakened by calcium deposits.

Sentences suggested by the participles:

The blood was clotted.

The vein was weakened.

Words modified by participles in the original sentence:

clotted modifies *blood*

weakened modifies *vein*

a. Fourscore and seven years ago, our forefathers brought forth upon this land a new nation, conceived in liberty and dedicated to the proposition that all men are created equal.

Sentences suggested by the participles:

_____

_____

Words modified by the participles in the original sentence:

_____

_____

b. I saw armed soldiers posted at every corner and accompanied, here and there, by dogs tied to nearby trees.

Sentences suggested by the participles:

_____

_____

Words modified by the participles in the original sentence:

_____

_____

c. The gift, given as charity, turned to lead in his folded fingers, and his outstretched arm stiffened and refused to obey his head.

Sentences suggested by the participles:

_____

_____

Words modified by the participles in the original sentence:

_____

_____

d. Several doubtful assumptions weakened the argument: the first was that children frightened by nightmares turn into sleepwalkers; the second was that stories overheard by accident automatically return as dreams; and the third was that worried parents incite restlessness in their children.

Sentences suggested by the participles:

_____

_____

Words modified by the participles in the original sentence:

_____

_____

e. Stolen kisses sometimes bring unexpected rewards.

Sentences suggested by the participles:

_____

_____

Words modified by the participles in the original sentence:

_____

_____

9. All verb forms, both whole verbs and verbals, have been underlined in the passage below. Decide which of these are whole verbs and whole verb phrases and underline these twice. Remember that the words of a verb phrase may be separated from each other by other words.

Here, in their kitchen, was her mother, a thin, pale, but kindly woman, peeling potatoes and washing lettuce, and putting a bit of steak or a chop or a piece of liver in a frying pan day after day, morning and evening, month after month, year after year. And next door was Mrs. Kessel doing the same thing. And next door Mrs. Cryder. And next door Mrs. Pollard. But, until now, she had not thought it so bad. But now—now— oh! And on all the porches or lawns all along this street were the husbands and fathers, mostly middle-aged or old men like her father, reading their papers or cutting the grass before dinner, or smoking and meditating afterward. Her father was out in front now, a stooped, forbearing, meditative soul, who had rarely anything to say—leaving it all to his wife, her mother, but who was fond of her in his dull, quiet way. He was a patternmaker by trade, and had come into possession of this small, ordinary home via years of toil and saving, her mother helping him. They had no particular religion, as he often said, thinking reasonably human conduct a sufficient passport to heaven, but they had gone occasionally to the Methodist Church over in Nicholas Street, and she had once joined it. But of late she had not gone, weaned away by the other commonplace pleasures of her world.

Theodore Dreiser, "The Second Choice"

10. Write sentences suggested by the passage above for the following verbals:

peeling _____

washing: _____

putting: _____

frying: _____

doing: _____

reading: _____

cutting: _____

smoking: _____

meditating: _____

stooped: _____

forbearing: _____

to say: _____

leaving: _____

saving: _____

helping: _____

thinking: _____

weaned: _____

Did you mark any of these words as parts of whole verbs in exercise 9? Why?

11. A sentence is a group of words that contains a subject and a whole verb and that makes sense by itself. Using that definition, carefully reread the sentences in the passage above and check to see whether each expression written as a sentence is in fact a sentence, according to our definition. On a separate sheet, write out any expression that is *not* a sentence, but that begins with a capital and ends with a period.

12. In the sentences below, find each whole verb and whole verb phrase, and underline each twice. Remember that a whole verb *states* action or information; whole verbs do not mean ''the act of,'' as *paying* does in this sentence:

Paying taxes depleted Fannie's bank account.

Depleted is the verb in that sentence. And remember that whole verbs *do not describe* other words, as verbals may. Look at the expression below:

Paid men

Paid is a participle describing *men*. In that expression, *paid* only *suggests* the sentence *Someone paid the men.*

a. The famed pianist Andre Watts will play Shubert again tonight at the theater designed by Anuskewicz.

b. She outlines their gripes with this administration.

c. The irony is that so little evidence remains of so many months of work.

d. The satisfaction of becoming more verbal seems to have been a real reward.

e. The days of the five-cent praline are gone forever.

f. The controversy simmered for years.

g. Opossums have long snouts, sharp teeth, and thick, ratlike tails.

h. It worked.

i. The braised turnips are not without appeal.

j. Lion cubs jostle one another with playful swats.

k. The prices are always discounted.

l. The surgeon, the anesthesiologist, and other attendants said the results were much better than expected.

13. Now find the subject or subjects of each of the verbs you have identified above. Underline each subject once. Draw an overline ⌐‾‾‾‾‾‾⌐ between each verb and its subject or subjects.

14. In the sentences below, find each whole verb and underline it twice.

a. A flock of mallard ducks returned here today.

b. Sticky-fingered Sam has already located the peanut butter.

c. Take a pen or pencil, a crayon or brush and, carefully keeping within the lines, color in the design.

d. Thus began a highly productive relationship.

e. Is the play over?

f. There is a film about birth control at your local health clinic.

g. There are many computerized devices on the market.

h. There are also two famous cast-iron mobiles.

i. There was some fighting among the males, and there was some tension at first.

j. There are tapestries along the passageways, all from French looms and all woven of silk thread.

k. There are some Italian wool leisure suits now available, imported from Milan.

l. Throughout the Western world there were outcries against the trial of one of the men and against the arrests of two others indicted for the same reasons.

m. On the fringes of some of the lots, there is nothing left but ash and broken glass.

n. It is unfair that we can't go.

o. It is reasonable to come to that conclusion.

p. It is possible to eat packaged macaroni and cheese and dream of oyster-stuffed sole.

q. It felt good to bathe.

r. It is easy to hook a rug.

s. Hooking a rug is easy.

15. Now find the subject or subjects of each of the verbs you have identified above. Underline each subject once. Draw an overline ⌐‾‾‾‾‾‾⌐ between each verb and its subject or subjects.

16. In the sentences below, find each whole verb and whole verb phrase, and underline each twice.

a. Showering her with affection did no good.

b. It did no good to shower her with affection.

c. To dream of a time when the accounts would once again be balanced relieved him of his distress.

d. Dreaming of a time when the accounts would once again be balanced relieved him of his distress.

e. It may prove costly to speak your mind.

f. Speaking your mind may prove costly.

g. That I can eat the way I do and want to be thin at the same time puzzles me.

h. It puzzles me that I can eat the way I do and want to be thin at the same time.

i. Eating all that horseradish before he sat down to dinner cost Pete his appetite.

j. Sometimes a plate of pig's feet hits the spot.

17. Now find the subject or subjects of each of the verbs you have identified above. Underline each subject once. Draw an overline between each verb and its subject or subjects.

18. Test the words in the subject column against the verbs provided in the verb column to see if the subject words and expressions work as subjects. If a word or expression will not work as a subject, cross it out and label it "nonsubject."

Possible subjects	_Verbs_
Himself	
Sam	
Sam's	
Sam's condition	
Sam's gear	needed attention.
Suddenly	
Afterwards	
Although	
Suitable	
And	

To paint a building
Painting a building   ⎫
I am painting a building ⎬   takes time.
By painting a building   ⎭

That Sam sails   ⎫
Whichever boat Sam sails |
Whatever Sam sails |
Which Sam sails   ⎬   presents a problem.
Whomever Sam sails with |
Whoever sails with Sam |
Whenever Sam sails   ⎭

19. In the following passage, underline each whole verb twice. Find the subject or subjects of each whole verb, and underline these once. Draw an overline between each whole verb and its subject or subjects.

One unversed in such matters can have no notion of the many and tragic things that can happen to a chicken. It is born out of an egg, lives for a few weeks as a tiny fluffy thing such as you will see pictured on Easter cards, then becomes hideously naked, eats quantities of corn and meal bought by the sweat of your father's brow, gets diseases called pip, cholera, and other names, stands looking with stupid eyes at the sun, becomes sick and dies. A few hens and now and then a rooster, intended to serve God's mysterious ends, struggle through to maturity. The hens lay eggs out of which come other chickens, and the dreadful cycle is thus made complete.

Sherwood Anderson, "The Egg"

20. In the following passage, underline each whole verb twice. Find the subject or subjects of each whole verb, and underline these once. Draw an overline between each whole verb and its subject or subjects.

I have quite forgotten what became of the king's nephews. But when the wicked Medea saw this new turn of affairs, she hurried out of the room, and going to her private chamber, lost no time in setting her enchantments at work. In a few moments, she heard a great noise of hissing snakes outside of the chamber window; and, behold! there was her fiery chariot, and four huge winged serpents, wriggling and twisting in the air, flourishing their tails higher than the top of the palace, and all ready to set off on an aerial journey. Medea stayed only long enough to take her son with her, and to steal the crown jewels, together with the king's best robes, and whatever other valuable things she could lay hands on; and getting into the chariot, she whipped up the snakes, and ascended high over the city.

Nathaniel Hawthorne, "The Minotaur"

21. Write the sentences suggested in the passage above by the verbals listed below.

   going: _____

   setting: _____

   hissing: _____

   wriggling: _____

   twisting: _____

   flourishing: _____

   to set off: _____

   to take: _____

   to steal: _____

   getting: _____

22. Now proofread your own first draft according to the proofreading guidelines in this chapter to make sure that you have followed the rule that a sentence must contain a subject and a whole verb.

In-Class Writing

1. Write a passage in which you describe three things you enjoy doing. Underline verbs twice, subjects once. Draw overlines between them. Label all verbals "verbal."

2. Write a sentence describing one of your fellow students, using two of the verbals below. Write three more sentences, using other verbals from the list, describing three other students in your class. Read your descriptions aloud and let your fellow students guess who you are describing in each sentence. Here are the verbals:

   reading, writing, sitting, thinking, hoping, working, leaning, breathing, dreaming, tapping, wearing, fearing, believing, smiling, scratching, staring, looking, expecting, ignoring, knowing, wondering, sleeping, resting, trying, worrying, planning, to understand, to answer, to hear, to appear, to seem, to attract, to ring, to escape

   Example: Following the teacher with her eyes, but really daydreaming about french fries, Marie is praying
   for the bell to ring.

3. Many verbs have only one form for the past. This form serves *either* as a past participle—a modifier—or as a whole verb. Some of these are listed below. Write a passage using *all* of these words. Use at least three of them as modifiers. Underline whole verbs twice, subjects once. Draw overlines between subjects and verbs. Label verbals "verbal."

arrived, borrowed, cleaned, danced, devised, earned, freed, held, ignored, lost, married, post-poned, used

Example: Paul and Mai, secretly married last year, borrowed my used Mustang to take a long-postponed honeymoon.

4. Write a ten-sentence description of your teacher. Tell not only how the teacher looks, but how the teacher *seems* to you—give your impression of this individual. Include at least one verbal in each of your sentences. Underline verbs twice, subjects once. Draw overlines between subjects and verbs. Label verbals "verbal."

5. Write a passage using the following words as *subjects* of verbs:

driving, thinking, speaking, remembering, wishing, staring, discovering

Underline verbs twice, subjects once. Draw overlines between subjects and verbs. Label verbals "verbal."

Exercises for Style

1. The passage below describes a place. Rewrite it three times, as directed.

The door opens on the right, which is a surprise. Inside there are four chairs, one on each side of the room. There is a large window opposite the door. There is another doorway off to the left, and through it a stairway is visible. In the center of the room there is a round table, and on it stands a tall vase. Someone is coming.

a. Rewrite the passage, adding verbals and whatever other words you may need, to create suspense.
b. Rewrite the passage, adding verbals and whatever other words you may need, to create a sense of joy.
c. Rewrite the passage, adding verbals and whatever other words you may need, to make the room unforgettable.

2. The sentences below contain verbals. On the lines beneath each sentence, rewrite the sentence, moving the verbal and whatever other words you have to move to create a certain effect or emphasis. Then write out what effect you have achieved or what you have emphasized by your change. If you choose not to change the sentence, use the lines to explain the effect or emphasis the sentence already has.

a. Followed by the women's eyes, six young men dressed for battle rode out of town.

_____

_____

Effect or emphasis: _____

_____

b. He gradually began to speed, lost in thought and exhausted by the long drive.

_____

_____

Effect or emphasis: _____

_____

c. The pot boiled on, untended, dried up, and finally began to char.

_____

_____

Effect or emphasis: _____

_____

d. Flexing her knees, raising her arms above her head, and curling her toes over the end of the board, Joanna got ready to dive.

_____

_____

Effect or emphasis: _____

_____

3. The draft that follows contains a number of verbals. Change some of these to verbs, and build sentences around them, in order to create a vivid picture for your reader.

Example: Large crowds fill department stores in the last few days before Christmas, *buying* millions of dollars worth of merchandise.

Revised: Large crowds fill department stores in the last few days before Christmas. *They buy* millions of dollars worth of merchandise, from candles to television cameras. They stand in one slow line to pay and in another even slower line to have their purchases wrapped.

Large crowds fill department stores in the last few days before Christmas, buying millions of dollars worth of merchandise. More and more, these large stores, located in shopping malls outside the towns and cities, are drawing away badly needed dollars from the communities where these unthinking shoppers actually live. The stores on their own main streets, decorated in last year's plastic candles and wreaths, stand open, hoping for the last-minute shoppers. The same merchandise sits on their shelves, costing a bit more, but waiting to be sold by a neighbor to a neighbor.

4. The passage below is ''choppy.'' Improve it by changing the verbs in some of the sentences to verbals and merging the resulting expressions with other sentences. You may move or cut out words to put the verbal expression into the sentence.

Example: Wade was a hard worker. He had been raised on a farm.

Revised: Raised on a farm, Wade was a hard worker.

Wade was not lucky. When I met him he was unemployed. He had been fired from his last job. He had spent the next few hungry months trying to find work. Finally he had decided to spend his last few dollars on a secondhand car. It was dented when he bought it, and almost out of gas. It broke down minutes after he closed the deal. His girlfriend had left him. She was looking for someone who was more fun to be with. He lived in a rented room. It overlooked the less prosperous bank of the Shonomac River. For the last two or three days of every month, his landlady followed him around. When he bought coffee, she warned him not to spend money on cake. When he stopped at a store window, she threatened to cut off his heat. And she always reminded him that it was cheaper to make lunch than to buy It.

Subordination

4

CAPSULE PREVIEW In this chapter you'll learn the difference between independent clauses and dependent (subordinate) clauses. Independent clauses are sentences; dependent clauses are sentence parts.

If you mistake dependent clauses for sentences, you may write fragments like those underlined in the following passage:

> There are not many foods that I won't eat. <u>Even if I don't particularly like them.</u> <u>When someone cooks me a meal and sets the table.</u> I feel grateful enough to eat it all. <u>No matter what is on the plate.</u>

Proofreading Techniques

To find and correct this kind of fragment, first locate the clauses; then decide which ones are dependent and which are independent. Underlining subjects and whole verbs will help you find the clauses:

There <u>are</u> not <u>many foods</u> that <u>I</u> <u>won't eat</u>. Even if <u>I</u> <u>don't</u> particularly <u>like</u> them. When <u>someone</u> <u>cooks</u> me a meal and <u>sets</u> the table. <u>I</u> <u>feel</u> grateful enough to eat it all. No matter <u>what</u> <u>is</u> on the plate.

Pinpointing subordinating conjunctions and relative pronouns shows which clauses are subordinate:

There <u>are</u> not <u>many foods</u> that <u>I</u> <u>won't eat</u>. Even if <u>I</u> <u>don't</u> particularly <u>like</u> them. When <u>someone</u> <u>cooks</u> me a meal and <u>sets</u> the table. <u>I</u> <u>feel</u> grateful enough to eat it all. No matter <u>what</u> <u>is</u> on the plate.

> Three of these "sentences" are really dependent clauses, not sentences. They're sentence parts, fragments that belong to nearby clauses.

DEFINITIONS

A clause is a group of words containing a subject and a verb.

A dependent clause is a clause that follows a subordinating conjunction or a relative pronoun. Dependent clauses are sentence *parts*.

An independent clause is an unsubordinated clause. An unsubordinated clause can stand alone as a sentence.

A simple sentence is a single independent clause standing alone as a sentence.

A compound sentence is a sentence containing more than one independent clause and no dependent clauses.

A complex sentence is a sentence containing one independent clause and one or more dependent clauses.

A compound-complex sentence is a sentence containing two or more independent clauses and at least one dependent clause.

Error: Sentence Fragment

Dependent clauses are clauses that have been reduced to sentence parts by subordinating conjunctions or relative pronouns. A dependent clause written as if it were a sentence is a sentence fragment:

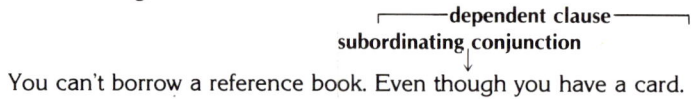

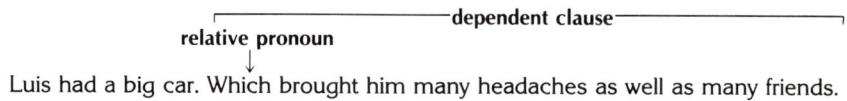

┌──────dependent clause──────┐
subordinating conjunction
↓
You can't borrow a reference book. Even though you have a card.

┌──────────────────────dependent clause──────────────────────┐
relative pronoun
↓
Luis had a big car. Which brought him many headaches as well as many friends.

RULE

A sentence must contain at least one independent clause.

Revision

Join the dependent clause to an independent clause:

You can't borrow a reference book even though you have a card.

Luis had a big car, which brought him many headaches as well as many friends.

Or, convert the dependent clause to an independent clause:

You can't borrow a reference book. The fact that you have a card doesn't matter.

Luis had a big car. It brought him many headaches as well as many friends.

Writing Assignment: First Draft

Topic: Personality

Subject: A notable character

Everyone has character traits. One person would give you the shirt off his back; another never trusts anyone. One is always contented; another is never satisfied. Bring to mind *one* person you know or know of who has a strong character trait. Then describe an incident involving that person and illustrating the trait. Finally, make a statement about that trait. (50–100 words)

---

1. The Process of Subordination

A clause is either independent or subordinate. Wherever you find a subject and a verb, then, you have either an independent or a dependent clause. Look at the following passage:

> Although he had tried to stop smoking each year in which he had developed a cough, Charles had had no success. Whenever he denied himself cigarettes for a day or for several days, he missed smoking so much that he felt sorry for himself. Inevitably, some small calamity would occur, such as having a flat tire while he was driving in the rain, and he would feel even sorrier for himself. In such a situation he would reason that he was not helping but punishing himself by not smoking. So he would renounce his good intention and go to the nearest tobacco shop, candy store, or cigarette machine, where he would buy a pack, tear it open, pull out the longed-for cigarette, and light it immediately.

In the first sentence, there are three subject-verb pairs: *he* (the first *he* in the sentence) *had tried; he* (the second *he* in the sentence) *had developed a cough;* and *Charles had had.* But not all three clauses formed by these subject-verb pairs are independent. Only the last clause makes sense by itself:

> Although he had tried to stop smoking each year in which he had developed a cough
>
> Charles had had no success.

If we punctuate the passage as though every clause were a sentence by itself, we will find other clauses that are not independent:

> Although he had tried to stop smoking each year. In which he had developed a cough. Charles had had no success. Whenever he denied himself cigarettes for a day or for several days. He missed smoking so much. That he felt sorry for himself. Inevitably, some small calamity would occur, such as having a flat tire. While he was driving in the rain. And he would feel even sorrier for himself. In such a situation he would reason. That he was not helping but punishing himself by not smoking. So he would renounce his good

intention and go to the nearest tobacco shop, candy store, or cigarette machine. Where he would buy a pack, tear it open, pull out the longed-for cigarette, and light it immediately.

Some of the sentences seem broken off, unconcluded. Taken out of the passage altogether, they are clearly incomplete:

Although he had tried to stop smoking each year.

In which he had developed a cough.

Whenever he denied himself cigarettes for a day or for several days.

That he felt sorry for himself.

While he was driving in the rain.

That he was not helping but punishing himself by not smoking.

Where he would buy a pack, tear it open, pull out the longed-for cigarette, and light it immediately.

The periods separating each clause in this repunctuated passage *fragment* it. The periods destroy relations between clauses so that some clauses become incomplete. When we test these clauses by the definition, ''a sentence is a group of words that contains a subject-verb pair and that makes sense by itself,'' we find that none of these clauses makes sense by itself; each seems to require some more information to complete it. Even the longest of these clauses, the last, raises questions. What is the place where he would buy a pack, tear it open, pull out the longed-for cigarette, and light it immediately? What happened where he would buy a pack, tear it open, pull out the longed-for cigarette, and light it immediately? What happened while he was driving in the rain? What happened whenever he denied himself cigarettes for a day or for several days?

Finally, look at the following clause:

that he was not helping but punishing himself by not smoking

This clause does not raise the same kind of question, but it is certainly incomplete. What is it about these clauses that makes them seem incomplete?

We already know that a subject-verb pair is the basis of any sentence. Because each of these clauses does contain a subject-verb pair, we can assume that some word or words outside the subject and verb makes the clause seem incomplete. Watch what happens in each clause when the word in front of the subject-verb pair is dropped.

~~Although~~ he had tried to stop smoking

Without *although* the clause makes sense by itself:

He had tried to stop smoking.

~~In which~~ he had developed a cough

Without *in which* the clause makes sense by itself:

> He had developed a cough.

> ~~Whenever~~ he denied himself cigarettes for a day or several days

Without *whenever* the clause makes sense by itself:

> He denied himself cigarettes for a day or for several days.

> ~~That~~ he felt sorry for himself

Without *that* the clause makes sense by itself:

> He felt sorry for himself.

> ~~While~~ he was driving in the rain

Without *while* the clause makes sense by itself:

> He was driving in the rain.

> ~~That~~ he was not helping but punishing himself by not smoking

Without *that* the clause makes sense by itself:

> He was not helping but punishing himself by not smoking.

> ~~Where~~ he would buy a pack, tear it open, pull out the longed-for cigarette, and light it immediately

Without *where* the clause makes sense by itself:

> He would buy a pack, tear it open, pull out the longed-for cigarette, and light it immediately.

Thus a word or phrase standing in front of a subject-verb pair might make the clause seem incomplete.

We must ask now which word or phrase standing in front of a subject-verb pair will make the clause incomplete. Look at these sentences:

> *Sadly,* he had often tried to stop smoking.
> *In the meantime,* he had often tried to stop smoking.
> *For the sake of his health* he had often tried to stop smoking.

None of these additions before the subject-verb pair seems to make the clause incomplete. The same is true for the following sentences:

Sometimes he denied himself cigarettes for a day or several days.

In a panic he denied himself cigarettes for a day or several days.

Despite his yearning he denied himself cigarettes for a day or several days.

Predictably, he felt sorry for himself.

Miserable without cigarettes, he felt sorry for himself.

Yesterday he was driving in the rain.

All alone he was driving in the rain.

Apparently he was not helping but punishing himself by not smoking.

In his opinion he was not helping but punishing himself by not smoking.

Frenzied, he would buy a pack, tear it open, pull out the longed-for cigarette, and light it immediately.

Glancing furtively right and left, he would buy a pack, tear it open, pull out the longed-for cigarette, and light it immediately.

None of these additions to the subject-verb pair makes the clause seem incomplete. Experiment yourself. There are many possible additions before any subject-verb pair, and only *some* of these—only *certain* words—will make the clause seem incomplete. We already know some of these words, but before we go on to find others, let us ask ourselves whether we need such words as *although, in which, whenever, that, while,* and *where* at all. Here is the original passage without these words:

[1]~~Although~~ he had tried to stop smoking each year ~~in which~~ he had developed a cough, Charles had had no success. [2]~~Whenever~~ he denied himself cigarettes for a day or for several days, he missed smoking so much ~~that~~ he felt sorry for himself. [3]Inevitably, some small calamity would occur, such as having a flat tire ~~while~~ he was driving in the rain, and he would feel even sorrier for himself. [4]In such a situation he would reason ~~that~~ he was not helping but punishing himself by not smoking. [5]So he would renounce his good intention and go to the nearest tobacco shop, candy store, or cigarette machine, ~~where~~ he would buy a pack, tear it open, pull out the longed-for cigarette, and light it immediately.

Surprisingly, omitting these words does not seem to alter our paragraph very much. Some of the information seems perfectly clear. We would not have difficulty understanding sentence 4 at all, for example, nor the expression in sentence 2 beginning "he missed. . . ." The missing word in both cases is *that,* and, in fact, in speech and in writing we often leave out *that* when it functions this way. The same is not true of the other expressions, however. For though we do *understand* the ideas in the sentences without these words, we do not know *how the ideas are related to each other.* Without these words we have clauses with no fixed relation to each other except that they are all

Exercise 1   about the same topic.

2. Subordinating Conjunctions

The words we have been experimenting with *establish relations* between clauses. The words *although, whenever, that,* and *while* belong to a group of words called *subordinating conjunctions.* Subordinating conjunctions make the clauses they head *dependent* on other clauses. Accordingly, we call clauses beginning with subordinating conjunctions *dependent* or *subordinate clauses.* The process of making one clause dependent on another is called *subordination.*

In effect, a subordinating conjunction marks a clause as a sentence *part.*

Whenever he denied himself cigarettes for a day or for several days, he missed smoking so much that he felt sorry for himself.

In the preceding example there are three subject-verb pairs—*he denied, he missed, he felt sorry*—which form the kernels of three clauses:

He denied himself cigarettes for a day or for several days.

He missed smoking so much.

He felt sorry for himself.

Subordinating conjunctions mark two of these clauses as dependent:

whenever he denied himself cigarettes for a day or for several days

that he felt sorry for himself

Once marked by subordinating conjunctions as dependent, these clauses can no longer stand alone as sentences. They appear incomplete in spite of their subject-verb pairs. They raise questions because the subordinating conjunctions signify that they are only *parts* of something else, and we have to know what the something else is to get a sense of completeness. *Whenever he denied himself cigarettes for a day or for several days* and *that he felt sorry for himself* seem complete only when joined to the independent clause *he missed smoking so much:*

Whenever he denied himself cigarettes for a day or for several days, he missed smoking so much that he felt sorry for himself.

The dependent clauses are *parts* of the independent clause. In the following passage, the subjects and verbs of subordinate clauses are marked with lower-case *s* and *v,* and the subordinating conjunctions are in heavy black type:

                                s   s   v

[1]Another common commercial situation **where** the uneasiness of customers plays a

       v   s   v   s

significant role is in the grocery. [2]James Vicary found **that** one reason **why** many young

    S   V   V
housewives prefer the supermarket to the small grocery is **that** in a small grocery, dealing

      V   ┌──S──┐
with a clerk, it is harder for them to conceal their ignorance about foods. ³The Jewel Tea

   S   V   S   V
Company found from a motivation study **that** this fearfulness is particularly common

     S   V   S V
when women confront the butcher in the meat department. ⁴They are afraid of the butcher

    S   V   S   V
because they know so little about cuts of meat. ⁵The Jewel stores, as a result, began

                                  S
training their butchers to show great sympathy and patience with women, and the strategy

 V
paid off with increased business for all departments of the store.

Vance Packard, The Hidden Persuaders

Sentence 1, with two subject-verb pairs, contains two clauses, one marked as a sentence part by the subordinating conjunction *where:*

> *where* the uneasiness of customers plays a significant role

The independent subject-verb pair is

> Another common commercial situation is

Sentence 2, with four subject-verb pairs, contains four clauses, three of them marked by subordinating conjunctions as sentence parts:

> *that* one reason why many young housewives prefer the supermarket to the small grocery is that in a small grocery, dealing with a clerk, it is harder for them to conceal their ignorance about foods

> *why* many young housewives prefer the supermarket to the small grocery

> *that* in a small grocery, dealing with a clerk, it is harder for them to conceal their ignorance about foods

The independent subject-verb pair is

> James Vicary found

Sentence 3, with three subject-verb pairs, contains three clauses, two of them marked by subordinating conjunctions as sentence parts:

> *that* this fearfulness is particularly common when women confront the butcher in the meat department

> *when* women confront the butcher in the meat department

The independent subject-verb pair is

> The Jewel Tea Company found

Sentence 4, with two subject-verb pairs, contains two clauses, one of them marked by a subordinating conjunction as a sentence part:

> *because* they know so little about cuts of meat

The independent subject-verb pair is

> They are

Sentence 5, with two subject-verb pairs, contains two clauses, but neither is marked by a subordinating conjunction as a sentence part. We can conclude that sentence 5 is in fact two sentences, two independent clauses, neither a part of the other. Sentence 5 is therefore a *compound sentence,* with the clauses joined by a comma plus a coordinating conjunction:

> The Jewel stores, as a result, began training their butchers to show great sympathy and patience with women, <u>and</u> the strategy paid off with increased business for all departments of the store.

The other sentences in the passage, because they contain dependent clauses, are *complex sentences.*

You should memorize the most commonly used subordinating conjunctions:

until	where	if	though
till	that	unless	even if
'til	how	provided that	even though
when	what	in case	although
since	whatever	so that	as . . . as
while	whichever	so . . . as	since
as	whenever		because
before	why		inasmuch as
whereupon	whether		than
after			

You should also ask yourself what each of these words actually means. When you do, you will learn something of the relations these words create.

The importance of each of these words is that it turns the clause it heads into a *part* of another clause, making it *dependent* on that other clause. This means that the clause it heads *cannot* stand alone. It must appear *in the same sentence* with the clause it depends on.

3. Relative Pronouns

Another word group, the group that the word *which* belongs to, also creates dependent clauses. The function of *which* and words like it is to replace in one clause a word that appears in another clause and to bind the two clauses into one sentence. Hence, we call *which* and words in its family *relative pronouns*. Here is how they work:

> Although he had tried to stop smoking each year in which he had developed a cough Charles had had no success.

The sentence above contains three clauses:

> although he had tried to stop smoking each year
>
> in which he had developed a cough
> Charles had had no success

Which, in the middle clause, *stands for and replaces each year* in the first clause. So the second clause means

> in each year he had developed a cough

Note that *which* is preceded by the preposition *in* just as *each year* would be. *Which* makes the second clause dependent on the first because the words it replaces are in the first clause. Here are two simpler examples:

> Opening the door, Ellen discovered the chair, *which* had been missing.

Without the relative pronoun replacement, we have two independent clauses:

> Opening the door, Ellen discovered the chair.
> The chair had been missing.

> The man *whom* she had seen crossing the street came to her door a few minutes later.

Without the relative pronoun replacement, once again we have two independent clauses:

She had seen the man crossing the street.

The man came to her door a few minutes later.

Relative pronouns allow us to write two pieces of information as one sentence, without repeating the noun common to both of them. Here is the list of relative pronouns:

Exercise 2–3
In-class writing 1–2

	who	which	when
ℵ	whom	⊤ that ℴ	where
ℴ	whose		

4. Three Ways to Make a Clause a Sentence Part

We now know the three ways in which clauses become sentence parts:

1. A whole verb can be reduced to a verbal—either a past participle, a present participle, or an infinitive—and inserted into another sentence. When this happens, the verbal does not function as a whole verb, but does *suggest* a sentence in which it functions as a whole verb (see Chapter 3, ''The Verb and the Subject''):

My old Sunday purse was filled with quarters.

They <u>dated</u> back to 1957.

We can change *dated* to *dating:*

My old Sunday purse was filled with quarters <u>dating</u> back to 1957.

The sun <u>was</u> <u>beating</u> down on our metal helmets.

It made us sweaty, drowsy, and careless.

We can change *was beating* to *beating:*

<u>Beating</u> down on our metal helmets, the sun made us sweaty, drowsy, and careless.

Your tents <u>will</u> <u>be</u> <u>nailed</u> to the platform.

They won't blow away.

We can change *will be nailed* to *nailed:*

<u>Nailed</u> to the platform, your tents won't blow away.

2. A clause can be subordinated as a sentence part by a *subordinating conjunction:*

You must oil the drill bit frequently.
It will snap without oil.

We can subordinate by using *if:*

If you don't oil the drill bit frequently, it will snap.

He solved the equation using real numbers.
That way we could see the logic in it.

We can subordinate by using *so that:*

He solved the equation using real numbers so that we could see the logic in it.

3. A clause can be subordinated as a sentence part by a *relative pronoun* replacing a noun common to both clauses:

Certain children spend a good part of the school day chewing on pencils.
They are anxious about something.

We can subordinate by using *who:*

Certain children, who are anxious about something, spend a good part of the day chewing on pencils.

The new bunk bed wobbles when you climb into it.
Its joints need glue.

We can subordinate by using *whose:*

Exercises 4–8
In-class writing 3–4

The new bunk bed, whose joints need glue, wobbles when you climb into it.

5. Conclusions

Dependent clauses begin with subordinating conjunctions or relative pronouns. A subordinating conjunction or relative pronoun beginning a clause reduces that clause to a subordinate clause.

Subordinating conjunctions and relative pronouns are dependent clause markers.

Sam ate.

An independent clause like the one above is no longer independent when headed by a subordinating conjunction or a relative pronoun:

> *Until* Sam ate . . .
> *Because* Sam ate . . .
> *That* Sam ate . . .
> *Which* Sam ate . . .

Like a phrase or a single word, a clause headed by a subordinating conjunction or a relative pronoun is a sentence *part:* either a *subject,* an *object,* a *complement,* or a *modifier:*

```
        ┌────── S ──────┐
        │     s    v    │
        Whatever Sam ate tasted salty.
```

```
         ┌──────── O────────┐
  S   V  │   s     v        │
  Sam ate what he could catch.
```

```
                    ┌──────── C ────────────┐
  S      V          │    s     v            │
  Sam would become whatever fate had in store for him.
```

```
      ┌────── M ──────┐              ┌────── M ──────┐
  S   │  s      v     │              │   s      v    │
  Sam, who could not swim, watched the waves rise as night blackened the water.
```

Now, let's review what you already know about sentence structure:

1. A sentence *must* contain a subject-verb pair.

    ```
      S   V
      Sam ate.
    ```

2. A sentence *may* contain an element that receives the action of the verb, an *object.*

    ```
      S   V   O
      Sam ate squid.
    ```

3. A sentence *may* contain an expression that identifies or modifies the subject of the verb, a *complement.*

    ```
      S   V     C
      Sam was despondent.
    ```

4. In addition, a sentence *may* contain modifiers for any or all of these sentence elements.

S ┌──── M ────┐ M V M O ┌── M ──┐
Sam, alone and adrift, often ate raw squid to stay alive.

Subject, verb, object, complement, and *modifier* are the basic sentence functions. Any sentence can be represented with this formula:

Subject Verb (Object) (Complement) (Modifier)

The formula can be abbreviated, S V (O) (C) (M).

Any of these sentence elements can occur any number of times in one clause. For one subject we might have one verb or five verbs or seventeen verbs; any verb might have one subject or ten subjects, any number of objects, any number of complements, or any number of modifiers. The formula for a sentence might be written as follows with *n* meaning "any number" and the parentheses showing that a sentence may or may not have that element:

$$S^n \quad V^n \quad (O)^n \quad (C)^n \quad (M)^n$$

Exercise 9

This formula can recur any number of times within the same sentence, because a sentence may contain more than one clause.

6. Arrangement of Sentence Elements

Given these facts, a sentence can grow indefinitely according to the following model:

┌──── S ────┐ V ┌──── O ────┐ ┌──── M ────┐
 s v o m   s v o m s   s v o m
svom   svom svom   svom svom svom   svom svom

This model could be repeated if the sentence contained more than one independent clause. Thus, knowing that a period goes at the end of a sentence is just the beginning; the work lies in identifying what kinds of clauses the sentence contains and determining how they are related to each other. Intricate patterns are common even in everyday sentences:

He knew that something that he had prayed for was about to happen when the wind shifted, and happen it did.

There are five clauses in this sentence:

Independent clauses: He knew ..., and happen it did.

Object of *knew:* that something was about to happen

Modifier of *something:* that he had prayed for

Modifier of *happen:* when the wind shifted

You can often tell what sentence part a clause plays by the subordinator in front of it. The chart below categorizes the subordinating conjunctions and relative pronouns according to the kind of dependent clause they typically mark. Notice that some subordinators occur in more than one category.

Subject	*Object/complement*	*Modifier*	
whoever	whoever, whomever	who, whom, whose	provided that
whatever	whatever	that	although
whichever	whichever	which	though
that	that	whether	because
whether	whether	why	if
what	what	where	as if
	why	when	as though
	wherever	how	as
		after	so that
		before	while
		since	once
		until	than
		unless	in order that

You'll be able to recognize the parts of a sentence more quickly if you memorize this list.

The dependent clauses in the sentences below are in italics, and their roles are marked:

      S   V   O
Whoever wants to learn has to ask questions.
   s   v

    V   C   S
It is important *that we keep most insects alive.*
               s   v   o   c

S   V   O
He says *whatever comes into his mind.*
       s   v   m

    S   S   S   V   C
An egg, some milk, and some flour become *whatever the chef cooks up.*
                                     s   v

    S   M   V   M   O
Merchants, *who work six days a week,* don't have easy lives.
         s   v   m

    S   V   M   M
Crowns are out of fashion, *since monarchs are rare nowadays.*
                       s   v   c   m

DEFINITION   **Clauses that act as *subjects*, *objects*, or *complements* are called noun clauses because they function as nouns function. Clauses that function as modifiers are adjective clauses if they modify nouns, or adverb clauses if they modify *verbs*, *adjectives*, or *adverbs*.**

7. A Note

Sometimes the subordinators *that* and *which* are omitted. Look at the sentence below:

The fin that Sam saw at sunset surfaced again on the water.

It might also be written

The fin Sam saw at sunset surfaced again on the water.

Either way, the sentence makes perfect sense; but the absence of the subordinator may leave you puzzled. It is clear that there are two subject-verb pairs, *the fin surfaced* and *Sam saw,* but it may not be clear at first glance that *Sam saw* is a subordinated clause, because there is no subordinator in front of it. If *that* or *which* is left out, you won't have any trouble putting it back in where it belongs. Sometimes, however, an unpracticed writer may replace the omitted subordinator with a comma:

Wrong: The fin, Sam saw at sunset surfaced again on the water.

Exercises 10–16
In-class writing 5

You may or may not sense something wrong with that sentence, but you can be sure that the comma does not improve it.

8. Proofreading Techniques

To proofread for sentence fragments

1. Find the clauses.
   a. Underline each verb in each sentence twice.
   b. Find the subject or subjects of each verb and underline each subject once.
   c. Draw an overline between subject and verb.

2. Separate dependent clauses from independent clauses.
   a. Put an arrow over each subordinating conjunction and relative pronoun and wherever *that* or *which* has been omitted.
   b. Now read the *independent* subject-verb pair in *each* sentence.

Here is a student passage that has already been proofread.

Topic: Hunger

Subject: Mouthwashes

Last week I watched a man slice an onion for a television audience, and dip one half into Lavoris and the other half into Listerine. The purpose of this ad was to show the smell-killing power of Listerine or Lavoris: I can't remember now which one was better. After the silly demonstration was over, I'm sure they threw the onion away. Whoever thought of displaying mouthwash this way wasn't starving. He or she probably went home to a dinner of oysters Rockefeller and filet mignon. In a starving country, he or she wouldn't even have a job. I'm sure they don't worry about mouthwash when there isn't even enough rice to go around. But in America, mouthwash is a big seller. We are constantly told what to put in our mouths so that we'll be ready for someone's kiss: gum, tablets, mouthwash, toothpaste, breath sprays. Manufacturers have every form but suppositories that could be slipped under the tongue to emit their smell-killing vapor as the day drags on. Our breath is not the only thing that might "offend." We have underarm deodorants, foot deodorants, and worse. We worry about how we smell because we don't have to worry about dinner. While we worry about who has body odor, we don't think about whose body is underfed.

Exercise 17

9. Using Grammar for Style

Much of the reason for having more than one clause in a sentence is precision. Using clauses as sentence parts makes it possible for us to say exactly what we mean. Instead of writing

> Dogs have fleas.

which is true but not precise, we can write

> Dogs *that roam outdoors* have fleas, *unless their owners protect them with flea collars and frequent baths.*

Use subordinators to make statements you can talk about.   You can see from these two sentences that the less you say, the more general your statement. *Dogs have fleas* means that *all* dogs have fleas, or that dogs generally have fleas, and that you know that for a fact. This would not be easy to prove. The second statement is a much more modest claim. *Dogs* is limited to a smaller group than all dogs by the relative clause *that roam outdoors,* and the clause *unless their owners protect them with flea collars* limits the whole statement to one you can talk about without being a dog or flea specialist.

Use key subordinators to explain.   Most people recognize the danger of writing statements like *dogs have fleas*. Dog owners will get angry: ''Your dog—not my dog!'' Analytical readers will be skeptical: ''How many fleas have you counted? And whose dogs were they on?'' Ordinary readers will yawn and turn the page. Nevertheless, many first drafts are written in this way. Some writers feel they've said it all, or at any rate said all they can say, because they don't know much about the subject. Gently confessing their lack of information, they write

> In my opinion, dogs have fleas.

Often, in that expression of opinion lies the key to explaining the claim. Here is an apologetic first draft that contains a claim the writer feels she has too little information to explain:

> I read in the paper not many weeks ago an announcement of the marriage of my best friend's younger sister. This girl is just sixteen. The boy she married is just seventeen. I don't think that marriage has much of a chance. *In my opinion, teen-agers are just too young to get married.*

Actually, since the writer *has* an opinion, she has what she needs to explain her claim. She's said *what* she thinks; now she can tell *why* she thinks that way, *how* her opinion differs from others, and *what* evidence she has that she's right:

why the writer feels this way

> Although I haven't read much about teen-age marriages nationwide, I do know about one between two other friends of mine. They ran off and got married two years ago. Their marriage has big problems. When the boy found that he couldn't earn enough to pay their rent and his fifteeen-year-old wife couldn't find a job, they had to move back to town to live with the girl's parents. Now they are children again, in a way, because they are dependent on her parents. They fight quite a bit about who lays down the law in the house, and they don't feel free to start a family yet. The girl doesn't want to finish school because she feels she's a married woman now, but she's bored at home and feels she has nothing to show for her marriage. The boy is jealous if she takes money from her parents because he feels he's man enough to support her himself.

how the
writer's
opinion
differs
from others

what
evidence
she has
that she's
right

I've heard people say, "Get married before you get used to being single." But most teen-agers must have money problems like my friends' because most are not ready to enter professions or start their own businesses yet. If they work, they have to take the lowest salaries because of their lack of experience. And most teen-agers who get married must have problems with their families because most families are against their children getting married before they get started on their careers. And how many mothers want to be grandmothers in their forties?

I think most people agree with me unless they are teen-agers who are thinking of getting married themselves. There are no ads in the papers telling teen-agers to get married before it's too late. Parents don't make big weddings for their teen-agers, and they don't drag their teen-agers to teen-age weddings and ask them why they don't do that. Most people want their children to have the chance to get to know as many future husbands or wives as they can, so they can make the best choice.

Using the key subordinating conjunctions *why, how* (how opinion differs), and *what* (what evidence) is a way of backtracking from a conclusion, your opinion, through the experiences and ideas that have given you that opinion. If you *do* have an opinion, a conclusion you've reached about something, then you've got plenty to back it up. Tell your reader what makes you think the way you do. When you write this information down, you have the support for your conclusion.

Use subordinating conjunctions for precision. Your readers expect you to speak with authority. If they didn't, they wouldn't waste their time reading what you have written, so you have to limit yourself to what you know. To do that, you need the set of subordinators that stake out the boundaries of your claims: *as, while, until, when, since, before, after,* and *once* place your statements in time by connecting them with other events:

> The chance for world peace ended forever *once the arms race began,* back *when gunpowder was discovered.*

> *Since the government of the United States established free public education for children,* parents have had the duty of seeing to it that their children get an education.

Unless, provided that, whether, although, though, if, and *in order that* modify your statements with certain conditions and circumstances so that you can say what you think, even if you're not one hundred percent sure it's true:

> Acne is not a curable disease, *unless some new treatment has been developed in the last five years.*

> *If most societies are like our own,* entry into adolescence is celebrated in a ritual of some kind.

These words pare statements down to the limits of what you know.

Because works differently. If you use *because* you must give a reason for what you are saying. Writers fear the word *because* when they think they may not have the answer.

They end up mentally bound and gagged, trying to think up statements that don't need explaining. Since practically everything of interest calls for some clarification, these writers find themselves unable to write. But used correctly, *because* can pry the lid off your thoughts and make your writing flow. Think of *why* as a routine question, one that will call up all the information you have. At the very least, it will tell you that you need more information—a situation you can remedy.

Use relative clauses to add interesting information. Relative clauses are the places for bits and pieces of information, the details that you can use to keep your readers reading:

> Mozart, *whose grave has never been found,* may have been murdered by Sogliere, a rival composer *who envied Mozart's genius.*

There are limits to precision. Since sentences can be subordinated as sentence parts, it is possible to write many words without having to insert a period. The effect is confusing rather than precise:

> America is the country where city people move away from strangers who greet them when they first come to the city because they know that, although some strangers may really mean no harm when they smile at you as you move away, others are truly crazy.

Even a short sentence can be overloaded with subordinated clauses:

> There are times *when, if because* there is no electricity there is no light, we go home.

Chapter 4 • Subordination

Exercises

1. In the passage below, many of the verbs are addressed to you, the reader, and so *you* is their subject. Find each verb and underline it twice. Find each subject and underline it once. Draw overlines between subject and verb. Write *you* above those verbs whose subject is you.

Let him give up certain vegetables for a while. If he suddenly turns against the vegetable that he loved last week, let him turn against it. If you don't make a fuss today, he will probably come back to it next week or next month. But if you insist on his taking it when he seems to dislike it, you only make him set his mind that that particular food is his enemy. You turn a temporary dislike into a permanent hate. If he turns down the same vegetable twice in succession, leave it out for a couple of weeks. It is naturally irritating to a mother to buy food, prepare it, serve it and then have it turned down by an opinionated wretch who loved the same thing a few days ago. It is hard for her not to be cross and bossy at such a time. But it is worse for the child's feeling about food to try to force or urge it. If he turns down half his vegetables for a while, serve him the ones that he does like. This is the wise and pleasant way to take advantage of the great variety of fresh and canned vegetables that we have. If he turns against all vegetables for a while but loves his fruit, let him have extra fruit. If he is taking enough fruit, milk and his vitamin drops, he is not missing anything that is in vegetables.

Benjamin Spock, *Baby and Child Care*

2. Reread the passage above and put an arrow over subordinating conjunctions and relative pronouns. Then, next to each of the subject-verb pairs listed below, write one of the following:

subordinated by (name the subordinating conjunction)
subordinated by (name the relative pronoun)
independent clause

you let: _____

he turns: _____

he loved: _____

you let: _____

you don't make: _____

he will come: _____

you insist: _____

he seems to dislike: _____

you make: _____

food is: _____

you turn: _____

he turns: _____

you leave: _____

to buy food, prepare it, serve it, and have it turned down is: _____

who loved: _____

for her not to be cross and bossy is: _____

to try to force or urge it is: _____

he turns down: _____

you serve: _____

he docs like: _____   _____

this is: _____

we have: _____

he turns but loves: _____

you let: _____

he is taking: _____

he is not missing: _____

that is: _____

3. Some of the sentences in the passage contain clauses subordinated by relative pronouns. They are written below. On the lines provided, write the word the relative pronoun stands for and then write the two clauses without the relative pronoun, as two separate sentences.

Example: If he suddenly turns against the vegetable *that* he loved last week, let him turn against it.

That stands for and refers to *vegetable.*

Clause 1: If he suddenly turns against *the vegetable,* let him turn against it.

Clause 2: He loved *the vegetable* last week.

a. It is naturally irritating to a mother to buy food, prepare it, serve it and then have it turned down by an opinionated wretch *who* loved the same thing a few days ago.

Who stands for and refers to _____

Chapter 4 • Subordination

    Clause 1: _____

    Clause 2: _____

  b. If he turns down half his vegetables for a while, serve him the ones *that* he does like.

    That stands for and refers to _____

    Clause 1: _____

    Clause 2: _____

  c. This is the wise and pleasant way to take advantage of the great variety of fresh and canned vegetables *that* we have.

    That stands for and refers to _____

    Clause 1: _____

    Clause 2: _____

  d. If he is taking enough fruit, milk and his vitamin drops, he is not missing anything *that* is in vegetables.

    That stands for and refers to _____

    Clause 1: _____

    Clause 2: _____

4. In addition to the use of subordinating conjunctions or relative pronouns, sentences may be reduced to sentence parts by reduction of a whole verb to a verbal. The sentence below contains a number of verbals. Write the sentence that each of these suggests.

    It is naturally irritating to a mother to buy food, prepare it, serve it and then have it turned down by an opinionated wretch who loved the same thing a few days ago.

  a. to buy food

    _____

  b. to prepare it

    _____

  c. to serve it

    _____

  d. to have it turned down

    _____

  e. opinionated

    _____

5. The passage below contains no punctuation. In order to determine which clauses are independent and which are sentence parts,

   a. find each verb and underline it twice.
   b. find each subject and underline it once.
   c. draw an overline between subject and verb.
   d. put an arrow over subordinating conjunctions.
   e. circle relative pronouns and draw arrows to the words they stand for.
   f. punctuate the passage so that each clause that is a sentence part *is* a part of the independent sentence to which it logically belongs.

It was an ordinary little room a clean white matting was on the floor gray paper spotted with pink and green flowers covered the walls in one corner under a white netting was a little bed the woodwork gaily painted with knots of bright flowers near it against the wall was a black-walnut bureau a worktable with spiral legs stood by the window which was hung with a green and gold window curtain opposite the window the closet door stood ajar while in the corner across from the bed was a tiny washstand with two clean towels.

Frank Norris, *McTeague*

6. Some of the following expressions are sentences; others are sentence parts. To the right of each expression indicate what it is by writing one of the following:

independent clause

clause subordinated by _____

verbal phrase

If the expression is either a verbal phrase or a subordinate clause, rewrite the expression as an independent sentence.

   a. which they did _____

   b. it was cold outside _____

   c. boys taking off their shoes _____

   d. until she met him at the beach _____

   e. her lips closed tight _____

   f. the faucet dripping _____

   g. her hair frizzing _____

   h. the bread plastered with mustard _____

   i. for Luis to cut the bread _____

   j. lasting less than a minute _____

k. the gifts were wrapped _____

l. before they realized it _____

m. things that are alive _____

n. down goes the curtain _____

o. looking into the distance _____

p. whether they sat down _____

q. for Julia to remember _____

r. since they drank _____

s. on the branches hung the lanterns _____

t. how they read _____

u. the woodchucks burrowing _____

v. because it rained _____

w. whose it was _____

7. The passage below contains a number of sentence fragments. Rewrite the passage, restoring the fragments to the sentences they belong to.

Although I have been aware since the day my first child was born that every day I should record what he did. I have never done it. I know that I will not remember his mannerisms as an infant. When he is a teenager loping through doorways and shaking the house when he raises his voice. I know that I will not remember how he learned to talk. Although I do remember the first sound. That he made that wasn't a cry. I had just laid him down to change him. He looked up at me and spoke. Something that wasn't a word. I don't remember how old he was then, but he must have been very small. I do remember his first word, *good*. He was walking around the living room. Holding onto whatever armchair or table he could reach. When he got to his uncle, who was drinking a scotch and water before dinner. He pulled himself up by his uncle's trousers and reached for his glass. With its clinking ice cubes. His uncle held it for him. And let him have a sip. He held his sip in his mouth and thought a minute. Then he swallowed and said, "Good."

8. Read this passage and

   a. find the verbs and underline them twice.
   b. find the subjects and underline them once.
   c. draw overlines between subject and verb.
   d. put arrows over each subordinating conjunction and relative pronoun.

Poor Jurgis was not very happy in his home life. Elzbieta was sick a good deal now, and the boys were wild and unruly, and very much the worse for their life upon the streets. But he stuck by the family nevertheless, for they reminded him of his old happiness; and when things went wrong he could solace himself with a plunge into the Socialist movement. Since his life had been caught up into the current of this great stream, things which had before been the whole of life to him came to seem of relatively slight importance; his interests were elsewhere, in the world of ideas. His outward life was commonplace and uninteresting; he was just a hotel porter, and expected to remain one while he lived; but meantime, in the realm of thought his life was a perpetual adventure. There was so much to know—so many wonders to be discovered! Never in all his life did Jurgis forget the day before election, when there came a telephone message from a friend of Harry Adams, asking him to bring Jurgis to see him that night; and Jurgis went, and met one of the minds of the movement.

Upton Sinclair, *The Jungle*

9. You are equipped now to determine *which* role—subject, object, complement, or modifier—the subordinated clause plays in the sentence of which it is a part. Recall the following definitions:

DEFINITIONS   A **subject** is the performer of the action of the verb, or the word the verb makes a statement about;

An **object** is the recipient of the action of the verb;

A **complement** identifies or describes the subject of the verb; and

A **modifier** is a word or expression that describes or defines another word or expression.

Name the role of the following subordinate clauses in the sentences from the passage above:

a. when things went wrong

Function: _____

b. since his life had been caught up into the current of this great stream

Function: _____

c. which had before been the whole of life to him

Function: _____

d. while he lived

Function: _____

e. when there came a telephone message from a friend of Harry Adams, asking him to bring Jurgis to see him that night

Function: _____

10. Insert the subordinators missing from the following sentences:

    a. The squid I ate this afternoon stayed in my stomach less than an hour.
    b. Everyone knows they throw dishes at each other.
    c. Here is the basted neck of lamb Buster ordered.
    d. The man she loves snores.
    e. The school Sarah left closed.
    f. Several people thought they saw it move.
    g. A sign written in Gaelic told us we should repent.
    h. The woman you want doesn't live here anymore.
    i. Some scratches on the rocks they dug up indicated they had found what they were looking for.
    j. Open the one I gave you.
    k. I believe I see a calico cat.
    l. We all think the begonia needs repotting.

11. The formula for a simple sentence is S V (O) (C) (M). The parentheses mean that the sentence may or may not contain objects, complements, or modifiers. On a separate sheet, write four simple sentences.

12. The formula for a compound sentence is any one of the following:

    S V (O) (C))M), coordinating conjunction S V (O) (C) (M).
    S V (O) (C) (M); S V (O) (C) (M).
    S V (O) (C) (M): S V (O) (C) (M).

That is, a compound sentence is a *series* of simple sentences, none of which is a part of any other, all of which are therefore independent. On a separate sheet, write three compound sentences.

13. In a complex sentence, at least one of the sentence parts—a subject, an object, a complement, or a modifier—is a dependent clause. On a separate sheet, write three complex sentences.

14. Write sentences conforming to these formats:

    a. S V and V O.

    _____

    b. S, S, and S V C.

    _____

    c. S V O, and S V O.

    _____

    d. S V, so S V.

    _____

    e. S V O M, M, and M.

    _____

    f. S V O, for S V O.

    _____

15. Identify each of the sentences in the exercise above as either simple, compound, or complex.

    a. _____

    b. _____

    c. _____

    d. _____

    e. _____

    f. _____

16. You should complete these exercises with a new insight: a clause is either independent or subordinate. Subordinate clauses are marked by subordinating conjunctions or relative pronouns. Remember that *that, which, who,* and *whom* are sometimes unstated. Put these conjunctions into your own writing where appropriate to guide you in your proofreading.

17. Now proofread your first draft according to the proofreading guidelines in this chapter, to determine that you have applied the rule that a sentence must contain at least one independent clause.

In-Class Writing

1. Write a short passage in which you tell why teachers should stop giving *D* as a grade or why they should continue to give it.

    a. Underline verbs twice, subjects once. Draw overlines between subjects and verbs.
    b. Label verbals "verbal."
    c. Put an arrow (↓) over each subordinating conjunction and relative pronoun, and wherever *that* or *which* is unstated.

2. Write a passage using *all* of the following subordinating conjunctions: *because, even if, so that, when, as, before, after, unless, how, why.*

    a. Underline verbs twice, subjects once. Draw overlines between subjects and verbs.
    b. Label verbals "verbal."
    c. Put an arrow over each subordinating conjunction and relative pronoun, and wherever *that* or *which* is unstated. Read your passage aloud to the class.

3. Write ten sentences that describe your clothing and also tell something interesting about it. Use a relative clause modifier—a clause subordinated by a relative pronoun—in each sentence.

   Example: My shoes, *which have walked the length of Manhattan Island and back every Saturday*

   for the last five months so that I can see my girlfriend, need *new soles.*

   a. Underline verbs twice, subjects once. Draw overlines between subjects and verbs.
   b. Label verbals "verbal."
   c. Put an arrow over each subordinating conjunction and relative pronoun, and wherever *that* or *which* is unstated.

4. Rewrite these ten sentences as twenty separate sentences.

   a. Underline verbs twice, subjects once. Draw overlines between subjects and verbs.
   b. Label verbals "verbal."
   c. Put an arrow over each subordinating conjunction and wherever *that* or *which* is unstated.

5. Write a passage in which you tell of a friend who accurately predicted something—someone who knew, for example, that he or she would win the lottery or lose some money, or take a trip by train, or have a terrible time, or see someone special at the fish market.

   a. Underline verbs twice, subjects once. Draw overlines between subjects and verbs.
   b. Label verbals "verbal."
   c. Put an arrow over each subordinating conjunction and relative pronoun, and wherever *that* or *which* is unstated.
   d. Read your passage aloud.
   e. Read the independent subject-verb pair in each sentence.
   f. Restore any fragments you find in this reading to the sentences to which they belong.

Exercises for Style

1. Use your own experiences and observations to limit the following statements with subordinated sentences (dependent clauses). Each completed statement should contain one independent clause and at least one subordinated clause.

   a. Accidents happen.
   b. A real friend is a friend for life.
   c. The truth hurts.
   d. You get what you pay for.
   e. The grade is a good measure of the student's work.

2. Choose one each of the paired statements below. Ask yourself why you believe the statements you've chosen, and complete them with clauses subordinated by *because*.

   a. Sixteen-year-olds should be taught to drive
      Sixteen-year-olds should not be taught to drive

   b. When you reach my age, your parents have just as much influence over you as they've always had
      When you reach my age, your parents have much less influence over you than they've had in the past

   c. President Carter was right to send soldiers to Iran to rescue the hostages
      President Carter was wrong to send soldiers to Iran to rescue the hostages

   d. Rebellion is a natural part of growing up
      Rebellion is an unnecessary part of growing up

3. a. Write a fifty-word description of your town or neighborhood, skipping every other line.
   b. Go back over your passage and add interesting details—things you remember, your impressions, current facts—to at least three of your sentences by means of relative clauses.
   c. Skipping every other line, write a fifty-word description of your last day of high school.
   d. Go back over your passage and add interesting details—what people were wearing, what people admired, what people were wishing for, what you remember about your classmates' pasts—by means of relative clauses *or* verbal phrases.

4. Choose one of the topics below.

   Jealousy
   Greed
   Forgiveness

   a. Write a fifty-word incident to illustrate it.
   b. Make a statement about it.
   c. Then write at least three sentences explaining *why* you think that way, three sentences explaining *how* your opinion differs from others on the same subject, and three sentences telling *what evidence* you have that you are right.

Coordination, Parallelism, and Comparison

5

CAPSULE PREVIEW   In this chapter you will see that a sentence may contain more than one independent clause. Such a sentence calls for specific punctuation so that the second independent clause won't be misread as a part of the first. Absent or misleading punctuation between independent clauses creates run-on sentences.

> Then everybody started to feel sick. We started to throw up some of us got dizzy and fell. We thought the food was poisoned. Then Abby raised a window and the telephone rang it was our neighbor saying that one of us had left the car on in our garage it is a part of our house. I ran down and turned it off, she saved our lives.

Proofreading Techniques

To find and correct run-on sentences, find the independent clauses as you did in Chapter 4. Working up to each period, count the clauses that precede it.

Then everybody started to feel sick. (one independent clause) We started to throw up

some of us got dizzy and fell. (two independent clauses) We thought that the food was

poisoned. (two clauses: one independent, one subordinate) Then Abby raised a window

and the telephone rang it was our neighbor saying that one of us had left the car on

in our garage it is a part of our house. (five clauses: four independent, one subordinate)

I ran down and turned it off, she saved our lives. (two independent clauses)

By counting the clauses in this way and noting which are independent and which are subordinate, you can see that three of these sentences are run-on sentences. They contain more than one independent clause, and the punctuation fails to tell that they do. Once you can find the clauses in your sentences and tell which ones are independent, you can easily punctuate to eliminate run-ons. This chapter tells how.

Error: Run-on Sentence

Sentences may contain more than one independent clause. A run-on sentence has more than one independent clause without the correct punctuation between them. There may be no punctuation between the independent clauses:

    ┌────**independent clause**────┐ ┌**independent clause**┐
    Mr. Roberts licked his plate his dog went hungry.

There may be only a comma between the independent clauses:

    ┌────**independent clause**────┐ ┌**independent clause**┐
    Mr. Roberts licked his plate, his dog went hungry.

Or, there may be only a conjunction between the independent clauses:

    ┌────**independent clause**────┐   ┌**independent clause**┐
    Mr. Roberts licked his plate so his dog went hungry.

RULE

Between any two independent clauses, there must be a semicolon (;), a colon (:), a comma followed by a coordinating conjunction (,and ,but ,so ,for ,or ,nor ,yet) or a period to create two separate sentences.

Revision

    Mr. Roberts licked his plate; his dog went hungry.

    Mr. Roberts licked his plate: his dog went hungry.

    Mr. Roberts licked his plate, so his dog went hungry.

    Mr. Roberts licked his plate. His dog went hungry.

Writing Assignment: First Draft

Topic: Dreaming

Subject: My role in a dream and in a daydream

The subject here is *your role* in the two kinds of dreams, so don't just describe a dream and a daydream. Tell *what you did* in the dream and *what you did* in the daydream. Then draw your idea from the similarities or the differences between how you acted in your dream and how you acted in your daydream. (50–100 words)

1. Simple, Compound, and Complex Sentences

You have seen that some sentences may contain more than one subject-verb pair; that is, more than one *clause*. In this chapter you will see how two or more independent clauses can occur in the same sentence as *coordinates*.

Before we turn to coordination, however, it is useful to recall how clauses, both independent and dependent, occur in three types of sentences.

A sentence that contains only one clause, only one subject-verb pair, is a *simple sentence*. A clause that forms a simple sentence is called an *independent clause*. Unlike dependent (subordinate) clauses, independent clauses can stand alone as sentences. And no matter how many clauses a sentence contains, it contains at least one independent clause.

A sentence that contains two or more independent clauses but no dependent clauses is called a *compound sentence*.

A sentence that contains both independent and dependent clauses is called a *complex sentence*.

$$
\begin{array}{cc}
\text{S} & \text{V}
\end{array}
$$
Simple sentence: The sea beneath him abounded with life.

$$
\begin{array}{cccc}
\text{S} & \text{V} & \text{S} & \text{V}
\end{array}
$$
Compound sentence: The sea beneath him abounded with life, but his own life seemed in danger.

$$
\begin{array}{cccc}
\text{S} & \text{V} & \text{s} & \text{v}
\end{array}
$$
Complex sentence: He could see that the sea beneath him abounded with life, but his

$$
\begin{array}{cc}
\text{S} & \text{V}
\end{array}
$$
own life seemed in danger.

Of these sentence types, only the complex sentence contains a dependent clause (the subject-verb pair marked with lower-case letters). Dependent clauses occur in four out of the five major sentence functions: as subjects, objects, complements, and modifiers. Since dependent clauses function in so many ways, we can expect complex sentences to come in a variety of forms.

$$
\overbrace{\underset{\text{s} \quad \text{v}}{\text{S}}}^{} \text{V}
$$
With a dependent clause as subject: *Wherever he looked* seemed frightening.

$$
\begin{array}{cc}
\text{S} \quad \text{V} & \overbrace{\underset{\text{s} \quad \text{v}}{\text{O}}}^{}
\end{array}
$$
With a dependent clause as object: He realized *that something large was in the water.*

$$\overbrace{\qquad\qquad}^{\text{C}}$$

With a dependent clause as complement: The apparition became *what he had always*

feared.

With a dependent clause as modifier: The rope *that secured his provisions* was the

only rope left.

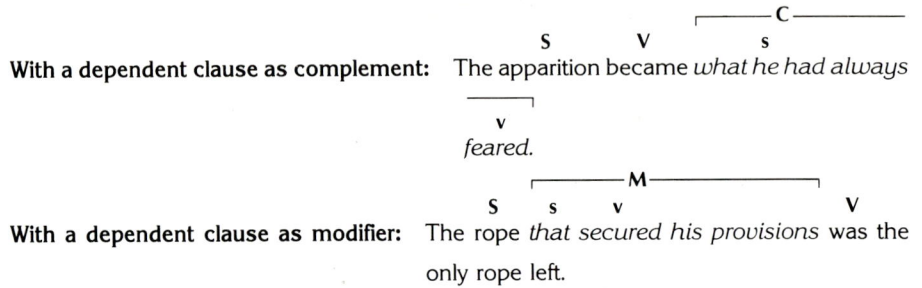

2. Coordination

What happens when a sentence contains more than one independent clause? We can easily write such a sentence:

Sam watched the fin the fish knew that he was there.

But this sentence reads oddly. The words ''the fin the fish'' are confusing because *the fin* and *the fish* belong to different clauses. *The fin* is a part of the first independent clause:

S V
Sam watched the fin

the fish is part of the second independent clause:

S V
the fish knew that he was there

Written without some signal that two independent clauses are present, the sentence must be reread. We might add the word *and* as a signal:

Sam watched the fin and the fish knew that he was there.

The sentence is now easier to read but still not perfect. *Sam watched the fin and the fish* might mean that Sam was watching two things. *And* always joins like to like, so we read the first available word after *and* that looks like the word in front of *and* as the other half of the pair *and* joins together. We will be misled, however, if *and* joins two clauses, as it does here, instead of just two words.

To signal two independent clauses joined in a sentence, you must insert a comma before *and:*

Sam watched the fin, and the fish knew that he was there.

The comma tells the reader that *and* doesn't just join two words; the comma splits *and* from *fin,* so the reader has to assume that *and* is not linking *fin* and *fish,* but two other words, phrases, or clauses. Thus, we join or coordinate an independent clause with another independent clause by using a comma and a coordinating conjunction.

You can also coordinate two independent clauses with a semicolon (;):

Sam watched the fin; the fish knew that he was there.

The semicolon makes the necessary stop signal between paired independent clauses and adds a note of drama: it tells the reader that these independent clauses are close enough in meaning to appear in the same sentence.

The colon (:) can do the same coordinating work and has an air of mystery because it directs attention to what follows it:[1]

Sam watched the fin: the fish knew that he was there.

Coordinating Conjunctions

Coordinating conjunctions join words, phrases, and clauses that have the same sentence function. The list of coordinating conjunctions is small:

and	for	neither . . . nor
or	yet	either . . . or
but	so	

Within the clause, coordinating conjunctions join subject to subject:

  S   S
The sea and *the sky* merged at dusk.

verb to verb:

    V   V
The wind *rose* and *whipped* a cold spray across Sam's face.

object to object:

                 O
His eyes straining against the darkness, Sam could see neither *the tiny lights of the*

      O
shoreline nor *the sweeping beam of the lighthouse.*

---

[1] Chapter 6 contains a more detailed discussion on use of the colon.

complement to complement:

$$\text{C} \qquad\qquad \text{C}$$
The timbers of the boat looked *weathered* but *sound.*

modifier to modifier:

$$\text{M} \qquad\qquad \text{M}$$
Far in the distance but *visible,* a thread of smoke unwound itself on the horizon.

DEFINITION **Coordinating conjunctions signal the sameness of sentence elements: they join words, phrases, or clauses that function in the same way. The words, phrases, or clauses joined by conjunctions are *coordinates.***

Series

DEFINITION **A string of two or more like words, phrases, or clauses is called a series.**

All of the elements in a series have the same sentence function.

$$\text{S} \quad \text{S} \quad \text{S} \qquad \text{S}$$
A series of subjects: *Fog, rain, cold,* and *darkness* had worn Sam down.

$$\text{V}$$
A series of verbs: After hours of pursuit, the dark form of the fish noiselessly *broke* the

$$\text{V} \qquad\qquad \text{V}$$
surface of the water, *rose* beside the boat, *showed* its blunted head,

$$\text{V}$$
and *plunged* once again into the blackness below.

$$\text{C} \quad \text{C} \quad \text{C} \qquad\qquad \text{C}$$
A series of complements: Sam felt *blank, grey, bodiless*—or *mindless:* he could no longer tell which.

$$\text{M} \qquad\qquad \text{M} \qquad\qquad \text{M}$$
A series of modifiers: *In his forearms, in his knees,* and *in his belly,* Sam felt small tremors: under the dark waters he could again see the dark form of the fish.

Exercises 1–2

The Role of the Comma in Series

In a series, the commas tell us that each element belongs on the same string. Commas work like the words *and, but,* and *or.* The commas in a series tell the reader that the elements in the sequence are alike—that they are *coordinates,* words functioning in the same way in the sentence. In the following example, the *coordinates* are marked with the symbol ⌣ :

> *In his forearms* and *in his knees* and *in his belly,* Sam felt small tremors: under the dark waters he could again see the dark form of the fish.

Thus, in the following sentence the comma tells us that the clauses are alike—both are independent:

> Sam watched the fin, and the fish knew that he was there.

But a comma can coordinate independent clauses only when followed by a coordinating conjunction.

3. Parallelism
___

The elements in a series must be alike in *function:* all subjects, all objects, all complements, all modifiers, or all verbs. They must also be alike in *meaning.* And they should be alike in *form,* though the form of the elements in a series may vary. Likeness of *function,* likeness in *meaning,* and likeness of *form* of the elements in a series make up what is called *parallelism.*

Likeness of Function

All of the examples we have seen so far have contained series in which each element functions as the other coordinates in the series do. This means that any one of them could function in place of any other in the sentence. If all are subjects, then any one of them is a subject; if all are objects, then any one of them is an object; and so on. We ought to be able to take out all but one element in any series and find that the one remaining functions exactly as its coordinates did:

<pre>
S   S   S   S
Fog, rain, cold, and darkness had worn Sam down.
</pre>

<pre>
S
Fog <s>rain, cold, and darkness</s> had worn Sam down.
</pre>

S
~~Fog,~~ Rain ~~cold, and darkness~~ had worn Sam down.

S
~~Fog, rain,~~ Cold ~~and darkness~~ had worn Sam down.

S
~~Fog, rain, cold, and~~ Darkness had worn Sam down.

A series that is not parallel is not well formed. If any elements in a series cannot function as the other elements in the series do, the series is not parallel.

S   S   S   M
Wrong: *Fog, rain, cold,* and *when night fell* had worn Sam down.

When night fell can't function as a subject of *had worn,* so it isn't parallel with *fog, rain,* and *cold,* which do.

Likeness of Form

Likeness of function, however, does not necessarily mean likeness of *form,* since each of the major sentence functions occurs in more than one form:

Subject	Verb	Object	Complement	Modifier
word	word	word	word	word
phrase	phrase	phrase	phrase	phrase
clause		clause	clause	clause

It is possible, then, to have a series of sentence elements that *function alike* but that are *not alike in form.* In the following example, all of the elements in the series are modifiers, but one is a phrase, while the others are single words:

Alone, hungry, and *losing hope,* Sam slept fitfully.

There is no single word for *losing hope,* so this modifier differs from the single-word form of the other modifiers. But it is disturbing to read a mixture of forms in a series where parallelism is possible:

word   word   ┌───── clause ──────┐
O   O   O
Wrong: Sam feared *hunger, cold,* and *that he would go mad.*

Hunger, cold, and *that he would go mad* are objects of *feared,* but the series is not well written because the forms of the objects are dissimilar. All of these objects can easily be written in the same form:

Sam feared hunger, cold, and madness.

The following example is similar:

Wrong: *Fog, raining, cold,* and *darkness* had worn Sam down.

The series is not well written because, though all of the words in the series are alike *in function*—each functions as a subject of *had worn*—and though each is a single word, the *forms* are different. The word *raining*, a *verbal*, is unlike the words *fog, cold,* and *darkness*, which are not verbals but nouns. Since *raining* has a noun form, *rain*, that is the form we must use if the series is to be parallel.

Likeness in Meaning

It is logical that the elements in a series should be alike in function and, as far as possible, in form. To be parallel, the elements in series must also be alike in meaning:

Wrong: *In his forearms, in his knees,* and *in the rumbling of his belly,* Sam felt small tremors.

In his forearms and *in his knees* tell *where* Sam felt the tremors. *In the rumbling of his belly* tells both *how and where* Sam felt the tremors. It therefore belongs to a category of meaning the other phrases do not belong to. This phrase is not parallel to the other two. As much as possible, you should try to keep the elements in your series within the same categories of meaning. This revision makes the series parallel:

In his forearms, in his knees, and *in his belly,* Sam felt small tremors.

Exercise 3

The general rule for parallelism is simple: elements in a series must be alike in function and should be as much alike in form and meaning as possible.

4. Comparison

Similar to a series, a comparison relates words or sequences of words to others like them. However, comparisons are built on modifiers—adjectives and adverbs—rather than on conjunctions.

Modifiers and Degree

Adjectives and adverbs are descriptive words: adjectives describe nouns; adverbs describe adjectives, verbs, verb forms, and other adverbs. Adjectives are words like *valiant, cool, amiable, red, broken, repaired, voluptuous;* adverbs are words like *fast, carefully, still, forthrightly, deep* (some of these words can function as adjectives as well). Most descriptive words can be expressed in four degrees: inferior, base, comparative, and superlative.[2]

Adjectives

Inferior	Base	Comparative	Superlative
less	equal	more	most
poor	good	better	best
less attractive	attractive	more attractive	most attractive

Adverbs

Inferior	Base	Comparative	Superlative
slow	fast	faster	fastest
carelessly	carefully	more carefully	most carefully
shallow	deep	deeper	deepest

Comparisons are built on the inferior, base, and comparative forms of adjectives and adverbs:

The meal she served was *as attractive as* she was.

Before Sam came to Thailand, he had never seen a pageant *more exciting than* the Easter Parade.

It is *likelier that Sam will call than* that he won't.

We compare like to like; that is, a noun to a noun, a verb to a verb, a noun clause to a noun clause, and so forth. If the reader can't tell what two expressions are being compared, then the point of the comparison will be lost. The words that signal comparison, *more . . . than, -er . . . than,* and *as . . . as,* divide the elements in the comparison so that you can tell what is being compared to what. In the first sentence of the previous example, *the meal* is compared to *she* in terms of *attractiveness;* in the second, the excitement of *a pageant* is compared to the excitement of *the Easter Parade,* and in the last sentence, the likelihood *that Sam will call* is compared to the likelihood *that he won't.*

As you can see in the last sentence of the example, the full content of the comparison is not always written out. Often part of the comparison is left out because it is "understood":

He is taller than I thought.

Exercises 4–6
In-class writing
1–2

In this example, *He* is not compared to *I.* Rather, *he is* is compared to something like *I thought he would be,* in terms of height.

---

[2]Some students of language argue that certain words are absolute—*perfect* and *dead,* for example—and that comparisons built on these words destroy their meaning: *deadest, more perfect.*

Faulty Comparisons

A sound comparison is true and revealing. Because it hits the nail on the head, a reader can easily see the truth in it. The problem for writers is that sometimes comparisons go astray. They can fail in two ways: some compare apples to oranges, and others are incomplete.

Wrong: This test is harder than when I went to high school.

The noun phrase *this test* is not comparable to the adverb clause *when I went to high school* because nouns can't be compared to adverb clauses. Look at the following revision:

Right: *This test* is harder than *the tests I took* when I went to high school.

Similarly, the following is also a faulty comparison:

Wrong: This test is harder than the English Channel.

Though its terms are both nouns, *the test* and the *English Channel* can't be compared in degree of difficulty without more explanation. We can guess what the writer means:

Right: Passing this test is harder than swimming the English Channel.

But a reader is more likely to notice the botched comparison than to follow what the writer is trying to say.

Incomplete comparisons are equally jarring:

Wrong: Franklin Roosevelt's policies were riskier.

Wrong: Bloomingdale's has better dresses.

Riskier than what? Better than whose? There are no rules governing what can be left out of a comparison and what can't. But the terms you are comparing must be clear. They may be contained in the sentence itself or in the surrounding sentences. As you reread what you've written, carefully state the terms of any comparisons: ask, "than what?" and "as what?" to be sure both terms are there.

Exercises 7–9

5. Proofreading for Faulty Comparisons

1. Find all comparison markers in your writing: *more . . . than, -er . . . than, less . . . than, as . . . as;* and mark these with vertical lines (‖).
2. Check to see that each comparison has two matching terms.
3. Put a plus sign (+) over coordinating conjunctions and check to see that the coordinates match.

Here is a sample of student writing already proofread:

Topic: Chores

Subject: A preferable chore

I know not many people would agree with me, but I prefer taking out the garbage to just

about any other chore in my daily routine. I have several reasons for this. First of all, most

of my other chores are either time consuming or boring or just plain hard. Second of all,

garbage disposal has improved a lot since the first days of my acquaintance with the job.

But let me talk first about what makes garbage pick-up better than washing dishes, better

than washing clothes, and better than what my mother calls "tidying up." After we eat

dinner, it is my job to wash the dishes. This does not just mean washing the dishes. This

means lifting my bloated self up from the table and taking in each and every dish, piece

of silverware, cup and saucer, and glass, and the salt and pepper shakers and the milk

pitcher and the sugar bowl. Then I have to put away the food that even I can't stand to

look at any more. The tops to the plastic dishes that I put this glop in are scarcer than

gold pieces. So it takes time to dig around in the cabinet for them, and when I find all I

need, I still have to wash the dishes. Taking out the garbage takes hours less time than

washing the dishes. Washing my clothes is as great a time consumer as washing the

dishes. First I have to find all my dirty clothes. I leave things under the bed, under my

pillow, hanging in my closet, and in the big hamper in the bathroom with everyone else's.

I have to sort mine out, and then sort them again for fabric and color. This takes hours, and the clothes smell. I can stand the smell of garbage better than the smell of dirty clothes. One is food; the other is me. Last, there is tidying up, the worst of all work. Picking up, hanging up, putting back on shelves, making up, I hate it all. It's more boring than licking envelopes, and it just takes a minute to wreck it. When I had to line the garbage cans with newspaper and spill the slimy mess down the incinerator shaft, these chores were better than the garbage patrol. But since the invention of plastic bags, garbage wins hands down.

Comparisons:

garbage pick-up to washing dishes, washing clothes, and tidying up
tops to gold pieces
taking out the garbage to washing the dishes
washing my clothes to washing the dishes
the smell of garbage to the smell of dirty clothes
tidying up to licking envelopes
these chores to the garbage patrol

Coordinates:

I know, but I prefer
time consuming or boring or hard
garbage disposal has improved. But let me talk
better than washing dishes, better than washing clothes, and better than what my mother calls "tidying up"
lifting and taking
each and every
cup and saucer, and glass, and the salt and pepper shakers and the milk pitcher and the sugar bowl
the tops are scarcer. So it takes time to dig
it takes time to dig, and I still have to wash
under the bed, under my pillow, hanging in my closet, and in the big hamper

to sort <u>and</u> sort

fabric <u>and</u> color

takes hours <u>and</u> the clothes smell

it's more boring, <u>and</u> it just takes a minute to wreck it

had to line <u>and</u> spill

these chores were. <u>But</u> garbage wins

6. Using Grammar for Style

Subordination and coordination are basic writing choices: any group of words is either a part of a sentence or a sentence by itself. Looking over a draft, you have the choice of leaving every sentence as it stands or making some of your sentences parts of other sentences. There are four ways to change a sentence to a sentence part:

1. You can change a verb to a verbal, making that sentence a verbal phrase. Then you put the verbal phrase into another sentence.
2. You can subordinate a sentence by putting a subordinating conjunction in front of it, making it a dependent clause. Then you can put the dependent clause into another sentence.
3. You can subordinate a sentence by changing a noun to a relative pronoun if the same noun appears in a nearby sentence, making the first sentence a relative clause. Then you can put the relative clause within the sentence that contains the noun.
4. You can coordinate one independent clause with another by changing the period to a comma followed by a coordinating conjunction: *,and ,but ,for ,so ,or ,nor* or *,yet.*

We have already seen how the changing of verbs to verbals and the use of subordination can create richer and more precise sentences, sentences that carry purposeful emphasis and transmit sharp pictures. Coordination has the same power.

Make an impression with appositives.   Often you want a word to touch your reader's imagination as you build an idea, or you want to add more meaning to a word. To do this, you can add information right next to it:

Her handbag, *a storehouse of the past,* gets heavier as the months go by.

The additional phrase *a storehouse of the past* is called an *appositive*. Appositives rename other words, giving a particular sense to their meaning. The appositive in the example reveals that the writer means *handbag* as a thing that holds other things, rather than as an accessory. *Storehouse of the past* gives a somewhat abstract meaning to *handbag,* as if the handbag could hold not only old bills, old photos, and old addresses, but also memories. Appositives can rename subjects, verbs, objects, complements, or modifiers:

>   **S**   **appositive**
> Horse racing, *the sport of kings,* is also the sport of cabbies stopping in the betting parlors on their lunch hours.

The appositive and the word *also* add to the sentence a contrast between cabbies and kings.

>   **V**   **appositives**
> Nureyev rotates, *whirls, spins, pirouettes* in the air, as if he were exempt from the law of gravity.

These appositives, each a faster movement than *rotate,* imitate the faster and faster turning of the dancer.

>   **O**   **appositives**
> Quickly they ate the bread, *someone's bounty, a blessing, a miracle.*

Similarly, *bounty, blessing, miracle* in this sentence build in intensity and suggest that as they ate, the people in the sentence grew more and more grateful for or amazed at the gift of bread.

>   **C**   **appositive**
> Dan seemed fearful, *imprisoned by his fantasies.*

Imprisoned by his fantasies carries the sense of fear as a paralyzing emotion and gives the picture of a trapped person.

>   **M**   **appositives**
> Martine, startled, *alarmed, frightened,* ran to the window.

Alarmed and *frightened* intensify the description of Martine's feeling.

Grammatically, appositives are coordinates of the words they add meaning to, and have the same sentence function. Stylistically, the original word provides the basic meaning, and the appositive supplies an impression.

Get an idea across with a simile.   Have you ever had to describe a person to someone who will need to recognize that person when you aren't there? Here's one attempt: ''Well, he's kind of short, and a little stout, with a paunch, you know, and a roundish face . . . and he's bald—in fact he looks like a mushroom! He reminds you of a mushroom!'' After scratching around for a while, this person decided to give up describing each feature and told instead what the stranger's looks *suggested.* Unusual though it was, this description worked: what the stranger suggested to one person, he also suggested to others, and as a mushroom, he was easy to recognize. Poets, good writers, and ordinary people speaking to each other often use odd comparisons to get an idea across:

He took one punch on the chin and went out *like a light.*

Outside it's *as black as a skillet* and as cold.

He kisses *like a fish.*

Like a light, as black as a skillet, and *like a fish* are all special forms of comparison called *similes.* A *simile* is a surprising comparison between unlike things. The surprise is that the comparison works. Good similes seem right even though they are unlikely comparisons, probably because they remind us of things that we've thought but never dwelled on or put into words. Although sometimes odd at first, a good simile describes a likeness we recognize.

To construct a good simile, you must know what you're talking about. Don't write, "Her eyes were like Venetian moonlight," if you've never been to Venice. In fact, stay away from the moon altogether; it's overused. The best material for similes comes from what you and your reader see every day close at hand: not moonlight in Italy, but a bookbag, kitchen chairs, a dresser drawer.

Use parallelism for emphasis.   Teachers warn students not to repeat. "Repet." written in the margin of your paper means you've used the same word or expression several times where you should have found other words. But when you're making a point, repetition can work for emphasis:

Spray paint on the trains, spray paint on the schools, spray paint even on historic landmarks is destroying the face of our city.

The repetition gives a sense of mounting anger. Parallel form works the same way:

When children are sick, mom gets the blame; when kids commit crimes, the parents are to blame; when a marriage breaks up, the couple are to blame: it's dangerous to start a family!

The definitions below will help you to recall the techniques discussed in this section:

DEFINITIONS   **An appositive is a word or expression that renames a word or expression immediately in front of it.**

A simile is an expression that shows a surprising likeness between two unlike things. Like ordinary comparisons, similes use *like* or *as.*

Chapter 5 • Coordination, Parallelism, and Comparison

Exercises

1. The coordinating conjunctions in the following passage are numbered. On the numbered lines following the passage, write the series that the numbered coordinating conjunction coordinates.

A holiday guaranteed to satiate the sweetest of teeth will be celebrated all over India this Saturday with lamp lighting, fireworks, and[1] the exchange of gifts and[2] pastries.

On this day, known as Diwali, or[3] the "festival of lights," Indians welcome Lakshmi, the goddess of wealth and[4] prosperity. All the homes, palaces, and[5] government buildings will be twinkling with thousands of oil-lit clay lamps, and[6] because it is said that the goddess overlooks homes that are dark, even the poorest families display candles.

Diwali heralds the new Hindu year and[7] the approach of winter, so[8] businessmen open new account books, and[9] winter crops are sown.

Indians buy new clothing, clean and[10] paint their houses, and[11] visit one another's homes to exchange good wishes and[12] feast on sweets.

Rosemary Black, "Indian Festival of Lights"

1. _____

2. _____

3. _____

4. _____

5. _____

6. _____

7. _____

8. _____

9. _____

10. _____

11. _____

12. _____

2. Find the coordinating conjunctions in the passage below and number them. Then list the elements in the series for each.

It would be too sad a story, if I were to tell you how Midas, in the fullness of all his gratified desires, began to wring his hands and bemoan himself; and how he could neither bear to look at Marygold, nor yet to look away from her. Except when his eyes were fixed on the image, he could not possibly believe that she was changed to gold. But, stealing another glance, there was the precious little figure, with a yellow tear-drop on its yellow cheek, and a look so piteous and tender, that it seemed as if that very expression must needs soften the gold, and make it flesh again. This, however, could not be. So Midas had only to wring his hands, and to wish that he were the poorest man in the wide world, if the loss of all his wealth might bring back the faintest rose-color to his dear child's face.

Nathaniel Hawthorne, *A Wonder Book*

1. _____

2. _____

3. _____

4. _____

5. _____

6. _____

7. _____

3. Each of the sentences below contains an underlined portion, which is to become the first element in a series. On the lines provided, rewrite the sentence, adding two elements that *function* like the underlined element, that are *logically like* the underlined element, and that are as *like it in form* as possible.

   a. At this moment her daydream vanished <u>abruptly</u>.

   Abruptly is a modifier telling how her daydream vanished. Add two more modifiers telling something about the vanishing.

   _____

   _____

   b. She <u>stopped and looked up</u>.

   Stopped and looked up is a series of verbs telling what she did. Add two more verbs to the series telling what else she did.

   _____

   _____

   c. She stood <u>in a dimly lit street</u>.

   In a dimly lit street is a modifier telling where she stood. Add two more modifiers telling more about where she stood.

   _____

   _____

d. Just above her head hung <u>a peeling metal sign</u> that had once said "Coke."

A peeling metal sign is the subject of *hung,* telling what hung. Add two more subjects for the verb *hung.*

_____

_____

e. She seemed to know <u>the building</u>.

The building is the object of the verb *seemed,* telling what she seemed to know. Add two more objects telling two more things she seemed to know.

_____

_____

f. She was standing outside the little grocery <u>where she had bought the sweet cream</u>.

Where she had bought the sweet cream is a modifier describing the grocery. Add two more modifiers describing *grocery* in this same form.

_____

_____

4. Complete the categories below with the appropriate forms. Note that some forms will require an additional word like *less, more,* or *most.*

Base	*Inferior*	*Comparative*	*Superlative*
dark			
shadowy			
lucid			
rapid			
good			
bad			
some			
deluded			
enthralling			
little			
surly			

Base	Inferior	Comparative	Superlative
strange			
enormous			
special			
able			
culpable			
likely			
homely			
awesome			
awful			
generous			
murky			
weird			
mad			
clearly			
accurately			

5. Find the elements of the comparisons in the sentences below. Write these elements on the lines beneath the sentences. Some parts of the comparison may be unstated in the sentence; state them on the lines below.

a. A chain smoker may have less willpower than a three-year-old.

_____

is compared to

_____

b. But the prospect of not smoking is not so dismal as you may think.

_____

is compared to

_____

c. You will eat rich desserts more appreciatively.

_____

is compared to

_____

    d. You can abstain better among nonsmokers.

    _____

    is compared to

    _____

    e. The smoker is more apt to take a doctor's advice than a relative's.

    _____

    is compared to

    _____

    f. A smoking clinic is more like a school or a business than a home.

    _____

    is compared to

    _____

6. The elements of the comparisons in the sentences above are given below. On the lines beneath them, tell *what* quality the comparison is based on.

    a. The willpower a chain smoker has is compared to the willpower a three-year-old has

    in terms of _____

    b. The real prospect of not smoking is compared to what you may think the prospect is

    in terms of _____

    c. The way you eat rich desserts now is compared to the way you will eat rich desserts

    in terms of _____

    d. How you behave among nonsmokers is compared to how you behave among smokers

    in terms of _____

    e. A smoker's taking advice from a doctor is compared to a smoker's taking advice from a relative

    in terms of _____

    f. A smoking clinic is compared to a school, a business, and a home

    in terms of _____

7. Write sentences comparing the nouns below in terms of the quality given. Use the comparative form of the quality.

    a. your biology text to your math text in terms of clarity

    _____

b. the buyer of stolen goods to the seller of stolen goods in terms of guilt

_____

c. movies to plays in terms of ability to hold your interest

_____

d. a computer to a slide rule in terms of accuracy

_____

e. your enemies to your friends in terms of resemblance to you

_____

f. sleeping to eating in terms of your enjoyment

_____

g. war to peace in your lifetime in terms of likelihood

_____

h. your thoughts to your feelings in terms of speed with which you become aware of them

_____

i. men to women in terms of generosity

_____

j. pets to plants in terms of your pleasure in raising

_____

8. Sentences like the following leave readers hanging. Rewrite the sentences, making the terms of the comparisons clear. Then tell what quality the comparison is based on.

a. We had a longer summer this year because of the strike.

_____

Elements are compared in terms of _____

b. I will have a much better chance of passing the course.

_____

Elements are compared in terms of _____

c. Sam is a more daring fisherman than before.

_____

Elements are compared in terms of _____

d. Sam and Migdalia have a much more secure marriage because they are adults.

_____

Elements are compared in terms of _____

e. Blondes have more fun.

_____

Elements are compared in terms of _____

9. Now proofread your first draft according to the guidelines in this chapter to find coordinated elements and to make sure that the elements in your series and comparisons are parallel.

10. Proofread your draft for sentence fragments and for subject-verb agreement, according to the proofreading guidelines in Chapter 3 and Chapter 4.

In-Class Writing

1. Write a short passage telling a story about the last time you were late. Write a second passage telling of the last time you waited more than fifteen minutes for someone.

   a. Write a sentence telling how you felt when you were late.
   b. Write a sentence telling how you felt when you were kept waiting.
   c. Write a sentence comparing being late to waiting, in terms of how easy each is for you.

   Example: It is |easier| for me to wait for someone |than| to be late myself.

   d. Write sentences comparing being late to waiting in terms of how disturbing each is to you and how frequently each happens to you.
   e. Mark off comparisons with vertical lines.
   f. Check to see that the terms of the comparisons can be compared.
   g. Read your passage to the class.

2. Write a passage about a visit to a creepy place, using the words below. What you should try to get across is what it was *like*.

   damp, faster, gloomier, lower, stony, dark, massive, more, as, longest, shorter, scarier, slippery.

   a. Add vertical lines to mark off the terms of the comparisons.
   b. Write the terms of the comparisons in the margin.
   c. Read your passage to the class.

3. Write a passage telling of a transaction you recently completed in which you traded something you had for something you wanted.

    a. Write five sentences comparing the item you gave away to the item you got.
    b. Add vertical lines to mark off the terms of comparisons.
    c. Write the terms of comparisons in the margin.
    d. Read your passage to the class.

4. Write a catalog of the items in your wallet or purse. Put a plus sign (+) over the coordinating conjunction and a check (√) over each coordinate.

    Example: In my wallet I have my I.D. card, a picture of my brother, my driver's license, small change, and

        four bills.

5. Now write a sentence about each item, telling what it consists of. Put a plus sign over the coordinating conjunction and a check over each coordinate.

    Example: My I.D. card has my picture on it, my name, my address, and my social security number.

6. Now write *one* sentence, combining the information in both catalogs.

    Example:

    In my wallet I have my I.D. card, which has my picture on it, my name, my address, and my social security number; a picture of my brother, which shows him with my dog and my house in the background; my driver's license; small change, which consists of a quarter, four nickels, and seven pennies; and four bills: three dollar bills and a ten-dollar bill.

    a. Use semicolons to punctuate the ''carrier'' series, which names the items themselves.
    b. Put a plus sign over each coordinating conjunction and number it.
    c. Put that number over the items it coordinates.

    Example:

    In my wallet I have my I.D. card, which has my picture on it, my name, my address, and my

    social security number; a picture of my brother, which shows him with my dog and my house

    in the background; my driver's license; small change, which consists of a quarter, four nickels,

    and seven pennies; and four bills: three dollar bills and a ten-dollar bill.

Chapter 5 • Coordination, Parallelism, and Comparison

Exercises for Style

1. Add appositives to the sentences below to create the meanings indicated.

   a. That lock gets stuck all the time.
   (Give *lock* the sense of an obstacle.)

   _____

   b. The Wildcats defeated the Cougars.
   (Give *defeated* the sense of complete victory.)

   _____

   c. My cousin's old motorboat needs a paint job.
   (Give *old* the sense of fragile.)

   _____

   d. I have been elected treasurer.
   (Give *treasurer* the sense of power beyond that of an ordinary treasurer.)

   _____

2. Write a short passage describing a chore you particularly dislike. Then go back through your passage and add appositives that suggest why you dislike it so much.

   Example: Yesterday, *Black Thursday,* I had to change the oil in my car, *the grease beast.*

   Humor is very much in order: try to amuse your readers, and appositives should come easily to mind.

3. Complete the following similes.

   a. The black plague spread over Europe in the fourteenth century like _____,
   killing almost one third of the population.

   b. We prepared the frog for dissection as if _____

   _____.

   c. Painting my room was as easy as _____.

   d. Finding the best energy source is like _____

   _____.

4. a. Write short descriptions of three other students in the class, using at least one simile each.
   b. Read these aloud and see if your classmates can identify the people you've described.
   c. Listen for the best description among all the readings. Write down why you like it. See if your classmates have chosen the same one.

The Comma and Other Forms of Punctuation

6

CAPSULE PREVIEW   Everything you have learned so far about sentence structure tells you that punctuation ought to signal something. When you are writing, though, you don't want to stop to figure out what each scratch and blot means—and you shouldn't. As you write, you put in punctuation because it seems needed. When you finish writing, however, you should try to read what you have written as your readers will. Your readers will need precise punctuation to guide them through your writing, so you must check to see that the marks that ''seemed right'' as you poured out your words truly *are* right. This chapter tells you what the various pieces of punctuation mean and how they work.

Proofreading Techniques

To punctuate accurately, you need to know, first, what the various marks of punctuation mean. Then you should go from mark to mark—from the first piece of punctuation in your paper to the last—and explain to yourself why each one is there. If you can't tell why you've used a certain mark of punctuation, it may be the wrong one, or it may not belong there at all. Examine the punctuation in the following passage and the comments that follow it.

> Last week several things happened to me; on Sunday especially. I moved into my own apartment for the first time in my life, I rented one downtown to be close to stores, and transportation since I don't have a car yet. When I rented it my mother asked me, "Are you sure you're ready to move out. You don't have to. I didn't have to move my parents are happy to have me live with them. But, after I thought about the pros and cons of moving it seemed to be the right thing to do. I can see them when I want to; and do what I want to do too.

Each mark of punctuation is reviewed below.

• *me*;—Semicolons coordinate clauses, but there is only one clause in the sentence.

Take out the semicolon and use a comma instead to tell the reader that *on Sunday especially* belongs to the first part of the sentence.

- *especially.*—The period indicates that an independent clause has been completed at this point.
- *life,*—Commas mark interruption, continuation, and coordination of structures within the sentence, but commas alone do not coordinate independent clauses. Change the comma to a semicolon.
- *stores,*—Only two words, *stores* and *transportation,* are coordinated here. *And* alone does the work. Take out the comma.
- *yet.*—The period follows the independent clause beginning with *I rented.*
- *me,*—The comma introduces a direct quote.
- *"Are*—Quotation marks open a direct quote; there should be another set of quotation marks at the end of the direct quote, after the period following *to.* Put it in.
- *out.*—The period following the independent clause beginning with *are you,* a question, is incorrect. Change the period to a question mark.
- *them.*—The period follows the independent clauses *I didn't have to move* and *my parents are.* There are two independent clauses here. Put in a semicolon after *move* to correct the run-on sentence.
- *But,*—This comma indicates a delay of the clause that *but* belongs to. Put in another comma just before that clause continues, between *moving* and *it.*
- *do.*—The period follows the independent clause *it seemed.*
- *to;*—A semicolon should coordinate two clauses, but there is only one clause here with two verbs, *can see* and (can) *do.* Take out the semicolon.
- *too.*—The period follows the independent clause that contains *I can see and do.*

Giving a strict accounting for each mark helps you to see the structure of your sentences and sometimes alerts you to omitted marks.

Errors

Mistakes in punctuation are like faulty directional signals: they misguide readers. A period at the end of a sentence fragment tells readers that the fragment is a sentence. The absence of a period, semicolon, colon, or comma plus conjunction between independent clauses makes readers think they are reading just one independent clause. Errors in punctuation occur when the writer puts a piece of punctuation where it doesn't belong or leaves it out where it is needed as a guide to the reader. To avoid these errors, writers need to know exactly what each piece of punctuation tells readers.

RULES

A period (.) follows an independent clause.

A question mark (?) follows a question, not a statement.

An exclamation point (!) follows something the writer reacted strongly to.

A colon (:) follows an independent clause and shows that more information about that clause is coming.

A semicolon (;) comes at the end of one independent clause and indicates that another follows in the same sentence, or it separates clauses or phrases in a series within the same sentence.

A comma (,) follows each word or phrase in a series of three or more, or follows a word and its appositive, or precedes and follows an interruption by another expression, or follows a modifier that will be followed by an independent clause or follows an independent clause that will be followed by a modifier.

A dash (—) indicates that the next piece of information is specific and is needed immediately.

Quotation marks (" . . . ") mean that the words between them repeat exactly what someone else said or wrote, or that the word or words have some special meaning.

Writing Assignment: First Draft

Topic: Household chores

Subject: A job worth doing

No household runs itself. Wherever people live, there is work to do to keep the place livable. Describe what happens when an essential task is not done in the place where you live; describe the task; then make a statement about this essential work. (50–100 words)

---

1. Introduction

So far we have studied several sets of words that are keys to the structure of sentences: coordinating conjunctions, subordinating conjunctions, and relative pronouns. Now we can look at other structural signals in sentences—punctuation marks. In general, punctuation alerts the reader that a sentence or a sentence part has come to an end or that it is being briefly interrupted.

2. End Punctuation

Period

A period at the end of a statement signals the completion of at least one independent clause. Beyond this minimum, there is theoretically no limit to the number of clauses, independent or dependent, that a sentence might contain. You only have to remember that the parts of a single sentence should be very closely related in meaning. The reader should not be subjected to very long sentences for no obvious reason. A good writer tries to set up ideas so that they can easily be understood. Sentence fragments and run-on sentences, like those in the following examples, distract readers by raising unnecessary questions:

> The plane landed without notifying the tower and then took off again. Confusing the flight controllers.

> Pilots normally file flight plans and planes are expected to fly plotted routes.

Exercises 1–2

Was it the landing or the take-off or both that confused the flight controllers? Do pilots file flight plans *and* planes? A misplaced period may signal the end of a sentence too early, creating a sentence fragment, or too late, creating a run-on sentence.

Question Mark

The question mark, like the period, must follow at least one independent clause. In some cases, most of the clause may be understood: *Who?* for "who was it?" *Why?* for "why did they do it?" and so forth. Question marks follow *direct questions*, that is, questions written in this pattern:

Auxiliary	Subject	Main Part of Verb
Has	the cell	divided?
(When) will	the subway	be completed?
(Why) has	the ambassador	failed to call?

Question marks do *not* follow *indirect questions. Indirect questions* are statements written in normal subject-verb order: the subject of the verb does not appear between the auxiliary and the rest of the verb:

> We don't know whether the cell has divided.

> No one can tell when the subway will be completed.

> Everyone is wondering why the ambassador has failed to call.

Exclamation Point

Exclamation points may follow whole sentences, but they also may follow single clauses, single phrases, or single words. That is, an exclamation point sometimes does not signal the end of a sentence:

> Our artillery fired on our own troops! and the casualties could not be moved to safer positions.

> The first snowfall! Everything is quiet under the blanket, and all nature is serene.

> Rattlesnakes! Five of them, a family, lay coiled, scarcely moving, on the ledge.

Exclamation points are rare in formal writing because their effect runs counter to the desired tone of carefully structured reasoning. Exclamation points signal sudden emotion or surprise, both of which the essayist creates sparingly. A writer does not want to seem unable to organize sudden impressions into ideas, or to delight in springing surprises on the reader, or to rant and rave in sudden bursts of conviction.

Colon

The colon is not end punctuation for a sentence, but it is for certain independent clauses. The colon sets up an ''as follows'' relationship between an independent clause or a word in it and a modifier or example outside and after the clause:

> The team needed spirit: a sense of working together, a sense that they were good together, a sense of purpose.

> The men at the front were all plagued by the same nightmare: that in the night, while they slept, a veil of poison gas would be flung over them, smothering them in its folds.

The independent clause should be completed *before* the colon, rather than by what follows the colon:

> **Wrong:**   His last wish was: that she marry again.

> **Right:**   His last wish was that she marry again: rejoicing and without regret.

3. Internal Punctuation: Coordination

Semicolon

Semicolons coordinate clauses. Normally, the semicolon stands between two independent clauses:

> The negotiators abandoned the talks; nobody knew when the talks would resume or whether they would at all.

These clauses need not be right next to each other:

> *The negotiators abandoned the talks,* although nothing had been resolved, or perhaps because nothing had been resolved; when the talks would resume, or whether they would at all, *nobody knew.*

Semicolons replace commas in a series when series elements contain commas:

> Everything for the picnic was packed and ready to go: the ham, potato salad, cheese, and bread; the soda, iced tea, and lemonade; the cups, paper plates, napkins, forks, knives, and spoons; the folding chairs, the card table, and the beach umbrella.

Semicolons may also stand between dependent clauses in a series:

> The immigrants knew where they had come from; why they had come; and even when they might return to their homeland.

They may occasionally even stand between long phrases in a series:

> Hoping to find the airport before nightfall; expecting to see the runway lights at any moment; and trying desperately to repair the radio, the pilot and crew suddenly saw the patchwork farms beneath them give way to the suburban hedgerows of rooftops and knew that they were safe.

Whether it stands between independent clauses, between dependent clauses, or between long phrases in series, the semicolon coordinates parallel structures—words, phrases, or clauses that function in the same way and have the same form.

Comma

Commas coordinate words and phrases in series, and, with coordinating conjunctions, coordinate independent clauses:

Words in a series:

The search uncovered bones, jewelry, pottery, and weapons.

All papers are due Monday, May 15, 1977.

We need time, not money.

The address is 16 Washington Place, Astoria, New York.

Phrases in a series:

The same kind of rock can be found in stream beds, in deserts, and under the sea.

We want to live in a warm climate, not in a hothouse.

Independent clauses in a series:

The cotton gin may have set back abolition by half a century, for its invention coincided with the opening up of new land for cultivation and the introduction of hardier strains of cottonseed, and the urge for expansion was tremendous.

Commas also set off appositives, words that rename other words:

The pituitary, a tiny gland located in the head, controls all of the glands in the body.

As a coordinate of the noun it renames, the appositive can switch places with it:

> A tiny gland located in the head, the pituitary, controls all of the glands in the body.

Or, it can replace the noun altogether:

A tiny gland located in the head controls all of the glands in the body.

4. Internal Punctuation: Interruption

Comma

Commas set off expressions that interrupt linked elements, as in the following examples:

Between subject and verb:
Sam, once he dared to open his eyes, *realized* that everything was all right.

Between verb and object:
Sam *realized,* once he dared to open his eyes, *that everything was all right.*

Between subordinator and subordinated clause:
Sam realized *that,* once he opened his eyes, *everything was all right.*

Commas set off words inserted between coordinate clauses:

Sam hoped that everything was all right, and, once he opened his eyes, *he realized that it was.*

5. Internal Punctuation: Delay

Commas may also be used to set off a word, a phrase, or a dependent clause that delays the independent clause. The insertion *once he dared to open his eyes* placed at the head of the sentence would be followed by a comma:

Once he dared to open his eyes, Sam realized that everything was all right.

The comma also sets off delayed modifiers, usually modifiers of the whole clause. In these sentences, the comma tells the reader that the modifier does not modify the word it follows, but something earlier:

He rode his horse in a blizzard that killed the animal.
He rode his horse in a blizzard, killing the animal.

In the first sentence, *that killed the animal* modifies the preceding word, *blizzard,* and so we understand that the blizzard killed the animal. In the second sentence, the comma between *blizzard* and *killing* tells us that the modifier does not modify blizzard, or at least not *blizzard* alone, but something earlier in the sentence. The second sentence says that the fact that he rode his horse in a blizzard killed the horse.

The comma, then, signals three sentence events: *coordination* of similar expressions, *interruption* by an expression inserted between linked elements, and *delay* of the independent clause or of a modifier.

6. Other Punctuation

Dash

A dash or a pair of dashes signals insertion of a word, a phrase, or a clause—even an independent clause—into another structure, much as commas do. But dashes give insertions dramatic emphasis:

> The trout swam upstream to their hatching grounds—they had no choice—and suffocated in the oxygen-poor waters polluted by the chemical plant on the shore.

Insertions between dashes are urgent messages that would be less effective if delayed. Here the independent clause *they had no choice* is inserted in the series *swam upstream and suffocated* in order to explain why the trout had to swim upstream, before the disastrous result is revealed.

Single dashes can provide strong contrastive emphasis, as follows:

> The House Ways and Means Committee proposed to encourage small-car purchases—not to punish large-car owners.

The effect of the same sentence written with a coordinating comma is much weaker:

> The House Ways and Means Committee proposed to encourage small-car purchases, not to punish large-car owners.

Like the exclamation point, however, the dash should be used only to good purpose—not to insert information that can be just as effective if deferred, and not to produce emphasis where none is called for.

Quotation Marks

Quotation marks signal the fact that a word, phrase, clause, sentence, or string of sentences is being included in a passage word for word, just as it was spoken or written elsewhere. When the quotation is itself a sentence or several sentences, it can stand alone, without being a part of a sentence in the passage:

> Then the new President spoke. "Ask not what your country can do for you; ask what you can do for your country."

Or, it may be included in a sentence in the passage:

> Then the new President said, "Ask not what your country can do for you; ask what you can do for your country."

Quotations of words, phrases, and dependent clauses cannot stand alone, but must be included in a sentence in the passage:

> Thomas Jefferson considered it "self-evident that all men are created equal," but he himself held slaves.

Punctuation within quotations.   Punctuation within the body of a quote should be retained as it was in the original, but the capital letter at the beginning of a quoted sentence may be reduced to lower case, and a final period at the end of a quoted sentence or a semicolon at the end of a quoted clause can be reduced to a comma if the sentence containing the quotation resumes at that point:

> Then the new President said, "ask not what your country can do for you; ask what you can do for your country," because he wanted to inspire us all to participate in our well-being as a nation.

Writers sometimes interrupt the quotation to insert their own words. The first part of the quotation then ends in a comma:

> "Ask not what your country can do for you," the new President said, "ask what you can do for your country."

Periods and commas following quotations always fall *inside* quotation marks, whether they are part of the quotation or not:

> When I was a child, every sixth-grader had to memorize at least the rest of the paragraph beginning "Fourscore and seven years ago."

> If you can remember "Fourscore and seven years ago," then you should know when Lincoln delivered the Gettysburg Address.

Question marks that are part of the quotation go inside quotation marks; those that belong to the sentence in which the quotation appears go outside quotation marks:

> What organization makes the bumper sticker that asks "Have you hugged your child today?" as a part of its public service advertising?

> How many sixth-graders today have even heard the words "Fourscore and seven years ago"?

You may choose to omit parts of the sentence or sentences you are quoting from. To signal an omission from a sentence, called an *ellipsis*, use three spaced periods:

Original: Thou hast most traitorously corrupted the youth of the realm in erecting a grammar-school; and whereas, before, our forefathers had no other books but the score and the tally, thou hast caused printing to be used; and, contrary to the king, his crown, and dignity, thou hast built a paper-mill.

Shakespeare, *Henry VI*

With ellipsis: Thou hast most traitorously corrupted the youth of the realm in erecting a grammar-school; and . . . thou hast caused printing to be used; and . . . thou hast built a paper-mill.

If you are quoting two or three sentences and you omit part or all of the second, signal the omission by *four* spaced periods. The first of these four periods is the period ending the first quoted sentence:

Complete quotation: Lincoln wrote: "I am not a Know-Nothing; that is certain. How could I be? How can anyone who abhors the oppression of Negroes be in favor of degrading classes of white people?"

With ellipsis: Lincoln wrote: "I am not a Know-Nothing; that is certain. . . . How can anyone who abhors the oppression of Negroes be in favor of degrading classes of white people?"

Punctuation outside quotations. Quotations of words, phrases, and dependent clauses can be inserted in sentences without any punctuation other than quotation marks around them:

The Monroe Doctrine introduced the concept of "manifest destiny" into American policy.

I hope I am never pushed to wonder whether "to be or not to be."

You can be sure that I will dump him "if he be not fair to me."

Quoted sentences may also be introduced without any punctuation other than quotation marks if the quoted sentence is subordinated in your sentence by a subordinating conjunction or relative pronoun:

Shakespeare may claim *that* "a rose by any other name smells as sweet," but nobody who has ever been stereotyped would agree with him.

If "the paths of glory lead but to the grave," why do people kill to be king?

Otherwise, a quoted sentence is introduced by a verb such as *stated, said, exclaimed, remarked,* and so on, followed by a comma or a colon:

Whoever said, "call me by my chosen name," would have given Shakespeare an argument.

Punctuation of Indirect Statements

You may choose to *report* a statement made or written elsewhere rather than *quote* it. Such a report is called an *indirect statement* because it is *not* a direct quotation. An indirect statement therefore is *not* enclosed in quotation marks:

> The new President says that we should not ask what our country can do for us but what we can do for our country.

In the report of the new President's statement, *you* in the original, referring to the audience of Americans, has become *we* because the writer is speaking as a member of that audience. In a similar change of perspective, you may shift the tense, or time, of the original statement:[1]

> The new President said that we should not ask what our country could do for us but what we could do for our country.

Exercises 3–7
In-class writing
1–3

> Thomas Gray claims that "the paths of glory lead but to the grave."
> Thomas Gray claimed that the paths of glory led but to the grave.

7. Proofreading Techniques

When you proofread for run-on sentences and sentence fragments, you proofread for much of the punctuation discussed here. When you have completed that, you should proofread sentence by sentence to *account for each piece* of punctuation you have written. You should be able to explain the function of each period, comma, semicolon, colon, exclamation point, question mark, dash, and quotation mark that you have used. This will assure you that each piece of punctuation is correct or else alert you to marks you can't explain, so that you can discuss the sentences in question with your instructor.

Here is a passage of student writing already proofread:

Topic: Begging

Subject: An encounter with a beggar

The last time I was asked for money, it took me a while to realize what was happening.

An old man came over to me, and I thought he was just one of those people who

wander the streets of downtown New York babbling to themselves and to anyone else

---

[1] See Chapter 7 for a full discussion of tense.

who will listen. He wasn't dressed in rags, and he wasn't unkempt, but he did walk over to me, a stranger, and start talking as if we had known each other for some time, or even as if he was just picking up the conversation after we had been separated for a few minutes. He was gesturing with his hands, and walking right beside me.

"I have a long way to go home," he said. "I live far away from here."

Then he looked at me, deep into my eyes, as if he expected me to understand something. So I spoke to him: "Where do you live?" I was really getting ready to go away from him, but I didn't want to be openly rude if I didn't have to. He said he lived in Brooklyn.

I said, "Brooklyn. That's a long way. I have a long way to go too. I live in Queens."

"It's a long way," he said. "It's too far to walk." Finally I began to understand. But he wasn't sure I did, so he said, "Subways cost money. Buses too. It's a long way." Then he held out his hand.

By this time we had been talking for a while. I still wanted to leave, but he had made it plain that he needed money, and why. I had too little change to give him the exact fare, so I gave him a dollar. Then I left—fast. I resented the whole thing. Why did he have to pick on me? What if he did this for a living? What if he was just taking me for a ride?

Here are the reasons for the numbered punctuation in the passage:

1. comma for delay of the independent clause *it took*
2. period following independent clause *it took*
3. comma plus *and* coordinating the independent clauses *man came* and *I thought*
4. period following independent clause *I thought*
5. comma plus *and* coordinating the independent clauses *he wasn't dressed* and *he wasn't*
6. comma plus *but* coordinating the independent clauses *he wasn't* and *he did walk and start talking*

7, 8. commas surrounding appositive *a stranger*

9. comma plus *or* coordinating the dependent clauses *as if we had known* and *as if he was picking*
10. period following the independent clause *he did walk and start talking*
11. comma signaling delay of *walking,* the coordinate of *gesturing*
12. period following the independent clause *he was gesturing and walking*

13, 15. quotation marks around direct statement

14. comma following a direct statement within another sentence
16. period following independent clause *he said*

17, 19. quotation marks surrounding direct statement

18. period following independent clause *I live*

20, 21. commas surrounding insertion *deep into my eyes*

22. period following independent clause *he looked*
23. colon following independent clause *I spoke* and introducing a direct statement specifying what was said

24, 26. quotation marks surrounding direct question

25. question mark following direct question
27. comma plus *but* coordinating independent clauses *I was getting* and *I didn't want to be*
28. period following independent clause *I didn't want to be*
29. period following independent clause *he said*
30. comma introducing direct statement

31, 36. quotation marks surrounding direct statement

32. period following sentence understood in conversation: *(You live in) Brooklyn*
33. period following independent clause *that is*
34. period following independent clause *I have*
35. period following independent clause *I live*

37, 39. quotation marks surrounding direct statement

38. comma following direct statement within another sentence
40. period following independent clause *he said*

41, 43. quotation marks surrounding direct statement

42. period following independent clause *it is*
44. period following independent clause *I began to understand*

45. comma plus *so* coordinating independent clauses *he wasn't* and *he said*
46. comma introducing direct statement
47, 51. quotation marks surrounding direct statement
48. period following independent clause *subways cost*
49. period following sentence understood in conversation: *Buses (cost) too*
50. period following independent clause *it is*
52. period following independent clause *he held*
53. period following independent clause *we had been talking*
54. comma plus *but* coordinating independent clauses *I wanted to leave* and *he had made*
55. comma plus *and* coordinating dependent clauses *that he needed money* and *why (he needed money)*
56. period following independent clause *he had made*
57. comma plus *so* coordinating independent clauses *I had* and *I gave*
58. period following independent clause *I gave*
59. dash followed by specifying information
60. period following independent clause *I left*
61. period following independent clause *I resented*
62. question mark following direct question
63. question mark following direct question
64. question mark following direct question

In proofreading your first draft, put a check over each piece of punctuation for which you can state the reason. Put an asterisk over any piece you can't account for and write a question in the margin asking about it.

In-class writing 4

8. Mechanical Forms

Apostrophe

Apostrophes have two functions: to mark *contraction* and *possession*. Use an apostrophe *to replace the missing letter or letters* when two words are contracted together, as in the list of contractions below:

she's	shouldn't	they're	won't	you'd
she'd	they'd	they've	wouldn't	you've
can't	doesn't	hasn't	he's	isn't
couldn't	don't	haven't	I'd	I've
didn't	hadn't	he'd	I'm	needn't

Note that the apostrophe does *not* mark the place where the words are joined (*can't, don't, doesn't*) but is written *where the missing letter or letters* would be (*he'd, I'm, you've*).

Use an apostrophe to mark possession:

Mrs. Bono's cat has kittens.

Mrs. Bono's means "belonging to Mrs. Bono" or "of Mrs. Bono." The apostrophe marking possession always follows the *last letter of the last word* in the expressions "belonging to ———" or "of ———." If you are not sure where to put the apostrophe, put the word in question into the blank:

The bedroom <u>of the children</u>

The children's bedroom

The legacy <u>of Mr. Samuels</u>

Mr. Samuels' legacy

The home <u>of the Samuelses</u>

The Samuelses' home

A champion <u>of the people</u>

The people's champion

Capitalization

Capitalize these words:

1. The first word of a sentence
2. The first word of a verse line:

   Like as the waves make towards the pebbled shore,
   So do our minutes hasten to their end;
   Each changing place with that which goes before,
   In sequent toil all forwards do contend.

3. Given names and titles attached to given names, but not ordinary (common) nouns. Use these paired lists as a guide:

Lower Case	Capital
she	Sarah
he	Luis
a museum	the Louvre
a state	Indiana
a people	Sumerians
a race	Mongolian
a tribe	the Ainu
a language	French
a princess	Princess Anne
an ambassador	Ambassador Young
a dean	Dean Shaughnessy
an archbishop	Archbishop Makarios

Lower Case	Capital
an assemblyman	Assemblyman Baer
a holiday or holy day	the Fourth of July
	Simhat Torah
a religion	Judaism
	Bahai
a region	the North
	the South
	the Middle East
	the Gold Coast

4. Institutions of government:

   the Supreme Court
   the Congress
   the Senate
   the House of Representatives

5. References to a monotheistic deity and to religious texts:

   God
   the Almighty
   the Eternal Spirit
   He, Him, His
   the Bible
   the Talmud
   the Book of Job

6. All words in the titles of works, except articles, conjunctions, prepositions, and the infinitive *to*, unless they are the first or the last word in the title:

   A Farewell to Arms
   To the Lighthouse

Underlining

Underline these elements:

1. foreign words, except those in use in everyday conversation:

   If we use <u>ad hominem</u> arguments, people will not respect our position.

   They formed an ad hoc committee.

2. the titles of books, works of art, and symphonies:

   <u>Totem and Taboo</u>, <u>The Assistant</u>, <u>Native Son</u>, the <u>Mona Lisa</u> the <u>Fifth Symphony</u>

3. the names of periodicals:

The New York Times, Essence, Ms., The Journal of the American Medical Association

and abbreviations of these titles in footnotes and bibliographies:

JAMA, PMLA

Titles of your own papers are *not* underlined or enclosed in quotation marks.

Abbreviation

Don't abbreviate words unless the abbreviation saves your reader from having to read a long formal given name over and over in your composition. You could abbreviate the American Society for the Prevention of Cruelty to Animals, for example, to its acronym, ASPCA, after writing it out in full once.

Abbreviations like *gov't* for *government; U.S.* for *United States; Mon., Tues., Wed.,* and so on for the days of the week; *Jan., Feb.,* and so on for months; *qt., in., ft.;* and other common abbreviations are *not* appropriate for formal composition.

In footnotes and bibliographies, however, dates, places, certain words, and sometimes titles of journals are regularly abbreviated: *ed.* for editor, edited by, and edition; *trans.* for translated by; *comp.* for compiled by; *TLS* for *Times Literary Supplement; MFS* for *Modern Fiction Studies;* and so on.

Numbers

Spell out numbers that can be written in one or two words. Write other numbers as numbers, unless they refer to the same category of things and people as other numbers that must be written out:

ten, eighty-eight, seventy-three

1887, 6¾, 774;

Wrong: The vote was 138 to seventy-seven.

Dates may be written several ways, but use the same form throughout your composition:

August 1970 or August, 1970

Exercise 8   August 3, 1973, or 14 August 1970

Chapter 6 • The Comma and Other Forms of Punctuation

Exercises

1. The periods in the following passage are numbered. On the numbered lines below, list the independent subject-verb pair preceding and following each period.

Experiments with animals, and a few observations on man, indicate that there is a basis of truth in the old wives' tales concerning the effects of the pregnant woman's emotional experiences on some of the characteristics of her child.[1] Many types of stress occurring during pregnancy leave their mark on the unborn child by stimulating the secretion of hormones that migrate across the placental barrier.[2] It has been shown in rats that hormones of the sexual, thyroid, and adrenal glands of the mother have a direct action on the central nervous system of the young and, if they act at a critical time, produce permanent effects on psychophysiological processes.[3] When the male hormone testosterone is injected into pregnant monkeys, the behavior of their female offspring is profoundly altered; although anatomically female, these young animals display activities similar to those of the male offspring.[4] Like the latter they engage in rough and tumble play, and they show little tendency to withdraw from the threats and approaches of others.[5]

Rene Dubos, *So Human an Animal*

1. Preceding independent subject-verb pair: _____

   Subsequent independent subject-verb pair: _____

2. Preceding independent subject-verb pair: _____

   Subsequent independent subject-verb pair: _____

3. Preceding independent subject-verb pair: _____

   Subsequent independent subject-verb pair: _____

4. Preceding independent subject-verb pair: _____

   Subsequent independent subject-verb pair: _____

5. Preceding independent subject-verb pair: _____

2. Read this unpunctuated passage. Put an arrow over all subordinating conjunctions and relative pronouns. Using periods, divide the passage into sentences. Make sure that each sentence contains at least one independent clause. Use commas to coordinate series of words and phrases, and commas followed by coordinating conjunctions to coordinate independent clauses.

Artists and scientists deal with the same world but they differ in their intellectual attitudes and in the techniques that they use to recognize and describe objects persons and events artists focus their attention on private experiences scientists on the generic aspects of nature this difference in attitude is so fundamental that the aspects of the world with which science and art are respectively concerned have little in common even when they are looking at the same plant animal or person artists and scientists become interested in entirely different manifestations of existence and think about different problems the scientist wants to know the components and structures of which the living organism is made the reactions which keep it alive the effects that environmental forces exert on it since he regards knowledge bearing on the elemental structures functions and responses that are common to all forms of life as the most fundamental aspect of reality he tends to minimize the differences between molecule microbe plant animal and man and to select for investigation whatever organism or substance happens to be most suitable for the analytical problem he has in mind

Rene Dubos, *So Human an Animal*

3. Convert the following statements to direct questions.

   a. The cat has a cold.

   _____

   b. One day we will have peace.

   _____

   c. Sarah hopes Sam will call.

   _____

   d. The baby's gift is in the car.

   _____

   e. She did not stop to ask what the trouble was.

   _____

   f. The time is ripe for an analysis of what intellect is.

   _____

   g. I know where I'm going.

   _____

   h. This airline, with thirty years of experience, can show you the best of Yugoslavia.

   _____

   i. A knowledge of the liberal arts is seen as a mark of social class.

   _____

   j. Tissue has its own intelligence: it can distinguish self from nonself.

   _____

k. When Louis stopped to think about it, he realized that he was not destined to become a commercial artist, but that instead he was going to become a cultural anthropologist.

_____

_____

Which of the clauses in the last two questions did you convert to direct question form? Can you tell why?

_____

_____

_____

4. The passage below is a conversation between two characters in Anton Chekhov's play *Uncle Vanya*. Sonya is speaking to Astrov. On a separate sheet, convert the conversation to *indirect* statements in the *present tense*, as if you are overhearing the conversation and reporting it to someone else while it is happening.

Example:

Sonya: You can go on drinking if you don't find it detestable.

Indirect statement: Sonya says that he can go on drinking if he doesn't find it detestable.

Note the change in the pronoun, from *you* in the direct statement, in which Sonya is speaking directly to Astrov, to *he* in the indirect statement, which is only a *report* of what she has said to him.

Sonya: You can go on drinking if you don't find it detestable, but I beg you, don't let my uncle drink. It's bad for him.

Astrov: All right. We won't drink anymore. I'll leave for my place right now. It's all settled and signed. It will be daylight by the time they've finished the harnessing.

Sonya: It's raining. Wait until morning.

Astrov: The storm is going past, we'll just catch the edge of it. I'm going. And please don't ask me to treat your father again. I tell him it's gout, and he says it's rheumatism. I ask him to lie down, he sits up. And today he won't speak to me at all.

Sonya: He's spoiled. Like something to eat?

Astrov: I think so, yes.

Sonya: I love to snack at night. I think we've something left on the sideboard. In his day and age, they say, he was tremendously successful with women, and the ladies simply spoiled him. Here, take some cheese.

5. The passage below records the conversation between Sonya and Astrov as indirect statements. On a separate sheet, convert their conversation to dialogue (direct statements) once again, but this time using quotation marks. More than one sentence may be enclosed within the same set of quotation marks, but everything within quotation marks is spoken by the same speaker.

Example: "It's raining. Wait until morning," Sonya says. Astrov replies, "The storm is going past; we'll just catch the edge of it."

Sonya says that Astrov can go on drinking if he doesn't find it detestable, but she begs him not to let her uncle drink. She claims that it's bad for him. He agrees, saying that they won't drink anymore. He tells her that he will leave for his place right now. He says that it is all settled and signed. And he tells her that it will be daylight before they finish the harnessing. Sonya points out that it is raining. She asks him to wait until morning. Astrov rejoins that the storm is going past; that they will just catch the edge of it. He tells her once again that he is going. And he adds, rather shortly, a request that she not ask him to treat her father again. He says that when he tells her father it's gout, he says that it's rheumatism. He says that when he tells her father to lie down, he sits up, and that today her father wouldn't speak to him at all. She replies that her father is spoiled and asks Astrov if he would like something to eat. He says that he thinks he would. She tells him that she loves to snack at night and says that she thinks that they have something left on the sideboard. Then she says that people say that in her father's day and age he was tremendously successful with women and that the ladies simply spoiled him. Then she offers Astrov some cheese.

6. In the passage below, the author tells in indirect statements what two characters are saying and thinking. Rewrite this passage, putting what the characters say and think into direct statements.

   Example: Harry asked Bill not to get him any coffee unless he already had some in the pot.

   Harry said, "Bill, don't get me any coffee unless you already have some in the pot."

   Bill insisted on showing the writer the first chapter of the novel he had recently begun. Lesser asked him not to just yet, but Bill said it would help him know if he had started off right. He said this was a brand-new book although there were some scenes from the other novel, brought from Mississippi to Harlem, where most of the action would take place. Bill asked Lesser to read the chapter in his presence. He sat in Harry's armchair, wiping his glasses and looking at a newspaper on his knees as the writer, chain-smoking, read on the sofa. Once Harry glanced up and saw Bill sweating profusely. He read quickly, thinking he would lie if he didn't like the chapter.

   Bernard Malamud, *The Tenants*

7. Account for each piece of punctuation numbered in the passage below by telling what its role is in the sentence or in the passage.

   I had all but forgotten that I had been born on a plantation and I was astonished at the ignorance of the children I met! I had been pitying myself for not having books to read? and now I saw children who had never read a book? Their chronic shyness made me seem bold and city-wise, a black mother would try to lure her brood into the room to shake hands with me and they would linger at the jamb of the door, peering at me with one eye, giggling hysterically? At night, seated at a crude table, with a kerosene lamp spluttering at my elbow, I would fill out insurance applications, and a share-cropper family, fresh from laboring in the fields, would stand and gape! Brother Mance would pace the floor, extolling my abilities with pen and paper! Many of the naive black families bought their insurance from us because they felt that they were connecting themselves with something that would make their children "write'n speak lak dat pretty boy from Jackson!"

   Richard Wright, *Black Boy*

8. Now proofread your first draft by numbering each mark of punctuation and giving the reason for each mark on numbered lines at the end of your passage.

In-Class Writing

1. Write a passage telling why you were late for something. Construct two of the sentences in this passage so that you can punctuate them with semicolons; construct one so that you can use a colon. Then write down a reason for each mark of punctuation that you use.

2. Turn to your neighbor. Ask where his or her favorite eating place is and why he or she likes to eat there. Write down the response as an indirect statement.

   Example: Miss Levine said that she likes the Hunan Garden best because . . .

   Write down a reason for each mark of punctuation that you use.

3. Now rewrite the passage above using direct quotation. Write down a reason for each piece of punctuation that you use.

4. Recall the last time you took a strong stand in opposition to a relative. It may have been about an everyday matter—you insisted that the television be turned off during dinner for example—or it may have been about a larger issue—perhaps you insisted that gambling should be legalized.

   a. Write a passage in which you describe the incident, telling what you said and what your relative said, using direct quotations.
   b. Write down a reason for each piece of punctuation that you use.
   c. Read your passage to the class.

Subject-Verb Agreement

7

CAPSULE PREVIEW This chapter deals with verb *tense*. By their tense, verbs tell *when* events happen—in the past, in the present, or in the future. A present tense verb also tells one thing more: whether or not its subject is third person singular—a "he," a "she," or an "it." When the subject of a present tense verb is a "he," a "she," or an "it," the verb or its auxiliary ends in -*s*.

Many dialects of English omit this -*s* from present tense verbs with third person singular subjects. Other dialects add it to present tense verbs with subjects other than third person singular. Either way is nonstandard and creates what is called a *subject-verb agreement error:*

> Every day the bus come late. No matter how early people gets to the stop, they has to wait. In bad weather, it seem like we waits longer.

The errors show a certain consistency: singular subjects add no -*s* to the verb; plural subjects add an -*s*. Standard English doesn't work that way, however, and readers of standard English quickly note the error.

Proofreading Techniques

To be certain that the verbs agree with the subjects in what you write, find each verb, and find its subject; decide whether the verb is present tense and whether the subject is a "he," a "she," or an "it."

3 sing. pres.

Every day the bus come late.

This verb is in the present tense and has a third person singular subject. The verb should end in -*s*; change it to *comes*.

plu. pres.   **plu. pres.**

No matter how early people gets to the stop, they has to wait.

People and *they* are plural subjects, so these present tense verbs should *not* end in -*s*. Change them to *get* and *have*.

> 3 sing. pres.   plu. pres.
> In bad weather, it seem like we waits longer.

It is singular, so this present tense verb should end in -*s*. Change the verb to *seems*. *We* is plural, so its present tense verb should *not* end in -*s*. Change it to *wait*.

Searching your writing for present tense verbs and then labelling them shows you where they are; finding the subjects of these verbs and then noting third person singular ones tells you which of your verbs should end in -*s*.

This chapter tells you how to identify present tense verbs and third person singular subjects.

DEFINITIONS

In active voice, the performer of the verb is the subject of the verb.

In passive voice, the performer of the verb is *not* the subject of the verb.

A direct object is a word or expression that receives the action of the verb, the thing acted upon by the verb.

An indirect object is a word or expression that partakes of the action of the verb but is not a direct recipient of the action of the verb.

The historical present is the present tense used to express past events.

Error: Subject and Verb Don't Agree

Sometimes writers omit the final -*s* on present tense verbs with ''he,'' ''she,'' or ''it'' subjects:

>   S   V   S   V
> Whenever Ann get paid, she save some of her salary.

>   S   V
> Now Arnold have made enough to start his own business.

RULE

When a verb is in the present tense, and the subject is third person singular—a "he," a "she," or an "it"—the verb or its auxiliary must end in -s.

Revision

Whenever Ann gets paid, she saves some of her salary.

Now Arnold has made enough to start his own business.

Writing Assignment: First Draft

Topic: Habit

Subject: The rut my mother (father, sister, brother, or friend) is in

Describe the person's routine, in detail, as it happens every day. Don't give your own thoughts about this routine, or about routines in general, until you've made your reader see the person you're writing about acting out the routine. (50–100 words)

---

1. More About Subjects

To check to see that your subjects and verbs agree, you must be able to (1) tell whether the subject you find is in fact a subject and (2) tell whether it's singular or plural. What kinds of expressions can be subjects?

A Word Can Be a Subject

Can any kind of word be a subject? Look at this set of words:

beauty	beautifully
to beautify	beautified
beautiful	beautifying
beautification	

Now try them as subjects:

Beauty takes time.

To beautify a home takes time.

Beautiful takes time

Beautification takes time.

Beautifully takes time

Beautified takes time

Beautifying a home takes time.

Beautiful and *beautifully,* both modifiers, don't work as subjects. Neither does *beautified,* a whole verb. The words that do function as subjects are words that *name:*

Beauty names the attribute.
To beautify names the process.

Beautification names the process.
Beautifying names the process in progress.

These words are *nouns*. Can any other words function as subjects?

This takes time.	A takes time
What takes time?	The takes time
It takes time.	And takes time
	In takes time

This, what, and *it* all function as subjects. They aren't nouns themselves, but clearly they stand for nouns. They are *pronouns.*[1]

This (courtship) takes time.

What (documentation) takes time?

It (giving birth) takes time.

A, the, and, and *in* are not nouns, nor do they stand for nouns. None of these words can function as a subject. Words that name or stand for names *can* function as subjects; whole verbs, modifiers, articles—*a, an* and *the*—conjunctions—*and, but,* and *or*—and prepositions—*in, above, around, from, to, for, on, at, with, by* and so on—cannot function as subjects.

A Phrase Can Be a Subject

Like words that name, phrases that name (*noun phrases*) can function as subjects. Whole verb phrases and modifying phrases (which include prepositional phrases) cannot.

Right:

Even short-lived, superficial beauty takes time to create.

For newlyweds to beautify a home takes time.

Nationwide beautification of parks takes time.

Tastefully beautifying a home takes time.

Wrong:

Beautiful as a picture takes time (modifying phrase)

Beautifully ever after takes time (modifying phrase)

Has been beautified takes time (verb phrase)

For a price takes time (prepositional phrase)

---

[1] See Chapter 10 for a full discussion of pronouns.

A Clause Can Be a Subject

You will recall that a clause is a group of words containing a subject and a verb. When a clause does not stand alone as a sentence, but instead functions as a *part* of another sentence, it is called a dependent clause. Dependent clauses that name can function as subjects, while dependent clauses that modify cannot.

Dependent Clauses That Name:

Whoever he chose made him happy.
Whatever he chose made him happy.
Whichever he chose made him happy.
That he had chosen made him happy.
Whether he chose or not made no difference.
What he chose made him happy.

Dependent Clauses That Modify:

Whom he chose	Since he chose	As if he chose
Which he chose	Until he chose	As though he chose
How he chose	Unless he chose	So that he chose
When he chose	Provided that he chose	While he chose
Why he chose	Although he chose	As he chose
Where he chose	Though he chose	Once he chose
After he chose	Because he chose	Than he chose
Before he chose	If he chose	

Words, phrases, and dependent clauses that name or stand for names can function as subjects, but whole verbs and words, phrases, and dependent clauses that modify cannot.

Exercises 1–3

2. Nouns

DEFINITIONS

A noun is any word, phrase, or dependent clause that names and that can function as a subject.

A gerund is the *-ing* form of the verb functioning as a noun.

A pronoun is a word that stands for a noun.

A noun clause is a dependent clause that functions as a subject or an object.

beauty, beautification	noun
to beautify	infinitive
beautifying	gerund
it	pronoun
whatever he chose	noun clause

Number: Singular and Plural Nouns

Many nouns, though not all, can name a thing in two ways: as a single item— a *singular* noun—or as more than one of a thing—a *plural* noun. The singleness or plurality of a noun is called its *number*.

Generally, the existence of singular and plural forms of a noun means that the thing named can be counted, that more than one such thing exists or can be imagined.

The ending *-en* marks the plural for a few nouns: *men, women, children, oxen, brethren,* for example. A few nouns have unique plural forms: *dice, feet, teeth,* for example; a few nouns have no distinct plural form: *sheep* and *deer* for example; both mean one as well as more than one of the animal. A few nouns have two plural forms, the singular form and the form ending in *-es: fish, fishes; buffalo, buffaloes*. The plural marker for most nouns, however, is *-s*.

This variety of plural endings can cause confusion, especially in the heat of composition. Unfortunately, no rules govern these forms; still worse, the problem of number doesn't end here, for a large number of nouns have plural meaning without plural endings.

Mass and Abstract Nouns.   One group of nouns, called *mass nouns,* names things that cannot be counted: *flour, sugar, water, humanity, mankind. Abstract nouns* name qualities and phenomena, which are also noncountable: *beauty, truth, reason, fear, bravery, grace, light, freedom, generosity, gravity, heat, cold,* and so forth. Mass and abstract nouns are considered *singular*.

Some of these mass and abstract nouns, however, have plural forms:

Small infants may be allergic to certain sugars.

"We hold these truths to be self-evident. . . ."

In their plural forms, these words aren't mass or abstract nouns anymore. They name countable things. *Certain sugars* refers to different kinds of sugars, and these kinds of sugars can be counted. *These truths* refers to the several separate truths Jefferson goes on to list.

Conversely, many nouns that form plurals normally with *-s* and are countable can be used, as mass and abstract nouns are used, to name the thing generally:

Countable	Noncountable (mass and abstract meaning)
Harry's debts mounted.	Harry is in debt.
Sue brought a quail home.	Quail is in season.
A selection of fine wines appears on the menu.	Bring wine when you come.

Collective Nouns.   A smaller group of nouns, called *collective nouns,* can mean more than one of the item they name even though they do not have plural endings: *people, committee, both, family, clergy, staff.*

The clergy in this parish have taken a vow of poverty.

Both need money.

Collective nouns are usually plural, but when the meaning "each and every one of them" is intended, some collective nouns can be singular:

(Each member of) The committee wants to vote again.

(Each member of) The staff needs a vacation.

Exercises 4–8 To sum up: mass and abstract nouns—things you can't count—are usually singular; collective nouns—which do not have plural endings—are usually plural.

3. Noun Modifiers

Even when a noun is clearly singular—*a tooth*—it may be modified by a phrase containing a plural form—*a tooth full of cavities*—and then accidentally treated as if it were a plural:

Wrong: A tooth full of cavities are more painful to fill than to pull.

Of cavities is a *prepositional phrase,* a modifier composed of a preposition followed by a noun. The question of number often arises with a noun modified by a prepositional phrase because the prepositional phrase introduces a second noun that may be singular or plural:

a house of cards

parking for trucks

some word about the troops

the field along the river banks

the action behind the scenes

the development over the next four years

a problem within our schools

Prepositional phrases even form chains of modifiers: the noun in one prepositional phrase is modified by another prepositional phrase:

a discussion in the privacy of the State Department offices

the meat between the slices of bread

a guide to the roadways of Paris

The prepositional phrase does not affect the number of the noun it modifies, however.[2] In spite of the plural nouns in these prepositional phrases, the nouns being modified are all singular. Thus, when a subject is modified by a prepositional phrase, look at the *subject itself*, not the modifier, to tell whether it is singular or plural.

4. Subject-Verb Agreement

In standard English verbs may also express number. This happens only when the verb is in present tense and only with one kind of subject, a singular noun in the third person, that is, a noun which refers neither to "I" (first person singular) nor "you" (second person singular), but is any word, phrase, or clause that can be understood as a "he," a "she," or an "it." Any whole verb in the present tense whose subject is third person singular has a final -s (sometimes -es) on the verb or on the first auxiliary of the verb phrase.

Present Tense

Active Voice

simple	he, she, it forgets
perfect	he, she, it has forgotten
simple progressive	he, she, it is forgetting
perfect progressive	he, she, it has been forgetting

Passive Voice

simple	he, she, it is forgotten
perfect	he, she, it has been forgotten
simple progressive	he, she, it is being forgotten
perfect progressive	he, she, it has been being forgotten

Whenever the subject is a third person singular noun—a "he," a "she," or an "it"—noun phrase, or noun clause, and the verb is present tense, the verb or the first auxiliary of the verb phrase ends in -s or -es:

Noun: Sam gets into more fights than conversations.

Noun phrase: The boy carrying that girl's books has been known to fall in love at the drop of a hat.

Noun clause: It has been true for some time that the boys in that family go on to college but the girls do not.

---

[2] There are exceptions: A number of children cry when their mothers leave them. In this sentence, *a number of children* is treated as plural.

Only present tense verbs whose subjects are third person singular end in *-s* or *-es* or have auxiliaries ending in *-s* or *-es*, with these exceptions:

he, she, it wa<u>s</u> (past tense)

I wa<u>s</u> (past tense)

When final *-s* or *-es* is added to present tense verbs whose subjects are third person singular, subject and verb are said to *agree*. Failure to add *-s* or *-es* to a present tense verb or auxiliary whose subject is third person singular creates a *subject-verb agreement error*.

5. The Meanings of Present Tense

To proofread for subject-verb agreement, you must be able to tell when a verb is in the present tense. To do that, you must know what present tense means.

Present tense does not only mean something happening this instant:

```
S           V
```
She always forgets the nice things I've done for her.

```
        S           V
```
The manuscript has been lost for many years now.

```
S    V
```
Irwin flies to California in four days.

In the first sentence, the forgetting happens "always" or at least regularly; in the second sentence, the loss happened many years ago, and the manuscript is still lost; in the last sentence, the flying has not yet happened. The tense that means "right now" is called the progressive present:

```
S     V
```
She is leaving home.

The verb in the example may also be read as an intended rather than a current event. However, for all present tense forms, "now" is a common reference point:

He knows when to keep his mouth shut (now, always, sometimes).

He has forgotten when to keep his mouth shut (now, by now, as of now).

He is forgetting when to keep his mouth shut (now, as of now).

He has been forgetting when to keep his mouth shut (up until now).

The problem is forgotten (now, as of now).

The problem is being forgotten (right now).

The problem has been being forgotten (for some time now).

Exercises 9–12
In-class writing
1–2

To tell whether a verb is present tense or not, you must decide whether it fits any of the meanings of the present tense. Ask yourself: Does the verb show that something happens now, always, or sometimes? by now, as of now, up until now, right now, for some time now? or does the verb mean that the event could happen now or in the immediate future?

6. Proofreading Techniques

To proofread for subject-verb agreement:

1. Find the verbs in each sentence and underline each twice.
2. Find the subject of each verb and draw an overline between subject and verb.
3. Determine whether each subject is singular or plural.
4. If a subject is third person singular, decide whether the verb is present tense or not. If it is, the verb or its first auxiliary must end in -s or -es.

Here is a sample of student writing already proofread:

Topic: Obedience

Subject: Obeying parents

I remember the last time my father gave me an order as if it were happening right now.

3 sing. pres.

We are all sitting down at breakfast. I think I am reading. My father is pretending to read,

3 sing. pres.   pres.   3 sing. pres.

but he is really very annoyed and doesn't know how to open up the subject. He doesn't

3 sing. pres.

want to seem petty, even though he is. I feel him looking over at me and holding himself

3 sing. pres.   3 sing. pres.

in at the same time. He looks at the food on his plate but he doesn't touch it because

3 sing. pres.   3 sing. pres.

he is too full of his rage. He is making little annoying noises, picking up his spoon and

tapping his plate, unfolding his paper, then folding it back again, pushing his cup and

                                                                        3 sing.   pres.

saucer back and forth across some spilt sugar. Finally my mother looks up from her plate,

    3 sing. pres.   pres.   3 sing. pres.   3 sing. pres.

which she has almost polished off, and asks him, "What's the matter?" I look up and he's

                                                    3 sing. pres.

looking straight at me. I decide to begin, because he looks like he will start to turn red

                                3 sing.   pres.   3 sing. pres.

from the pressure any minute. That makes me all the more casual. "It's my friend, Ma,"

                            3 sing. pres.
                                                      (you)

I say, and before I say anything else, he's bellowing, "Get him out of this house! You get

                    3 sing. pres.

him out of this house *today!* This is not a boardinghouse!" My friend Charles had been

staying with us because he'd left home, but he hadn't found an apartment. He'd been

                                        3 sing. pres.

sleeping on the floor of my room for four days. But Charlie is a responsible guy, and my

                                                                                3 sing.

father knew it. What he resented was Charlie getting something for nothing. My father

pres.

hates for things to come easily to anybody. When he said that, Charles came into the

room and announced that he would be leaving that morning because he had found an

apartment. Out of the blue, I said I was going to move in with him. I did, and now, because

                            3 sing.   pres.

I am on my own, my father doesn't give me orders at all. You owe obedience only when

Exercise 13
In-class writing
3–4

you don't support yourself.

Chapter 7   Subject-Verb Agreement

Exercises

1. Write five sentences with single-word subjects.

2. Write five sentences with phrases as subjects.

3. Write five sentences with clauses as subjects.

4. Read the following sentences and decide whether the underlined noun in each is *mass* or *abstract* or *countable*. Put your answer in the margin next to the sentence.

_____ a. In his speech before Congress, the President urged moderate spending.

_____ b. Speech seems to be a uniquely human ability.

_____ c. Tom's speaking out last night was a mistake.

_____ d. Speaking out is the duty of responsible people.

_____ e. To speak out is the duty of responsible people.

_____ f. Agreement has been reached on this proposal.

_____ g. An agreement has been reached on this proposal.

_____ h. Agreeing with you is sometimes possible.

_____ i. The thought of the Greeks underlies Western civilization.

_____ j. The thought for today is ''give generously.''

_____ k. The Romans respected the thinking of the Greeks.

_____ l. Sarah loves doing good for her fellow man.

_____ m. The kids are planning big doings at the Center this week.

_____ n. Philip is a help to me.

_____ o. Help is on the way.

_____ p. The furniture is on the way.

_____ q. Give me a helping of the strawberry mousse.

_____ r. He gave a speech about helping others.

_____ s. She gave me a kiss for helping her to move.

_____ t. Learning a language by reading it is best.

_____ u. The candidate's learning was impressive.

_____ v. The deed is done.

_____ w. Sheila's idea became <u>the basis</u> of the plan.

_____ x. A penny for your <u>thoughts</u>.

_____ y. There is <u>a lesson</u> in all this.

5. On the lines below, justify your answers to question 4: for example, "This noun is a *mass noun* in this sentence because it names something that is noncountable"; or ". . . is an *abstract noun* because it names action or a quality of some kind"; or ". . . is a *countable noun* because we can insolate distinct items."

a. speech: _____

b. speech: _____

c. speaking out: _____

d. speaking out: _____

e. to speak out: _____

f. agreement: _____

g. an agreement: _____

h. agreeing: _____

i. the thought: _____

j. the thought: _____

k. the thinking: _____

l. doing: _____

m. doings: _____

n. a help: _____

o. help: _____

p. the furniture: _____

q. a helping: _____

r. helping: _____

s. helping: _____

t. learning _____

u. learning: _____

v. deed: _____

w. the basis: _____

x. thoughts: _____

y. a lesson: _____

6. Read the passage below and, on the lines beneath it, identify each noun as either mass, abstract, collective, or countable, and tell why it is.

The American farmer's boy is the descendant of Founding Fathers who themselves were rebel sons. They had refused to hide behind any crown or cross. They were heirs of a reformation, a renaissance, the emergence of nationalism and of revolutionary individualism. They had before them a new continent which had not been their motherland and which had never been governed by crowned or ordained fathers. This fact permitted an exploitation of the continent which was crudely masculine, rudely exuberant, and, but for its women, anarchic. The Americans have, if any people has, fulfilled Chekhov's dream. They have made conquered earth comfortable and machinery almost pleasant, to the ambivalent envy of the rest of the world. Protestantism, individualism, and the frontier together created an identity of individual initiative which in industrialization found its natural medium.

Erik Erikson, *Childhood and Society*

reformation: _____

renaissance: _____

emergence: _____

nationalism: _____

individualism: _____

Americans: _____

people: _____

earth: _____

machinery: _____

envy: _____

rest: _____

world: _____

Protestantism: _____

individualism: _____

frontier: _____

identity: _____

initiative: _____

industrialization: _____

medium: _____

7. The nouns listed below are abstract in the passage above. Write sentences next to each of these in which these nouns are countable.

nationalism: _____

initiative: _____

8. Read the passage below and then find and underline each verb twice, each subject once. Draw overlines between subject and verb. Then mark each subject singular or plural by writing *sing.* or *plu.* over it.

Watch a baby at the creeping stage when his mother is washing the dishes. He plays contentedly with some pots and pans for a while. Then he gets a little bored and decides to explore in the dining room. He creeps around under the furniture there, picking up little pieces of dust and tasting them, carefully climbing to his feet to reach the handle of a drawer. After a while he seems to feel the need of company again, for he suddenly scrambles back into the kitchen. At one time you see his urge for independence getting the upper hand, at another the need for security. He satisfies each in turn. As the months go by he becomes more bold and daring in his experiments and explorations. He still needs his mother, but not so often. He is building his own independence, but part of the courage comes from knowing he can get security when he feels he needs it.

I am making the point that independence comes from security as well as from freedom, because a few people get it twisted around backward. They try to "train" independence into a child by keeping him in a room by himself for long periods even though he is crying for company. I think that when the issue is being forced this hard, a child is not learning anything very good.

Benjamin Spock, *Baby and Child Care*

9. Identify the tense—simple, perfect, or progressive present—of each of these verbs taken from the passage above. Use the chart on page 154.

watch: _____

is washing: _____

plays: _____

gets: _____

decides to explore: _____

creeps: _____

seems to feel: _____

scrambles: _____

see: _____

satisfies: _____

go: _____

becomes: _____

needs: _____

is building: _____

comes: _____

feels: _____

needs: _____

am making: _____

comes: _____

get: _____

try to ''train'': _____

is crying: _____

think: _____

is being forced: _____

is not learning: _____

10. The following verbs from the passage above do not end in -*s*, though they are in the present tense. Next to each, explain why.

watch: _____

see: _____

go: _____

get: _____

try to ''train'': _____

think: _____

11. These verbs, taken from the passage above, are all present tense. Write the meaning that the verb has in the passage on the line next to it: tell whether it means that the event happens now, always, or sometimes; by now, as of now, up until now, right now, for some time now; or that the event could happen now or in the immediate future.

watch: _____

is washing: _____

plays: _____

gets: _____

decides to explore: _____

creeps: _____

seems to feel: _____

scrambles: _____

see: _____

satisfies: _____

go: _____

becomes: _____

needs: _____

is building: _____

comes: _____

feels: _____

needs: _____

am making: _____

comes: _____

get: _____

try to "train": _____

is crying: _____

think: _____

is being forced: _____

is not learning: _____

12. The passage below is written in the past tense. Cross out the underlined verbs and write present tense forms above them, so that the events are represented as happening before your eyes. Then find the

subject of each verb, underline it once, and draw an overline from it to the verb or verbs of which it is the subject. See that present tense verbs whose subjects are third person singular end in -*s*.

The dentist crossed the city, going back to the music store. It was a little after eleven o'clock. The night was moonless, filled with a gray blur of faint light that seemed to come from all quarters of the horizon at once. From time to time there were sudden explosions of a southeast wind at the street corners. McTeague went on, slanting his head against the gusts to keep his cap from blowing off, carrying the sack close to his side. Once he looked critically at the sky.

"I bet it'll rain tomorrow," he muttered, "if this wind works round to the south."

Once in his little den behind the music store, he washed his hands and forearms and put on his working clothes, blue overalls and a jumper, over cheap trousers and vest. Then he got together his small belongings—an old campaign hat, a pair of boots, a tin of tobacco, and a pinchbeck bracelet which ... he believed to be valuable. He stripped his blanket from his bed and rolled up in it all these objects, together with the canvas sack, fastening the roll with a half hitch such as miners use, the instincts of the old-time boy coming back to him in his present confusion of mind. He changed his pipe and his knife—a huge jack-knife with a yellow bone handle—to the pockets of his overalls.

Frank Norris, McTeague

Note: Two aspects of this change in tense are important. The first is that the verbals do not change. You'll learn more about why they don't in a later chapter. The second is that the verbs in the quoted statement do not change. The quotation marks mean that the statement is written exactly as spoken.

13. Now proofread your first draft to make sure that you have followed the rule that when the verb is present tense and the subject is third person singular—a *he*, a *she*, or an *it*—the verb or its auxiliary must end in -*s*.

In-Class Writing

1. Write a passage telling what you usually do from the time you leave your last class of the week until you go to bed.

   a. Underline verbs twice, subjects once.
   b. Draw overlines between subject and verb.

2. Rewrite the passage above as if you were someone else, changing *I* to *he* or *she*.

   Example: pres.
   I leave my physics class and walk to the bus stop at the college gate.

   pres.
   She leaves her physics class and walks to the bus stop at the college gate.

a. Underline verbs twice, subjects once. Draw overlines between subject and verb.
b. Label each present tense verb. Check to see whether the subject is third person singular or not. Make sure that all present tense verbs or their auxiliaries whose subjects are third person singular end in -s.

3. Write a passage in which you tell how you prepare your breakfast each morning. Underline verbs twice, subjects once. Draw overlines between subject and verb.

4. Rewrite the passage above, changing your first person *I* to third person *he* or *she*. Change the verbs to agree with their subjects.

5. Write a passage using the following verbs *in these forms: drinks, washes, think, carries, watch, expects, hope, wins, congratulate.*

a. Underline verbs twice, subjects once. Draw overlines between subject and verb.
b. Label present tense verbs. Check their subjects. Make sure that all present tense verbs or their auxiliaries whose subjects are third person singular end in -s.

6. Write a passage depicting the ordinary furniture in your classroom suddenly doing odd things before your eyes.

Example:

The blackboard is turning yellow and melting onto the floor. The teacher's desk is expanding like a balloon with him sitting on top of it. The doorway is stretching to the ceiling, getting narrower as it does.

a. Underline verbs twice, subjects once. Draw overlines between subject and verb.
b. Label present tense verbs. Check their subjects. Make sure that all present tense verbs or their auxiliaries whose subjects are third person singular end in -s.
c. Read your passage to the class, emphasizing the endings on your words.

Verb Tense and Voice

8

CAPSULE PREVIEW   In this chapter you will see that verbs give three kinds of information: they tell *what* happens, *when* it happens (tense), and *whether* or not the action is performed by the subject (voice). Here you will find the tenses listed and defined, so that you can check your writing to see that the tenses of your verbs carry the meanings you intend.

In any piece of writing, once you establish a specific tense, a time frame, you may have reason to move out of it and into a new tense. If, however, you are not careful to match the tenses of your verbs to your intended meanings, you may confuse your reader:

> As the hours passed, certain strange things begin to happen. A bad smell had started to come up from the basement; the furnace pipes start to knock; and the doors of the kitchen cabinets shook open.

Proofreading Techniques

To catch and correct tense shift errors like those in the preceding example, you must be able to *name the tense* of your verb; *tell what the tense means;* and *tell how the tense matches* your meaning:

           simple past   **simple pres.**   **perfect**

As the hours passed, certain strange things begin to happen. A bad smell had

   past   **simple pres.**

started to come up from the basement; the furnace pipes start to knock; and the doors

                  simple past

of the kitchen cabinets shook open.

passed—simple past tense because these events happened in the past.

begin—simple present. Does not fit the time set by the preceding verb; change to simple past tense, *began*.

had started—perfect past. Does not fit because it means the starting up happened before "things began to happen." Change to simple past, *started*.

start—present. Does not fit the past time set for these events; change to simple past, *started*.

shook—simple past; fits the time set for these events.

You can catch and correct errors in tense by accounting for the tenses used. This chapter tells you what the various tenses mean.

Error: Tense Shift

Tense indicates time. An error in tense, therefore, indicates the wrong time. The first verb you use in your writing sets the time of the events you are describing. Your reader expects you to continue in that time, unless there is a good reason for changing it. Sometimes, though, in the heat of composition writers skip out of the tense they've been using for no apparent reason:

>   **past tense**   **past tense**   **past tense**   **past tense**
> Stephen <u>went</u> into the kitchen. He <u>knew</u> his mother <u>would be</u> home any minute. He <u>heard</u>
>
>   **present tense**   **present tense**
> her key in the door. Then he <u>rushes</u> to the refrigerator, <u>takes</u> out an ice cream bar, and
>
>   **present tense**
> <u>downs</u> it in three bites.

RULE   **Don't shift tense unless you have a reason.**

Revision

>   **past tense**   **past tense**   **past tense**   **past tense**
> Stephen <u>went</u> into the kitchen. He <u>knew</u> his mother <u>would be</u> home any minute. He <u>heard</u>
>
>   **past tense**   **past tense**
> her key in the door. Then he <u>rushed</u> to the refrigerator, <u>took</u> out an ice cream bar, and
>
>   **past tense**
> <u>downed</u> it in three bites.

1. Introduction

We saw in Chapter 3 that verbs state action or information; that they do not function as subjects, objects, or modifiers; and that they have *tense*. Tense tells *when* the action takes

---

Writing Assignment: First Draft

Topic: Pleasure

Subject: A treat at age ten; a treat some years later

As we grow our notions of pleasure change. Try to remember a treat you looked forward to when you were ten. Then summon up the greatest treat you can think of now. Describe what thrilled you when you were ten; then describe what pleases you most today and make a statement about pleasure. (50–100 words)

---

place or *when* the information was given. We ordinarily think of verbs as past, present, or future, but verbs also express subtler distinctions. We have already seen that the present tense does not simply mean right now. Look at the complete list of tenses below and try to tell what they mean:

Past

simple	I saw
perfect	I had seen
simple progressive	I was seeing
perfect progressive	I had been seeing

Present

simple	I see
perfect	I have seen
simple progressive	I am seeing
perfect progressive	I have been seeing

Future

simple	I will see
perfect	I will have seen
simple progressive	I will be seeing
perfect progressive	I will have been seeing

2. Past Tense

Simple Past

It is clear that past tense verbs express events that have already happened, events that are in the past. The question is, what do these past tense verbs mean? Consider the following:

a. I saw him yesterday.

b. I saw him often yesterday.

c. I saw him practicing his jumpshot yesterday.

The verb in sentence *a* expresses a single event that happened at one point in the past:

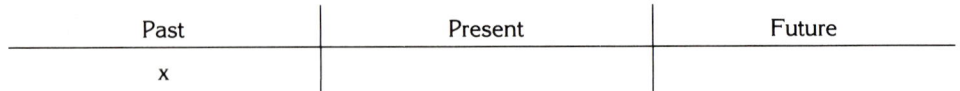

Past	Present	Future
x		

The same verb in sentence *b* expresses an event repeated several times in the past:

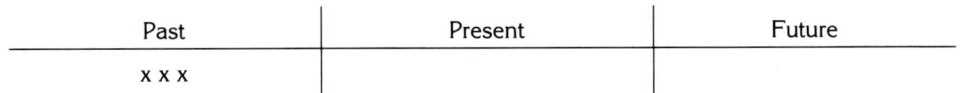

Past	Present	Future
x x x		

The same verb in sentence *c* expresses an event taking place over a period of time in the past:

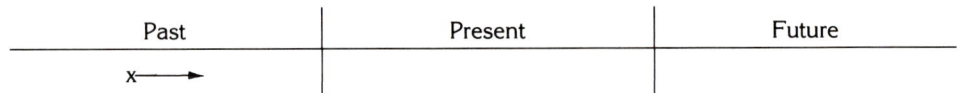

Past	Present	Future
x——▸		

The verb *saw* does not change form to express these meanings, but it can express any one of them as suggested by the context.

Perfect Past

The perfect past form *had seen* is similarly flexible:

a. I had seen him yesterday.

b. I had seen him often yesterday.

c. I had seen him practicing his jumpshot yesterday.

In addition to the meanings it shares with the simple past form *saw*—that the seeing happened at one point in the past; that the seeing happened at several points in the past; and that the seeing happened over a period of time in the past—the perfect past form *had seen* implies another point of reference in the past:

a. I had seen him yesterday, so I *didn't expect* to see him again so soon.

b. I had seen him often yesterday, so I *thought* he was up and around in earnest.

c. I had seen him practicing his jumpshot, so I *knew* he wasn't sick.

d. I had seen him before *eleven o'clock.*

The expecting happened after the seeing; the thinking happened after the seeing; the knowing happened after the seeing, and eleven o'clock was after the seeing. The reference point in the past occurs *after* the event in the perfect past, so the scheme for the perfect past looks like this:

Past		Present	Future
X	X		
event in perfect past	later event or time		

The word *perfect,* from the Latin word *perfectus,* meaning "completed," is a clue to all of the perfect tenses: all of these tenses indicate that something has been *completed* by or before a certain time. The perfect past form indicates that something has been completed by or before a certain time in the past. Thus, the seeing in sentence *a* happened and was over by the time *didn't expect* happened; the seeing in sentence *b* happened and was over by the time the thinking happened; the seeing in sentence *c* happened and was over by the time the knowing happened; and the seeing in sentence *d* happened and was over by eleven o'clock.

Progressive Past

The progressive tenses all share the meaning "in progress." Progressive past forms like *was seeing* and *had been seeing,* for example, mean that the event was in progress over a period of time in the past.

Through the miracle of time lapse photography, I was seeing an orchid unfold in ten seconds.

The perfect progressive past tense shares with the other perfect tenses the meaning that an action is completed by a certain time, so an event in the perfect progressive past is in progress in the past and then completed before or by a time or event that happens later in the past:

I realized then that I had been seeing not my son but my twin sons born.

This is the sequence of events in that sentence:

Exercises 1–2
In-class
writing 1

Past		Present	Future
X	X		
I had been seeing	I realized		

3. Present Tense

Simple Present

You have already learned much about the present tense in Chapter 7 in connection with subject-verb agreement. In the present tense, -s appears on the verb or on its auxiliary when the subject of the verb is third person singular—a *he,* a *she,* or an *it.* You also learned the meaning of present tense verbs, and you can identify present tense verbs in your own sentences. Here, we will examine the present tense in the context of the other tenses. Consider these sentences:

a. I see a storm on the horizon.

b. I see Sam every day.

c. I taste, I smell, I feel, I hear, and I see through my five senses.

d. At noon tomorrow I see my advisor and get my SAT scores.

In these sentences, the verb *see* has some relation to present time, to *now:*

I see a storm on the horizon (at this moment, right now).

Past	Present	Future
	X	

But *see* does not always mean right now:

I see Sam every day.

Past	Present	Future
X X X X X X X X X X X X X X X	X X X X X X X X X X X X X X X X	– – – – – – – – – – – ▶

In this sentence *see* expresses an event that happens over and over and that is expected to continue: the event happens *now*, as it always happens and is expected to continue to happen in the future.

Similarly, *see* in sentence *c* expresses an event that is *always* true:

I taste, I smell, I feel, I hear, and I see through my five senses.

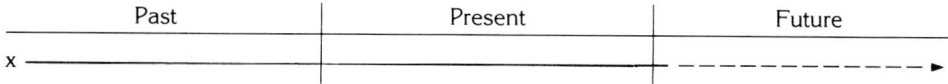

Past	Present	Future

x

Finally, in sentence *d see* expresses an event that has not yet occurred, but that will occur in the immediate future:

At noon tomorrow I see my advisor and get my SAT scores.

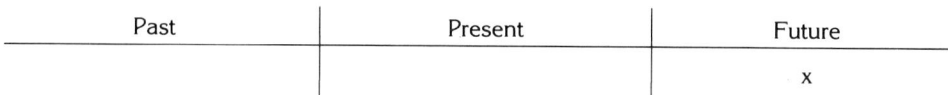

Past	Present	Future
		x

Perfect Present

The perfect present, like the other perfect tenses, signifies completion of the event, in this case completion of the event before now or by now: that is, the event has been going on "up to this time." We can observe this shift in meaning from simple present to perfect present by inserting the perfect present into the four sample sentences:

  a. I have seen a storm on the horizon.

(The sense is that the seeing has already happened or that it has happened before.)

  b. I have seen Sam every day.

(The sense here is that the seeing has happened up to now.)

  c. I have tasted, I have smelled, I have felt, I have heard, and I have seen through my five senses.

(The sense here is that these things have gone on up to now, or that the person speaking has just demonstrated each sense.)

We cannot make the insertion in sentence *d*, however:

At noon tomorrow I have seen my advisor and get my SAT scores.

The perfect present, meaning *completion by now* or *duration up to now,* cannot be used to indicate a future event.

Because the perfect present implies completion before now or by now, or duration up to now, the perfect present verges on the present or moves into it:

I have seen a storm on the horizon.

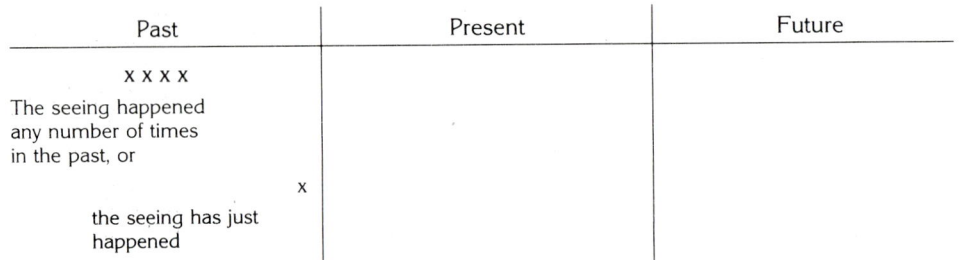

Past	Present	Future
x x x x
The seeing happened
any number of times
in the past, or

the seeing has just
happened | | |

I have seen Sam every day.

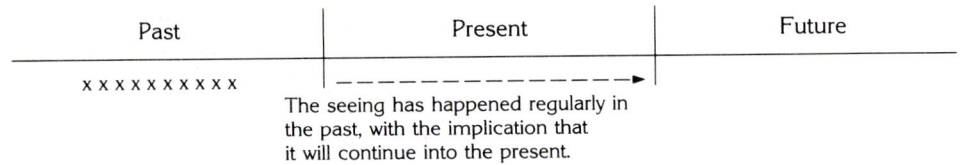

Past	Present	Future
x x x x x x x x x x
The seeing has happened regularly in
the past, with the implication that
it will continue into the present.		

I have tasted, I have smelled, I have felt, I have heard, and I have seen through my five senses.

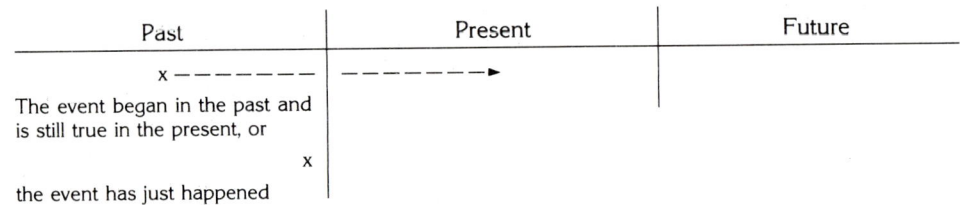

Past	Present	Future
x — — — — — —
The event began in the past and
is still true in the present, or

the event has just happened | — — — — — — ►| |

Progressive Present

Like the other progressive forms, the progressive present means that the event is "in progress" at a given time:

I am seeing Sam every day.

This sentence means that the seeing is going on at the present moment. The perfect progressive present means that the seeing began in the past and is going on in the present:

I have been seeing Sam every day.

Exercises 3–5
In-class writing
2–3

Because this is a perfect form, however, it may mean that the seeing has now ended:

I have been seeing Sam every day, but now I won't see him anymore.

4. Future Tense

The future tense is the clearest of all; the event has not yet happened.

a. I will see that sign (in a moment, tomorrow, next week, in six months, and so on).

The perfect future tense means that the event has not yet happened, but will be completed by or at a certain time in the future:[1]

b. I will have seen that sign before I leave this evening.

The progressive future means that the event has not yet happened but will be in progress at some time in the future:

c. I will be seeing that sign in a moment.

Only the perfect progressive future, a tense form rarely used or seen, is layered with meanings:

d. I will have been seeing that sign for seven years next October.

The sense here is that the event *has* already begun and that *by* a certain time it will have gone on *for* some time but will not yet be completed for good.[2] We seldom use this tense, though, because we rarely feel called upon to express future events with such precision. It is interesting, too, that we can use the other future tense forms without modification:

a. I will see that sign.

b. I will have seen that sign.

c. I will be seeing that sign.

The future perfect progressive, however, requires modification to complete its meaning:

Incomplete: I will have been seeing that sign.

---

[1] The perfect future may, however, also mean that the event has already begun:

I will have seen that sign seven times this year when I see it tomorrow.

[2] Using this tense, we could, however, write a sentence in which the event has not yet begun:

I will have been seeing that sign for only a few weeks when it becomes obsolete next month under the new charter.

The future tense often occurs with present tense forms expressing future events:

a. I will see the patient when I *have had* a chance to rest.

b. I will have seen the patient before the X-ray department *closes*.

c. I will be seeing the patient while she *is* still under anesthesia.

d. I will have been seeing that patient for ten years when he *comes* in next Wednesday.

Exercise 6
In-class writing
4

5. Summary

Past Tense

Simple Past: I saw

The seeing happened at one point in the past; or the seeing happened several times in the past; or the seeing took place over a period of time in the past.

Perfect Past: I had seen

The seeing happened once in the past before another event or time in the past; or the seeing happened several times in the past before another event or time in the past; or the seeing happened over a period of time in the past before another time or event in the past.

Progressive Past: I was seeing

The seeing was in progress over a period of time in the past.

Perfect Progressive Past: I had been seeing

The seeing was in progress over a period of time in the past and was completed by or before a certain event or time in the past.

Present Tense

Simple Present: I see

The seeing is a recurring event: it happens now as it has happened in the past and is expected to recur in the future; or the event is always true; or the seeing is happening right now; or the seeing has not yet occurred, but will occur in the immediate future.

Perfect Present: I have seen

The seeing began in the past and is completed by or at the present; or the seeing happened several times in the past and may continue into the present; or the seeing began in the past and is still happening; or the event began in the past and is still occurring.

> **Progressive Present:** I am seeing

The seeing is going on right now.

> **Perfect Progressive Present:** I have been seeing

The seeing began in the past and is going on in the present; or the seeing began in the past and is no longer true as of now.

Future Tense

> **Simple Future:** I will see

The seeing has not yet happened.

> **Perfect Future:** I will have seen

The seeing has not yet begun, but will be completed at some time in the future; or the seeing is happening in the present and will be completed in the future.

> **Progressive Future:** I will be seeing

The seeing has not yet begun, but will be in progress at some time in the future.

> **Perfect Progressive Future:** I will have been seeing

The seeing has already begun and by a certain time in the future will have gone on for a certain time, but will not necessarily be completed for good. This form can also be used to express an event that has not yet begun.

Exercises 7–11

6. Active and Passive Voice

All of the tense forms we have been examining are in the active voice. This means that the performer of the action stated by the verb is the subject of the verb. It is also possible to express certain events by using the recipient of the action of the verb as the subject of the verb. When the recipient of the action of the verb is the subject of the verb, the verb is in the *passive voice:*

                                    S   O
                            (performer) **V**   (recipient)
Active: Twelve <u>students</u> saw the <u>autopsy</u>.
                                    S
                            (recipient)   **V**
Passive: The <u>autopsy</u> was seen by twelve students.

Passive voice verbs are always made up of some form of the verb *be* acting as an auxiliary to a past participle. In the sentences above, *students saw* is in the active voice, and *autopsy was seen* is in the passive voice. When the verb is in the active voice, the subject of the verb is "active,"—it performs the action of the verb. When the verb is in the passive voice, the subject of the verb is "passive"—it does not perform the action of the verb.

   Any verbs that can take objects (see Chapter 2) can be written in the passive voice. Thus we can change the verb *see* to passive voice throughout all of the tenses:

Past

Active	*Passive*
They saw me	I was seen
They had seen me	I had been seen
They were seeing me	I was being seen
They had been seeing me	I had been being seen

Present

Active	*Passive*
They see me	I am seen
They have seen me	I have been seen
They are seeing me	I am being seen
They have been seeing me	I have been being seen

Future

Active	*Passive*
They will see me	I will be seen
They will have seen me	I will have been seen
They will be seeing me	I will be being seen
They will have been seeing me	I will have been being seen

   Verbs that don't take objects that receive the action of the verb directly (*direct objects*) may be changed to passive voice if they take objects that are related to the action but not direct recipients of it (*indirect objects*):

   S   V   indirect object
   Sam accounted for <u>his absence</u>.

           S   V
   His absence is accounted for.

Notice that in these passive constructions we do not know who or what is actually performing the action: who is doing the seeing or who is doing the accounting. When the performer is not the subject of the verb, it may be elsewhere in the sentence:

> S   V   **performer**
> His absence was accounted for by <u>Sam</u>.

Or it may not appear at all. If we want to conceal the performer of the deed, then we can shift our sentences into passive voice. Using the passive voice excessively causes suspicion, however: people want to know who or what is responsible for the action we describe. In any case, even if you wrote a whole essay in the passive voice, you would probably find that not every verb converts smoothly to the passive form:

>   S   V   O
> **Active:**   I thought <u>that you knew</u>.

>   S   V
> **Passive:** <u>That you knew</u> was thought by me.

And some cannot be made passive at all:

> **Active:** John Donne slept.
>
> **Passive:**   ———

Exercises 12–13
In-class writing
5–6

Transitive and Intransitive Verbs

Slept in the example above cannot be changed to passive voice because *sleep* does not ever have objects, direct or indirect. *Sleep* belongs to a class of verbs called *intransitive verbs*. Intransitive verbs do not have objects: they do not express actions that act upon anything else. *Salivate, transpire, walk, run,* and *rise,* for example, belong to the class of intransitive verbs. *Walk* and *run* are perhaps marginally transitive in sentences like

> New Yorkers walk their dogs.
>
> Lewis ran the mile.

In these sentences the verbs can be understood as actions performed by a performer on a recipient. No one, however, can salivate or transpire anyone or anything else:

> **Wrong:** Pavlov salivated his dogs.
>
> **Wrong:** The muggers transpired the mugging.

These verbs are always intransitive.

A large number of verbs are *both* transitive and intransitive, as *bled* is in this sentence:

```
       S    V                               S    V    O
Sam bled from the snakebite, and the doctor bled him further.
```

Some verbs are always transitive:

```
                    S                    V
Right:   The people of Englewood have elected a mayor.
```

```
                    S                    V
Wrong:   The people of Englewood have elected.
```

Only transitive verbs can occur in the passive voice, because only transitive verbs have objects:

```
                  S                 V          O
Active:   The people of Englewood have elected a mayor.
```

```
            S        V
Passive:   A mayor has been elected by the people of Englewood. (Elect is transitive.)
```

```
                 S     V       O
Active:   A wealthy man founded the town.
```

```
            S       V
Passive:   The town was founded by a wealthy man. (Found is transitive.)
```

Exercises 14 16

```
                 S    V
Active:   The old hound s belly sagged to the floor. (No passive form; sag is intransitive.)
```

7. Looking at Time

We can see now that a verb not only states an event but also tells when the event occurs (tense) and whether or not the subject of the verb is the performer of the action (voice). Tense is a way of describing events so that we can understand their sequence—then, before then, after then, before now, after now, and so forth—and also the range of time over which statements are true or valid—always true, true right now, no longer true, true up until that point, true after that point, and so forth. Tense forces us to think statements through. When we write a verb, we have to ask whether the statement containing it is true over the range of time represented by the verb. You have to ask yourself, ''Can I write, 'The people of Nyack vote Republican,' meaning that this is always true, or should I limit my statement to concrete fact: 'The people of Nyack have voted Republican for the last fourteen years'?'' You will find a large part of what you want to prove to your readers in the verbs of your first draft because the verbs state events and facts.

Tense also allows you to choose your vantage point. You can write in the past, the present, or the future:

Past tense:

Agriculture *was* one part of the biological revolution; the domestication and harnessing of village animals *was* the other. The sequence of domestication *was* orderly. First *came* the dog, perhaps even before 10,000 B.C. Then *came* food animals, beginning with goats and sheep. And then *came* draught animals such as the onager, a kind of wild ass. The animals *added* a surplus much larger than they *consumed*. But that *was* true only so long as the animals *remained* modestly in their proper station, as servants of agriculture.

J. Bronowski, The Ascent of Man

Present tense:

Agriculture *is* one part of the biological revolution; the domestication and harnessing of village animals *is* the other. The sequence of domestication *is* orderly. First *comes* the dog, perhaps even before 10,000 B.C. Then *come* food animals, beginning with goats and sheep. And then *come* draught animals such as the onager, a kind of wild ass. The animals *add* a surplus much larger than they consume. But that *is* true only so long as the animals *remain* modestly in their proper station, as servants of agriculture.

The present tense is the tense of general truth. In the present tense version, the author is writing both as if the events are happening as he writes and as if things always happen this way. Shifting the passage from the past to the present is like shifting from still photographs to motion pictures: suddenly the events are happening while the audience is watching.

By skillfully shifting tense *within* a passage, it is possible to bring together past events and present time, to make comparisons, as H. G. Wells does in this passage:

Past tense

So long as there *was* no actual violence, the senate and the financiers *kept* on in their own disastrous way. Only when they *were* badly *frightened would* governing cliques or parties *desist* from some nefarious policy and *heed* the common good. The real method of popular expression in Italy in those days *was* not the *comitia tributa,* but the strike and insurrection, the righteous and necessary methods of all cheated or suppressed peoples. We *have seen* in our own days in Great Britain a decline in the prestige of parliamentary government and a drift towards unconstitutional methods on the part of the masses through exactly the same cause, through the incurable disposition of politicians to gerrymander the electoral machine until the community *is driven* to explosion.

Present tense

For insurrectionary purposes a discontented population *needs* a leader, and the political history of the concluding century of Roman republicanism *is* a history of insurrectionary leaders and counterrevolutionary leaders. Most of the former *are* manifestly unscrupulous adventurers who *try* to utilize the public necessity and unhappiness for their own advancement. Many of the historians of this period *betray* a disposition to take sides, and *are* either aristocratic in tone or fiercely democratic; but indeed, neither side in these complex and intricate disputes *has* a record of high aims or clean hands. The senate and the rich Equestrians *were* vulgar

Historical present

Past tense
━━
Present tense
━━

and greedy spirits, hostile and contemptuous towards the poor mob; and the populace *was* ignorant, unstable, and at least equally greedy. The Scipios in all this record *shine* by comparison, a group of gentlemen.

In his summary of the last century of the Roman republic, Wells shifts tense to good purpose. He begins in the past tense to tell events that happened centuries ago in Rome: *was, kept, were frightened, would desist, would heed,* and *was* again; then he moves to the perfect present *have seen* to compare the situation in Rome then to the situation in Great Britain at the time he is writing. The next two verbs, *is driven* and *needs,* are simple present, expressing what is always true. With these present tense forms, in the context of the comparison he is drawing between Great Britain and Rome, Wells is saying that some things do not change; some political realities are ever present: look at Rome then and at Great Britain now. Although he then returns to the Roman past, Wells continues in the present tense: *are, try, betray, has,* deliberately bringing that past into the present, as if it is happening while he is writing, for his readers' close inspection. This change in perspective makes use of the *historical present.* The effect is to strengthen Wells' comparison: Great Britain now, compared to ancient Rome as if it were now. With *were* and *was,* Wells briefly returns to the past tense he began in, only to switch again to the present tense *shine,* to tell what he thinks *now* about Rome *then.*

Thus the meaning of the tense of the verb is very much a part of the meaning of any statement. For that reason, you have to be careful. Avoid stating a general truth as if it were a momentary fact:

Wrong: Children all over the world *are needing* a high proportion of protein in their diets.

Or expressing an event of limited duration as if it were a general truth:

Exercise 17

Wrong: Havana cigars *are* contraband for almost twenty years now.

8. Proofreading for Verb Tense

You already know all the techniques you need to proofread for correct verb tense:

1. Find and underline twice each verb in each sentence.
2. Find the subject or subjects of each verb and underline each once. Draw overlines between subject and verb.
3. Label each verb with its tense: *perf. past, pres., prog. fut.,* and so on.

To be sure that you are using the tense you need, you must know what meaning you intend and compare that meaning to the verb you have written. Use the list of meanings on pages 176–177 to determine whether the tense you have chosen matches the meaning you intend for each verb you've written. Pay special attention to the time sequence your verbs establish. No hard and fast rule can be set down with respect to the sequence of tenses in any given sentence, except that the reader should not have to puzzle over what happened first, or whether one event is simultaneous with another. Thus you can't proofread for tense sentence by sentence; you must first read the whole piece and then reread it, stopping yourself at each verb to make sure that its tense fits your purpose. Wherever you notice a shift, present to past or vice versa, write the reason for the shift at the end of the paper.

Here is a student passage already proofread:

Topic: Freedom

Subject: The freest time of day

that

From the time I roll over in my bed and turn on the television set for some morning news,

that

to the time I put away the last dish after dinner, I am running. I have a job that I go to

+

three mornings a week, and the other two mornings I have classes. I work as a messenger,

that

+

so I actually do run from the time I get my first address until I'm finished at noon. Then

I have a very fast lunch, which is from a bag if I've had time to make it before I leave, or

from a cellophane wrapper if I haven't. I don't have time to sit down in a luncheonette,

+

so I have a package of corn chips, which keeps my mouth busy enough to fool my stomach

that

into thinking I've had lunch. I ate corn chips or candy bars on a regular basis in high

school when I had swim practice while everyone else got to eat lunch. The sugar gave

+

me energy, or at least that was what I told myself. At school I have classes without a break

until three. I planned it that way to get out while there is still some daylight to enjoy. I

thought when I registered that I could get in some handball if I got out by three. But what

usually happens is that somebody else needs some of my time when I get home. If my

father is home, he asks me to help him on the truck, or else wants my help fixing
something. If my mother is home, she needs bread for dinner and eggs for breakfast, so
I have to go to the store. So my free time doesn't come until everyone has eaten and is
falling asleep in front of the television set.

Here is an account of the tense and meaning of each verb in the passage:

Verb	Tense	Meaning
roll	simple present	happens every day
turn	simple present	happens every day
put	simple present	happens every day
am running	progressive present	happens throughout the day every day
have	simple present	now
go	simple present	happens regularly
have	simple present	happens regularly
work	simple present	now
do run	simple present	happens regularly
get	simple present	happens regularly
am finished	simple present	happens regularly
have	simple present	happens regularly
is	simple present	always
have had	perfect present	completed before *is*
leave	simple present	happens regularly
haven't (had)	perfect present	completed before *leave*
don't have	simple present	always
have	simple present	happens regularly
keeps	simple present	always
have had	perfect present	up until that moment
ate	simple past	took place over a period of time in the past (in high school)
had	simple past	took place in high school
got to eat	simple past	took place in high school
gave	simple past	took place in high school
was	simple past	took place in high school
told	simple past	took place in high school
have	simple present	now (in college)
planned	simple past	at one point in the past
is	simple present	every day
thought	simple past	at one point in the past
registered	simple past	at one point in the past
could get	past conditional	(see Chapter 9)

Verb	Tense	Meaning
got	past conditional	(see Chapter 9).
happens	simple present	every day
is	simple present	happens regularly
needs	simple present	happens regularly
get	simple present	always
is	simple present	happens regularly
asks	simple present	happens regularly
wants	simple present	happens regularly
is	simple present	happens regularly
needs	simple present	happens regularly
have to go	simple present	always
doesn't come	simple present	always
has eaten	perfect present	happens before *doesn't come*
is falling	progressive present	going on regularly

Exercises 18–19

9. Using Grammar for Style

Tense is so much a part of our thought, our speech, and our ideas, that we don't think about it. But we may notice tense when a newscaster says, "He played major roles in Hollywood and on the Broadway stage." We know before we hear the announcement that the star has died. Although we don't think about it, tenses make statements, as we have seen, and they also transmit feeling.

When you've finished your first draft, experiment with your tenses. Your subjects determine your tenses, and you can't change them at will. Nevertheless, tense can be used to serve style: newspaper headlines, for example, are usually in present tense—"Storage Tanks Explode"—though the events they report are in the past. The present tense headline announces the recent past as *now*, rather than as *over*, to give a sense of up-to-the-minute information. Whether we know much about the past or not, most of us want to know what is going on around us now. Present tense headlines give us the secure feeling that we know what's happening while it's happening.

Although you won't know until you've read your first draft whether you can strengthen what you've written through some change in verb tense or voice, you should know that tense and voice do affect style. In general, the longer the verb phrase, the weaker the sentence. Compare:

Some small countries have been building nuclear reactors.

Some small countries are building nuclear reactors.

The long verb phrases of the passive voice may be the reason many readers feel that the passive is weaker than the active voice:

By the time the repairman sends his bill, the club's money will have been spent.

By the time the repairman sends his bill, the club will have no money.

In general, it is awkward to maintain the future tense throughout long passages:

> First your application will go to our personnel manager. She then will send it to a committee of department managers, who will decide which of your skills they can use. Then they will forward your application to the vice president, who will check your salary request with our budget. Our president will consider his recommendation, and then your application will go to our board of directors, who will decide your fate.

Use the present tense instead:

> First your application goes to our personnel manager. She then sends it to a committee of department managers, who decide which of your skills they can use. Then they forward your application to the vice president, who checks your salary request with our budget. Our president considers his recommendation, and then your application goes to our board of directors, who decide your fate.

The present tense replaces the verb phrases with single words, and that accounts for some of the improvement: instead of eight *wills* there are none. The big change, though, is that in the second version the action happens as we read. We feel closer to unfolding action than to events that will happen. Yet none of the meaning is lost: we know that these events have not happened yet and that they will.

Chapter 8 • Verb Tense and Voice

Exercises

1. Identify each of the *past tense verbs* in the passage below as simple past, perfect past, progressive past, or perfect progressive past.

As the writing tells, at the age of ten Alexander was lying in a bed adorned with paintings; a costly embroidered silk, lined with marten's fur, was his coverlet. At night there came to him a dream, a mysterious vision, that he was eating an egg, and it rolled from his hands and broke on the paved floor. A dreadful serpent issued from it; never had man seen so loathsome a shape. It passed round the bed three times, then withdrew to its shell and fell dead at the entrance. That was a great marvel.

R. S. Loomis, trans., "The Youth of Alexander the Great"

a. _____ tense _____

b. _____ tense _____

c. _____ tense _____

d. _____ tense _____

e. _____ tense _____

f. _____ tense _____

g. _____ tense _____

h. _____ tense _____

i. _____ tense _____

j. _____ tense _____

k. _____ tense _____

l. _____ tense _____

2. The past tense verbs in the passage above are listed below. Next to each, write out the *meaning* each of the past tense verbs has in the passage.

Example: *was lying*—progressive past: for a certain period of time, when he was ten years old, Alexander lay on a bed.

a. was lying—progressive past: _____

_____

b. was—simple past: _____

_____

c. came—simple past: _____

_____

d. was eating—progressive past: _____

_____

e. rolled—simple past: _____

_____

f. broke—simple past: _____

_____

g. issued—simple past: _____

_____

h. had seen—perfect past: _____

_____

i. passed—simple past: _____

_____

j. withdrew—simple past: _____

_____

k. fell—simple past: _____

_____

l. was—simple past: _____

_____

3. Rewrite the passage above, changing the past tense verbs to present tense.

4. Reread both passages. What effect does changing the passage from past tense to present tense have?

5. The participles in the Loomis passage are listed below. Write sentences suggested by the participles.

a. adorned: _____

b. embroidered: _____

c. lined: _____

Tell when each of these events occurs in the passage, with respect to the whole verbs in the sentence:

d. With respect to *was lying,* when did the adorning happen?

_____

e. With respect to *was,* when did the embroidering happen?

_____

f. With respect to *was,* when did the lining of the coverlet happen?

_____

Write in each of the three participles (5a, b, and c) in the correct position on the chart below, with respect to the tense of the whole verbs.

Past	Present	Future
was lying		
was		

6. Read the following passage and find each verb. Above each verb, give its tense and tell whether it is simple, perfect, progressive, or perfect progressive.

Physical and biological technologies have alleviated pestilence and famine and many painful, dangerous,

and exhausting features of daily life, and behavioral technology can begin to alleviate other kinds of ills.

In the analysis of human behavior it is just possible that we are slightly beyond Newton's position in the

analysis of light, for we are beginning to make technological applications. There are wonderful possibilities—

and all the more wonderful because traditional approaches have been so ineffective. It is hard to imagine

a world in which people live together without quarreling, maintain themselves by producing the food,

shelter, and clothing they need, enjoy themselves, and contribute to the enjoyment of others in art, music,

literature, and games, consume only a reasonable part of the resources of the world and add as little as

possible to its pollution, bear no more children than can be raised decently, continue to explore the world

around them and discover better ways of dealing with it, and come to know themselves accurately and,

therefore, manage themselves effectively.

B. F. Skinner, *Beyond Freedom and Dignity*

7. Present tense verbs in the Skinner passage are given below. Next to each, tell what meaning the verb tense has in the passage: now, always, sometimes; by now (already), as of now, up until now, right now (beginning or ongoing in the present), for some time now (a continuous or recurring event), just now; or the event will happen in the near future.

a. have alleviated—perfect present: _____

_____

b. is—simple present: _____

_____

c. are—simple present: _____

_____

d. are beginning—progressive present: _____

_____

e. are—simple present: _____

_____

f. have been—perfect present: _____

_____

g. is—simple present: _____

_____

h. live—simple present: _____

_____

i. maintain—simple present: _____

_____

j. need—simple present: _____

_____

k. enjoy—simple present: _____

_____

l. contribute—simple present: _____

_____

m. consume—simple present: _____

_____

n. add—simple present: _____

_____

o. bear—simple present: _____

_____

p. continue—simple present: _____

_____

q. discover—simple present: _____

_____

r. come to know—simple present: _____

_____

s. manage—simple present: _____

_____

8. The verbs above are listed again below, along with the meaning of the tense of each in the passage. On the line provided beneath each verb, write your own sentence using the verb in the same sense.

   Example: have alleviated—by now, as of now

   Today, credit cards have alleviated the shopper's need for ready cash.

   a. have alleviated—by now, as of now

   _____

   b. is—now, as of now

   _____

   c. are—now, as of now

   _____

   d. are beginning—right now, as of now

   _____

e. are—now, as of now

_____

f. have been—up until now

_____

g. is—now, always

_____

h. live—always, in the near future

_____

i. maintain—always, in the near future

_____

j. need—always

_____

k. enjoy—always, sometimes

_____

l. contribute—always

_____

m. consume—always

_____

n. add—always

_____

o. bear—always

_____

p. continue—always

_____

q. discover—always

_____

r. come to know—always

_____

Chapter 8 • Verb Tense and Voice

s. manage—always

_____

9. Rewrite the Skinner passage, changing the present tense verbs to past tense. Change the verbs *can begin to alleviate* and *can be raised,* to *could begin to alleviate* and *could be raised.*

10. The sentences below are written in the simple past tense. Rewrite them as indicated. Beneath each rewrite, tell what the new sentence means. Put an *X* next to any sentence produced that doesn't sound like good English.

a. Sam loved fishing.

simple present: _____

meaning: _____

perfect present: _____

meaning: _____

progressive present: _____

meaning: _____

perfect progressive present: _____

meaning: _____

b. The rainfall was good.

simple present: _____

meaning: _____

perfect present: _____

meaning: _____

progressive present: _____

meaning: _____

perfect progressive present: _____

meaning: _____

c. Sale prices brought people to town.

simple present: _____

meaning: _____

perfect present: _____

meaning: _____

progressive present: _____

meaning: _____

perfect progressive present: _____

meaning: _____

d. He who stole my purse stole trash.

simple present: _____

meaning: _____

perfect present: _____

meaning: _____

progressive present: _____

meaning: _____

perfect progressive present: _____

meaning: _____

11. The passage below is written in the present tense. Rewrite the passage using future tense forms of the verbs.

> By the end of the first month a whole embryo is formed. From head to heel it is a quarter to half an inch long. It is the size of half a pea, fragile as jelly and almost without substance. One can hardly see the fine detail of its structure. But the body has a head with rudimentary eyes, ears, mouth, and a brain that already shows human specialization. There are simple kidneys, a liver, a digestive tract, a primitive umbilical cord, a blood stream and a heart. The heart is usually beating by the twenty-fifth day. It is only a primitive heart, a U-shaped tube two millimeters long. But the twenty-five-day-old embryo is so small that the minute heart forms a large bulge on its body. This heart, in proportion to the size of the body, is nine times as large as the adult heart. After a few days of practice it pumps sixty-five times a minute to circulate the newly formed blood that is needed to nourish the embryonic tissues. The blood flows through the embryo in a simple closed system of vessels that is separate from the mother's blood circulation.
>
> Geraldine Lux Flanagan, *The First Nine Months of Life*

a. What differences do you find between the passages?
b. What impression does each passage leave you with?
c. Which version seems the better one? Why?

12. Fill in the following chart for the verb *eat*. Then copy the categories onto two other sheets of paper and complete them for the verbs *deny* and *make*.

Chapter 8 • Verb Tense and Voice

	Active Voice	**Passive Voice**
	Past Tense	
simple		
perfect		
progressive		
perf. prog.		
	Present Tense	
simple		
perfect		
progressive		
perf. prog.		
	Future Tense	
simple		
perfect		
progressive		
perf. prog.		

Note that you will have an easier time figuring out the passive form if you write each active voice entry as a short sentence with an object:

Active Voice	**Passive Voice**
Past Tense	
Sam ate the prunes	The prunes were eaten
Sam had eaten the prunes	The prunes had been eaten

13. All of the tense forms for *eat* are listed below. On the line following each form, write the *meaning* of the verb.

   Example: Sam has been eating prunes: perfect progressive present

   Sam began to eat prunes in the past and is still eating them; he is likely to go on eating prunes as he has in the past; he started eating prunes a while ago and has just stopped.

   a. Sam ate prunes: simple past

   _____

b. Sam had eaten prunes: perfect past

_____

c. Sam was eating prunes: progressive past

_____

d. Sam had been eating prunes: perfect progressive past

_____

e. Sam eats prunes: simple present

_____

f. Sam has eaten prunes: perfect present

_____

g. Sam is eating prunes: progressive present

_____

h. Sam has been eating prunes: perfect progressive present

_____

i. Sam will eat prunes: simple future

_____

j. Sam will have eaten prunes: perfect future

_____

k. Sam will be eating prunes: progressive future

_____

l. Sam will have been eating prunes: perfect progressive future

_____

m. Prunes were eaten: simple past

_____

n. Prunes had been eaten: perfect past

_____

o. Prunes were being eaten: progressive past

_____

p. Prunes had been being eaten: perfect progressive past

_____

q. Prunes are eaten: simple present

_____

r. Prunes have been eaten: perfect present

_____

s. Prunes are being eaten: progressive present

_____

t. Prunes have been being eaten: perfect progressive present

_____

u. Prunes will be eaten: simple future

_____

v. Prunes will have been eaten: perfect future

_____

w. Prunes will be being eaten: progressive future

_____

x. Prunes will have been being eaten: perfect progressive future

_____

14. Read the passage below. On the lines beneath it, list all of the whole verbs in it and identify the tense and voice of each. List objects of the verb, direct and indirect.

The wireless telegraph was given spectacular publicity in 1910 when it led to the arrest at sea of Dr. Hawley H. Crippen, a U.S. physician who had been practicing in London, murdered his wife, buried her in the cellar of their home, and fled the country with his secretary aboard the liner *Montrose.* The secretary was dressed as a boy, and the pair traveled as Mr. Robinson and son. Captain George Kendall of the *Montrose* became suspicious of the Robinsons, having read in the English papers about the Crippen case.

The *Montrose* was one of the few ships then equipped with Marconi's wireless. Binding his wireless operator to secrecy, Captain Kendall sent a message to Scotland Yard, and the Yard sent Inspector Dews on a faster liner to race the *Montrose* across the Atlantic. Inspector Dews, dressed as a pilot, boarded the *Montrose* before it reached port, and arrested Crippen. Eighteen months after Crippen's arrest, an act was passed in the British Parliament making it compulsory for all passenger ships to carry a wireless.

Marshall McLuhan, *Understanding Media*

Verb	Tense	Voice	Objects
a.			
b.			
c.			
d.			
e.			
f.			
g.			
h.			
i.			
j.			
k.			
l.			
m.			
n.			
o.			
p.			

15. The tense, voice, objects, and subjects of the verbs in the McLuhan passage are listed below. Convert each construction to the other voice, or explain why no conversion is possible.

$$\text{Example:} \quad \overset{S}{\text{the telegraph}} \;\; \overset{V}{\text{was given}} \;\; \overset{O}{\text{publicity}} \text{: simple past, passive}$$

$$\overset{S}{\text{the press}} \;\; \overset{V}{\text{gave}} \;\; \overset{O}{\text{publicity}} \;\; \overset{IO}{\text{to the telegraph}}$$

The subject "the press" does not appear in the passage but is understood and can be supplied, as can the subject "someone" or "something" for many of the passive constructions.

a. the telegraph was given publicity: simple past, passive

_____

b. it led to the arrest: simple past, active

_____

c. who had been practicing: perfect progressive past, active

_____

d. who murdered his wife: simple past, active

_____

e. who buried her: simple past, active

_____

f. who fled: simple past, active

_____

g. the secretary was dressed: simple past, passive

_____

h. the pair traveled: simple past, active

_____

i. Captain Kendall became: simple past, active

_____

j. the *Montrose* was: simple past, active

_____

k. Captain Kendall sent a message: simple past, active

_____

l. the Yard sent Inspector Dews: simple past, active

_____

m. Dews boarded the *Montrose:* simple past, active

_____

n. it reached port: simple past, active

_____

o. Dews arrested Crippen: simple past, active

_____

p. an act was passed: simple past, passive

_____

16. All of the verbs and verbals in the McLuhan passage are listed below. Enter each under either the heading *Transitive* or *Intransitive*. Under the heading *Object*

   a. list any direct objects the verb has in the passage; or
   b. write "transitive/intransitive" if the verb *can* have an object but has none in the passage; or
   c. write "intransitive" if the verb never takes objects.

   Example:

Verb	Transitive	Intransitive	Object
was given	was given		publicity
had been practicing	had been practicing		trans./intrans.

   a. was given _____

   b. led _____

   c. had been practicing _____

   d. murdered _____

   e. buried _____

   f. fled _____

   g. was dressed _____

   h. traveled _____

   i. became _____

   j. having read _____

   k. was _____

   l. equipped _____

   m. binding _____

   n. sent _____

   o. sent _____

   p. dressed _____

   q. boarded _____

   r. reached _____

   s. arrested _____

   t. was passed _____

   u. making _____

   v. to carry _____

17. Read the passage below. Find each verb and underline it twice.

Johannes Brahms wrote enough string quartets, he said, to paper his room. Of these he submitted only three for publication, the three that we know. One night in a Vienna cafe, a young composer was complaining of the poor reception his first opera had had from the critics. "Ach!" Brahms said. "It is customary to drown the first litter."

Brahms had a right to say it; he had destroyed his own offspring when he considered them unworthy. The point to bear in mind, I think, is that, to hit the target, a man has to shoot off much ammunition. One of the marks of true genius is a quality of abundance. A rich, rollicking abundance, enough to give indigestion to ordinary people. Great artists turn it out in rolls, in swatches. They cover whole ceilings with paintings, they chip out a mountainside in stone, they write not one novel but a shelf full. It follows that some of their work is better than other. As much as a third of it may be pretty bad. Shall we say this unevenness is the mark of their humanity—of their proud mortality as well as of their immortality.

Catherine Drinker Bowen, "The Nature of the Artist"

On a separate sheet, copy out each verb and state its tense and voice. Beneath this information, write what the verb means in the passage.

18. Now proofread your first draft according to the proofreading guidelines in this chapter for errors in verb tense.

19. Proofread your draft for sentence fragments, run-on sentences, errors in parallelism, and errors in punctuation.

In-Class Writing

1. Write a passage telling about a recent assignment, job, or other obligation for which you were unprepared, although you knew you should have been prepared.

   a. Underline verbs twice, subjects once. Draw overlines between subject and verb.
   b. Label the tense of each verb.
   c. Check the endings of each verb to make sure that these are the tenses you want for the meanings you intend.

2. Write a passage describing a lucky break you recently had.

   a. Underline verbs twice, subjects once. Draw overlines between subject and verb.
   b. Label the tense of each verb.
   c. Check the endings of each verb to make sure that these are the tenses you want for the meanings you intend.

3. Rewrite the passage above, changing the verbs to progressive present tense, as if the lucky break is happening right now.

   a. Underline verbs twice, subjects once. Draw overlines between subject and verb.
   b. Check for subject-verb agreement.
   c. Read your passage aloud to the class, emphasizing the endings on your words.

4. Ask your neighbor in class what he or she will be doing tomorrow at this time. Write down what you are told.

   a. Underline verbs twice, subjects once. Draw overlines between subject and verb.
   b. Label the tense of each verb.
   c. Check the endings of each verb to make sure that these are the tenses you want for the meanings you intend.

5. Write a passage describing the place you liked best when you were a child.

   a. Underline verbs twice, subjects once. Draw overlines between subject and verb.
   b. Label the tense of each verb.
   c. Check the endings of each verb to make sure that these are the tenses you want for the meanings you intend.

6. Write a passage describing the place in the passage above as it probably looks today.

   a. Underline verbs twice, subjects once. Draw overlines between subject and verb.
   b. Label the tense of each verb.
   c. Check the endings of each verb to make sure that these are the tenses you want for the meanings you intend.
   d. Check for subject-verb agreement.
   e. Read this passage aloud to the class, emphasizing the endings on your words.

Exercises for Style

1. Drop something on the floor. Write a description of how your classmates respond, first in the present tense, then in the past tense. Read these passages, then choose one of the statements below and write your explanation for your choice:

   Results of a study should be written in the past tense.

   Results of a study should be written in the present tense.

2. Write a passage of about fifty words describing how you think someone you love will look ten years from now using the future tense with *will*.

    a. Rewrite the passage using the present tense with future meaning.

    b. Write a brief passage telling which description you prefer and why.

3. Collect and read five advertisements. Briefly write out what tense each advertisement is written in and tell why you think the advertiser has chosen that tense.

Verb Form and Mood

9

CAPSULE PREVIEW   This chapter shows how verb form changes as verb tense changes. If you look at the tense models in the last chapter, you will see that these changes in the verb are systematic. This chapter explains the system.

If you aren't aware of this system, you may use nonstandard forms of verbs. These may sound all right when you read them aloud, since very often verb endings are slurred or not pronounced, but *readers* notice missing endings, just as they do misspellings, and the effect is disturbing:

> Smart people don't always show that they're smart in school. My friend Paul has learn German on his own overseas well enough to write it, but he failed it twice in school here before he was ship to Europe.

Proofreading Techniques

To restore omitted endings on verbs, find each verb, look at its ending, and see that that ending matches the tense and subject of the verb or that it matches its auxiliary. Chapter 7, ''Subject-Verb Agreement,'' and Chapter 8, ''Verb Tense and Voice,'' explain how subject and tense govern verb endings. This chapter shows how auxiliaries govern verb endings.

Smart people don't always show that they're smart in school. My friend Paul has learn

German on his own overseas well enough to write it, but he failed it twice in school

here before he was ship to Europe.

don't show—the auxiliary *do* is followed by the base form of the verb.

has learn—the auxiliary *has* is followed by the past participle: change *learn* to *learned*.

failed—tense is simple past.

was ship—the auxiliary *was* is followed by the past participle or the present participle: change to *was shipped*.

You keep track of the forms of your verbs by explaining *why* they end the way they do.

This chapter also tells about verb forms used to express *mood*. Mood is that meaning in the verb that tells whether the event is actual, possible, conditional, or contrary to fact.

Error: Verb Form

Sometimes writers omit endings on parts of verb phrases:

> **verb phrase**
> Patricia *hasn't talk* to her counselor yet.

> **verb phrase**
> I *have just been interview* today.

RULE

In verb phrases the auxiliary determines the ending of the verb form that follows it. Verb forms that follow *have, has, had,* and *having* end in -ed, -en, -d, or -t. Verb forms that follow *is, am, are, was, were, been,* and *being* end in -ed, -en, -d, -t, or -ing.

Revision

Patricia hasn't talk*ed* to her counselor yet.

I have just been interview*ed* today.

Writing Assignment: First Draft

Topic: Possessions

Subject: What I would acquire if I were rich, or what I would keep if I were poor

Some people dream of wealth; others fear sudden poverty. We can all imagine something we would acquire if we became rich, or something we would hold on to, even if we suddenly lost everything. Imagine yourself suddenly changed: made abruptly rich or suddenly poor. Describe the thing you would acquire or the thing you would safeguard if a sudden change occurred. Then make a statement about what you are determined to possess. (50–100 words)

1. Introduction

Because verbs are affected by person, tense, and voice, they follow patterns: a system governs the forms of verbs.

2. Verb Forms Reviewed

In Chapter 3 we briefly discussed the basic single-word forms in which any given verb appears. Most verbs in English have either four or five forms. These two verbs are typical of each kind:

Four Forms

walk—simple present, used with all but third person singular subjects
walks—simple present, used with third person singular subject
walked—past tense and past participle
walking—present participle

Five Forms

eat—simple present, used with all but third person singular subjects
eats—simple present, used with third person singular subject
ate—simple past tense
eating—present participle
eaten—past participle

Comparing the two, we can see that the verb with five forms has a separate form for the past participle. Those with four forms use the same form for the past tense and the past participle, *walked,* in our example. Five-form verbs have one form for the past tense, here *ate,* and another for the past participle, *eaten.* Many irregular verbs, verbs that follow a different pattern from most verbs, have five forms like *eat;* some have four forms; and a few do not follow a pattern at all. Here is a list of the forms of common irregular verbs for reference:

Common Irregular Verbs

Simple Present	Simple Present (Third Person Singular	Simple Past	Present Participle	Past Participle
awaken	awakens	awakened	awakening	awakened
beat	beats	beat	beating	beaten
begin	begins	began	beginning	begun
bend	bends	bent	bending	bent
bleed	bleeds	bled	bleeding	bled
bring	brings	brought	bringing	brought
build	builds	built	building	built
burn	burns	burned	burning	burnt (-ed)

Simple Present	Simple Present (Third Person Singular)	Simple Past	Present Participle	Past Participle
burst	bursts	burst	bursting	burst
catch	catches	caught	catching	caught
choose	chooses	chose	choosing	chosen
come	comes	came	coming	come
cost	costs	cost	costing	cost
creep	creeps	crept	creeping	crept
cut	cuts	cut	cutting	cut
deal	deals	dealt	dealing	dealt
do	does	did	doing	done
draw	draws	drew	drawing	drawn
drink	drinks	drank	drinking	drunk
eat	eats	ate	eating	eaten
find	finds	found	finding	found
flee	flees	fled	fleeing	fled
forbid	forbids	forbade	forbidding	forbidden
forget	forgets	forgot	forgetting	forgotten
give	gives	gave	giving	given
go	goes	went	going	gone
hear	hears	heard	hearing	heard
hide	hides	hid	hiding	hidden
hit	hits	hit	hitting	hit
hurt	hurts	hurt	hurting	hurt
lay	lays	laid	laying	laid
lead	leads	led	leading	led
lend	lends	lent	lending	lent
let	lets	let	letting	let
lie	lies	lay	lying	lain
meet	meets	met	meeting	met
mow	mows	mowed	mowing	mown
put	puts	put	putting	put
read	reads	read	reading	read
rid	rids	rid	ridding	rid
ride	rides	rode	riding	ridden
ring	rings	rang	ringing	rung
rise	rises	rose	rising	risen
run	runs	ran	running	run
saw	saws	sawed	sawing	sawn
say	says	said	saying	said
sell	sells	sold	selling	sold
shut	shuts	shut	shutting	shut
slay	slays	slew	slaying	slain
speak	speaks	spoke	speaking	spoken
spin	spins	spun	spinning	spun
split	splits	split	splitting	split
stand	stands	stood	standing	stood
steal	steals	stole	stealing	stolen
strive	strives	strove	striving	striven

Simple Present	Simple Present (Third Person Singular)	Simple Past	Present Participle	Past Participle
swim	swims	swam	swimming	swum
wake	wakes	woke	waking	waked
write	writes	wrote	writing	written

Only the simple present and the simple past tense forms are whole verbs. The present participle, the past participle, and the infinitive forms do not function as whole verbs:

Wrong: Handcuffed and trembling, the prisoner *walking* the last mile.

Wrong: For the first time, experimenters *seen* the structure of a bacterium.

Wrong: They *been* here and gone.

Wrong: Sam *to run* the last mile tomorrow.

Because they don't have fixed tense, verbals don't function as whole verbs. The verbals in the example might follow several possible auxiliaries:

Handcuffed and trembling, the prisoner is
         was
         will be *walking* the last mile.

For the first time, experimenters have
           will have *seen* the structure of a bacterium.

They have
     will have *been* here and gone.

Sam was
    is *to run* the mile tomorrow.

Exercises 1–2

3. Auxiliaries

Auxiliaries, a class of words introduced in Chapter 3, establish tense and person and are added to participles to form whole verbs. All but the auxiliaries *been, being,* and *having,* which are participles, are whole verbs that can stand alone as well:

am	have	do
are	has	did
is	had	does
was	having	
were		
been		
being		

To the class of auxiliaries also belongs a set of words that add a different kind of meaning, as we will see in the section on mood in this chapter. These are the *modal auxiliaries:*

may	would
might	shall
must	should
can	ought to
could	used to
will	

Auxiliaries combine with verbals in fixed ways. The verb form that follows an auxiliary is always the same: the present participle, the past participle, or the infinitive (with or without *to*).

Auxiliary	**Verb Form that Follows**	**Ending In**
am		
are		
is	present participle	*-ing*
was	or	
were	past participle	*-ed, -en,*
been		*-d,* or *-t*
being		
have		
had	past participle	*-ed, -en,*
has		*-d,* or *-t*
having		
can		
could		
may		
might		
must		
ought (to)	the infinitive,	
shall	usually without *to*	
should		
used (to)		
will		
would		
do		
did	the infinitive,	
does	without *to*	

You can easily remember which verb form follows which auxiliary if you recall the verb phrase, *will have been being seen:*

Will is followed by *have:* the verb form that follows a modal auxiliary is the infinitive, usually without *to.*

Have is followed by *been:* the verb form that follows any form of *have* is the past participle.

Been is followed by *being; being* is followed by *seen:* the verb form that follows any form of *be* is either the present participle or the past participle.

Thus the verb phrase *will have been being seen* demonstrates the ''verb form that follows'' rule:

the verb form that follows modal auxiliaries is the unchanged, base spelling of the verb—the infinitive without *to;*

the verb form that follows *have* auxiliaries is the past participle, usually ending in *-ed, -en, -d,* or *-t;*

Exercise 3
In-class writing 1

the verb form that follows *be* auxiliaries is either the present participle, ending in *-ing,* or the past participle, ending in *-ed, -en, -d,* or *-t.*

4. Verb Characteristics of Verbals

Verbals Have Subjects

We know that verbals don't function as whole verbs because they lack fixed tense. Yet it is also true that verbals share a number of characteristics with whole verbs. Consider the following sentences:

Wrong: Walking along the beach, broken shells poked our feet.

Right: Scattered along the beach, broken shells poked our feet.

As soon as we read the participle *walking,* we wonder who is walking along the beach; and as soon as we read the participle *scattered,* we wonder what is scattered along the beach. Both walking and scattered seem to demand performers. Expecting to find out who is walking in the first sentence, we find only *broken shells,* which can't walk. Shells are not possible performers for the action *walking.* Whoever is doing the walking is not in the sentence. By contrast, the second sentence meets our expectation of a performer for the participle *scattered.* Rewritten, the second sentence reads:

Broken shells scattered along the beach poked our feet.

We can see in this version that *scattered along the beach* is a modifier of *broken shells. Walking,* however, can't be a modifier of *broken shells:*

Wrong: Broken shells walking along the beach poked our feet.

Whoever it is that *walking* modifies is not in the sentence, so *walking* is what is called a *dangling modifier* or *dangling participle.* Our sense that *walking* ''dangles,'' that it doesn't belong to *broken shells,* but to something else, comes from the fact that participles have performers or subjects, just as verbs do. *Walking* dangles because the subject is missing.

The subject-participle relationship is a strong one:

Wrong: Tired and frustrated, the contract fell through, and Esther took the rest of the day off.

Here too we expect to learn what subject is *tired and frustrated*. In this sentence, the answer seems to be *the contract*. When we come to *Esther*, we know that she must be the subject, but the sentence as written is misleading because the first noun following the participles doesn't make sense as the subject of the action they describe. These participles are modifiers. The sentence contains an appropriate noun for them to modify, a suitable subject, but the modifiers are misplaced; so we come to an inappropriate subject, *the contract*, before we come to the intended one, *Esther*. The sentence should read:

The contract fell through, and, tired and frustrated, Esther took the rest of the day off.

Thus, the first available subject for *tired and frustrated* is capable of fatigue and frustration.

The fact that participles have subjects is one that you knew even if you weren't aware of it:

Wrong: I saw eating an apple.

Right: I saw John eating an apple.

Right: The idea of working pleases legislators.
(This means that legislators do the working.)

Right: The idea of young people working pleases legislators.
(This means that young people do the working.)

Even infinitives have subjects:

Wrong: An oil slick caused to topple over.

Right: An oil slick caused the truck to topple over.

Sometimes infinitives appear without *to*, but they still have subjects:

              S   infinitive
Sam sees *Esteban leave* every day.

              S infinitive
Peter hears *Paul confess,* even in his dreams.

               S infinitive
Lenore feels the *baby move* whenever she sits down to read.

S infinitive

Wanda lets *Fred go* wherever he wants to.

S   infinitive

Ella Fitzgerald's voice makes the *glass shatter.*

Infinitives without *to* look very much like whole verbs. But there is a difference: infinitives, unlike the whole verbs in these sentences, don't change. Although the sentences are in present tense and the subjects of these infinitives are third person singular, the infinitives do not end in -*s*.

Moreover, though verbals have subjects, these subjects differ from those of whole verbs. We can see this when we use pronouns as subjects:

Right: I saw *him* eating an apple.

Wrong: I saw *he* eating an apple.

Right: The idea of *them* working pleases legislators.

Wrong: The idea of *they* working pleases legislators.

Right: She lets *her* go wherever she wants to.

Wrong: She lets *she* go wherever she wants to.

He, they, and *she* are subjects for whole verbs; *him, them,* and *her* are subjects for verbals.

Verbals Can Have Objects and Complements

Knowing that verbals have subjects as whole verbs do, you should not be surprised to find that verbals can also have objects and complements. Objects of verbals receive the action named by the verbals; complements of verbals describe or identify the noun modified by the verbal:

participle   object
Pounding his gavel, Judge Gesell brought the court to order.

participle object   participle object
Pumping iron means *lifting weights.*

participle complement
Feeling expansive, Forrest ordered drinks for the house.

participle complement
Declared the winner again, Stevie Wonder offered the Grammy to another composer.

infinitive   object
The candidate promises *to repeal the tax*.

infinitive   complement
Veronica plans *to become a law enforcement officer.*

Verbals Have Relative Tense

After reading this heading, you probably suspect that there are no real differences between verbs and verbals. There are, but your suspicions are well founded: the differences are subtle.

Verbals lack fixed tense, but they do have relative tense: we can tell when they happen with respect to the whole verb in the clause. The present participle always happens *at the same time* the whole verb happens. Compare these sentences:

Pounding his gavel, Judge Gesell *brought* the court to order.

Pounding his gavel, Judge Gesell *brings* the court to order.

Pounding his gavel, Judge Gesell *will bring* the court to order.

Whether the whole verb is *brought, brings,* or *will bring,* the judge's pounding happens at the same time. The past participle adapts to the whole verb in the same way:

Declared the winner again, Stevie Wonder *offered* the Grammy to another composer.

Declared the winner again, Stevie Wonder *offers* the Grammy to another composer.

Declared the winner again, Stevie Wonder *will offer* the Grammy to another composer.

In each of these sentences, Stevie Wonder is declared the winner before he makes his offering. The past participle *happens before* the whole verb.

To summarize:

Verbal	*Relative Tense*
present participle	happens at the same time as the whole verb
past participle	happens before the whole verb

Verbals Can Have Auxiliaries

Both the past participle and the infinitive appear sometimes with auxiliaries, and still remain verbals. This happens when the auxiliary is itself a participle—*having* or *being*—and when the infinitive contains auxiliaries:

Having deposited her eggs and concealed them with dirt, the spider walks away from her young forever.

Being asked all these questions makes me nervous.

Having been chosen the winner, the young violinist played an encore with tears in her eyes.

Exercises 4–5   Jenny was delighted *to have been* first in line at her nursery school graduation.

5. Nonverb Characteristics of Verbals

Although verbals share nearly all of the characteristics of verbs, they are different from verbs. Verbals cannot function as whole verbs, and whole verbs cannot function as verbals do. In terms of the forms used in major functions in the sentence—subject, verb, object, complement, and modifier—the distinction between verbs and verbals is absolute.

Whole verbs function only as verbs:

Base form:	walk	see	say	feel	sleep
Simple present:	walks	sees	says	feels	sleeps
Simple past:	walked	saw	said	felt	slept

Verbals function as subjects, complements, objects, and modifiers:

Present participle:	walking	seeing	saying	feeling	sleeping
Past participle:	walked	seen	said	felt	slept

A sampling of the sentences we have seen so far shows that none of the verbals functions as a whole verb:

   M   S   V   O
Scattered along the beach, broken shells poked our feet.

       S   V   M   M   S   V   O
The contract fell through, and, *tired and frustrated,* Esther took the rest of the day off.

   M   S   V   O
Pounding his gavel, Judge Gesell brought the court to order.

   S   V   C
Pumping iron means *lifting weights.*

But infinitives may be added to whole verbs:

      S   V   O
An oil slick *caused* the truck *to topple* over.

(The sense is "caused to topple.")

      S   V   O
The candidate *promises to repeal* the tax.

                    V   **C**

Veronica *plans to become* a law enforcement officer.

6. Errors in Verb Form

Because forms of the verb function as subjects, objects, complements, and modifiers, and also as whole verbs, and because many verb forms vary from a regular pattern, errors in verb form are easy to make. Sometimes writers use a participle as if it were a whole verb:

Wrong: My parents and I *seen* a great movie rated PG.

Or, they may drop the ending of a past tense verb or a participle:

Wrong: Last week the Senate *was ask* to pass a bill *design* to control pollution of rivers by industry.

Occasionally writers form the past participle of an irregular verb as if it were a regular verb:

Wrong: After they were fed the drug, the guinea pigs *lied* down and slept for hours.

7. Proofreading for Errors in Verb Forms

1. Find each verb and underline it twice. Be sure that you have found and underlined all auxiliaries to verbs as well.
2. Find the subject of each verb and underline it once.
3. a. For each verb phrase, check to see that the verb form that follows *am, are, is, was, were, been,* and *being* is the past or present participle. The past participle usually ends in *-ed, -en, -d,* or *-t.* The present participle ends in *-ing.*
   b. Check to see that the verb form that follows *have, has, had,* or *having* is the past participle.
   c. Check to see that the verb form that follows *can, could, may, might, must, ought to, shall, should, used to, will, would, do, did,* or *does* is the unchanged base form of the verb.

8. Mood

One set of auxiliaries can produce statements that have meaning different from any we have studied so far. These are the modal auxiliaries:

can	should
could	will
may	would
might	ought to
must	used to
shall	

All of the verb meanings we have studied so far fall into a category called *indicative mood*, in which all statements are understood as "actual," even statements about future events. The indicative mood covers events that have happened, are happening, or will happen. But a large part of our thought, speech, and writing concerns events that we can only speculate about. These events have not happened and will not or may not happen; they are not actual and may never be. Statements about such events are in the *subjunctive mood*. Consider the following:

    a. When I drink this cocktail, I will throw up.

    b. If I drink this cocktail, I will throw up.

    c. If I drank this cocktail, I would throw up.

Sentence *a* is "actual": the drinking is going to happen, and so is the result; sentence *b* is also "actual," in the sense that it is possible that the drinking will happen, and if it does, then the result will also happen; but sentence *c* is not actual at all. Although it contains no negative like *not* or *never*, the sentence strongly implies that the drinking *will not* happen and that the result, therefore, will not happen either. Sentence *b*, therefore, although in the indicative mood, is halfway between the indicative and subjunctive statements; it concerns an event that happens or is true *under a certain condition*.

Conditional Statements

The difference between sentence *b* and sentence *c* is slight and not obvious at first. Both are conditional statements. The difference is that in sentence *b* the drinking *might* happen, but in sentence *c* the drinking probably *will not* happen. Sentence *b* is neutral: it is as likely as it is unlikely to happen or to be true. Thus a prosecuting attorney at a murder trial might say of the accused: "If his fingerprints *match* those on the gun, then that man *is* the killer." And the defense attorney might retort in the subjunctive: "If his fingerprints *matched* those on the gun, then that man *would be* the killer," asserting, by implication, that his client's fingerprints *do not* match those on the gun and that he is therefore *not* the killer.

Compare these indicative conditional and subjunctive conditional statements:

Indicative conditional: The uterus *will respond* as if an embryo *is* present. (given a certain condition)

Subjunctive conditional: The uterus *would respond* as if an embryo *were* present. (given a certain condition, but the condition has *not* been met)

Indicative conditional: They *may come,* even if we *try* to stop them.

Subjunctive conditional: They *might come* even if we *tried* to stop them. (but we won't try)

There is a structural difference between indicative conditional and subjunctive conditional statements. The subjunctive conditional uses past tense forms: *drank, would throw up, matched, would be, would respond, were, might come, tried.* The indicative conditional, however, uses present and future tense forms: *drink, will throw up, match, is, will respond, is, may come, try.*

Subjunctive Mood

The word *subjunctive* means ''less than joined.'' If we understand that to mean ''less than actual,'' we have a general idea of what kind of statement the subjunctive mood defines. This ''less than actual'' feature is found in conditional statements in which the condition is most likely *not to be met,* in statements outright contrary to fact, and to some extent in statements of wishes, requests, and commands.

Contrary-to-Fact Statements. Like the subjunctive conditional, the contrary-to-fact statement is created by past tense forms that do not express past time:

I *wouldn't marry* him even if he *had* a job. (He doesn't have a job.)

He acts as if he *didn't want* the money. (He does want the money.)

If we *were* lucky, *would* we *be paying* this parking fine? (We aren't lucky.)

Wishes, Requests, Commands. Wishes, requests, and commands use past and present tense verbs that do not carry their usual tense meanings:

The taxpayers wish that the election *were over.*

I wish you *were* here.

I wish that you *could come.*

I asked that Sam *be present* to witness the signing.

The passengers asked that the boat *remain* in the harbor for one more fabulous night.

The investigating committee will demand that they *be given* access to the record.

The judge ordered that she *be remanded* to jail.

Yvonne insists that she *be allowed* up past her bedtime.

Be quiet.

Subjunctive Verb Form

As we have seen, subjunctive conditional and subjunctive contrary-to-fact statements are created by past tense verbs that do not express past time. Wishes, requests, and commands are expressed by past and present tense verbs that do not carry their usual tense meanings, and by a specifically subjunctive verb, *be*. Verbs in subjunctive statements, unlike verbs in indicative statements, do not change with respect to person:

Yvonne insists that she *be allowed* to stay up past bedtime.

Exercises 7–9   Yvonne insists that her friends *be allowed* to stay up past bedtime.

9. Errors in Mood

As you might expect, errors in mood occur where the distinctions between indicative and subjunctive are least obvious—in conditional statements. The most common error occurs in a statement in which the moods are mixed, the *if* clause in one mood, the *then* clause in the other:

Wrong: If I drink this cocktail, I would throw up.

Right: If I drank this cocktail, I would throw up.

Right: If I drink this cocktail, I will throw up.

Wrong: The uterus would respond if an embryo is present.

Right: The uterus would respond if an embryo were present.

Right: The uterus will respond if an embryo is present.

Mistakes in mood are difficult to identify because *indicative* conditional statements *can* use one tense in the *if* clause and another in the *then* clause:

If his fingerprints *matched* those on the gun (in the lab tests you ran yesterday), then the man *is* the killer.

Moreover, *would* and *could* occur as ordinary past tense verbs in indicative statements:

When I *broke* my leg, Bob *would go* to the store for me.

In-class writing
2–4   Sam *knew* that he *could win*.

10. Proofreading for Mood

There are no precise rules for identifying errors in mood other than reading sentence by sentence to determine whether the sentence is clearly indicative or subjunctive as written. Generally, a past tense verb that does not mean past time is subjunctive, and the sentence should therefore be appropriate for use of the subjunctive: it should be a conditional statement with a strong implication that the *condition is not met,* or a contrary-to-fact statement, or a wish.

Here is a student passage already proofread:

Topic: Grades
Subject: Rewards for grades

If a final A were worth a dollar, nobody would bother.¹ You wouldn't get people interested in making grades for money until you got up around a hundred dollars.² College students wouldn't be interested in competing for less than that, because money doesn't go far these days.³ On the other hand, the higher the prize, the more problems you might get.⁴ A few students might be tempted to cheat on exams or papers.⁵ You as the teacher would have to be on guard against these tactics.⁶ You would have to walk up and down the aisles during any tests you gave.⁷ But I don't know how you could prevent cheating on papers unless you had all the writing done in class.⁸ That would be a problem if you wanted a long paper or a research paper.⁹ Then there would be other students who would feel just the opposite and not want to compete at all.¹⁰ Two friends might not want to be forced to have their skills compared in a contest atmosphere.¹¹ You might have people refusing to write for you at all.¹² This might be especially true between a girl and her boyfriend.¹³ Suppose the girl knew that she was a better writer than her boyfriend, but that she didn't want to have a victory at his expense, especially a financial one.¹⁴ She might write poorly just to prevent an uncomfortable conflict.¹⁵ Other students might figure that, based on their past performance in English courses, they didn't have a chance for the prize, so their writing wouldn't be any different with the offer than it would be without it.[16]

Then it wouldn't be worth the expense.[17] And you would have to consider the expense,

because you might have the opposite problem of an unusually large number of hotshot

writers in your class, all of whom could do A work.[18] In that case you are talking about

real money.[19] If you happened to have as many as ten in your class, you would stand to

lose one thousand dollars.[20] And that brings up a final problem, as I see it: you.[21] How

would you keep yourself honest when you graded papers?[22] You might suddenly feel a

strong tendency to raise standards and give mainly B's and C's.[23] You might do us out

that   that

of A's we really deserved.[24] I can believe you would try to be honest, but I can't believe

you wouldn't start to count your pennies and sharpen your red pencil if what you thought

was going to be two or three hundred dollars started to look closer to one thousand.[25]

In the end you might have a riot in the class or a rotten egg thrown at you.[26] If I were you,

I'd leave well enough alone.[27]

The following account tells which mood each sentence is written in and why.

1. subjunctive—the statement is contrary to fact.
2–13. subjunctive conditional—the condition is not met.
3. *doesn't go:* indicative—the statement is a fact.
14. subjunctive conditional: the condition is not met. The clause containing *suppose* is subjunctive—the statement is a command.
15–18. subjunctive conditional—the condition is not met.
19. indicative—the statement is a fact.
20. subjunctive conditional: the condition is not met.
21. indicative—the statement is a fact.

22–24. subjunctive conditional—the condition is not met.

25. subjunctive conditional—the condition is not met. The verbs *can believe* and *can't believe* are indicative—the statements are facts.

26. subjunctive conditional—the condition is not met.

27. subjunctive—the statement is contrary to fact—and subjunctive conditional—the condition ''if an offer of one hundred dollars is made for each final A'') is not met.

Exercises 10–11

Exercises

1. The forms of three verbs are listed below. On a separate sheet, write a sentence for *each* form of *each* verb: three sentences using simple present forms, three sentences using third-person-singular simple present forms, and so on. Remember that the present and past participles are verbals and cannot function as whole verbs.

Simple Present	Simple Present, Third Person Singular	Present Participle	Simple Past	Past Participle
put	puts	putting	put	put
begin	begins	beginning	began	begun
am, are used	is used	being used	was, were used	been used

2. Write out the forms indicated for the following verbs:

a. *Active voice*

   1. go: simple past _____

   2. go: perfect past _____

   3. come: progressive past, third person singular _____

   4. come: progressive past, plural _____

   5. run: perfect progressive past _____

   6. say: simple present _____

   7. say: simple present, third person singular _____

   8. flee: perfect present _____

   9. flee: perfect present, third person singular _____

  10. hear: progressive present _____

  11. hear: progressive present, third person singular _____

  12. sell: perfect progressive present _____

  13. sell: perfect progressive present, third person singular _____

  14. burn: simple future: _____

  15. bend: perfect future _____

  16. build: progressive future _____

  17. deal: perfect progressive future _____

  18. spin: simple past _____

  19. strike: perfect past _____

20. swim: progressive past, first person singular _____

21. swim: progressive past, second person singular _____

22. begin: perfect progressive past _____

b. *Passive voice*

1. bring: simple past _____

2. bring: simple future _____

3. catch: perfect past _____

4. rid: progressive past, third person singular _____

5. rid: progressive past, plural _____

6. burst: perfect progressive past _____

7. cut: simple present _____

8. cut: simple present, third person singular _____

9. hit: perfect present _____

10. hit: perfect present, third person singular _____

11. put: progressive present _____

12. put: progressive present, third person singular _____

13. split: perfect progressive present _____

14. split: perfect progressive present, third person singular _____

15. lead: simple future _____

16. lead: simple future, third person singular _____

17. meet: perfect future _____

18. read: progressive future _____

19. find: perfect progressive future _____

20. ring: simple present, third person singular _____

21. drink: perfect present, third person singular _____

22. choose: progressive present, first person singular _____

23. choose: progressive present, second person singular _____

24. choose: progressive present, third person singular _____

25. forbid: perfect progressive present, first person and second person singular _____

_____

26. forbid: perfect progressive present, third person singular _____

27. awaken: simple future _____

28. awaken: perfect progressive future _____

3. Each of the verbs in the passage below has been put in parentheses in the infinitive form. Supply the correct form in the space above it.

The daughter of Hamilcar was not (to alarm) by the clamorings of the populace; she was (to trouble) by

loftier anxieties—for her great serpent, the black Python, was (to fail): and for the Carthaginians a serpent

(to be) not only a national but a personal fetish. They (to believe) every serpent to be an offspring of the

slime of the earth, inasmuch as it (to emerge) from its depths, and (to need) no feet to walk upon; its

movements (to be) as the undulations of streams; its temperature (to be) ancient darkness, clammy and

fecund; and the orb that it (to describe) when biting its tail, the complete planetary system, the intelligence

of Eschmoun.

Salammbo's serpent had many times of late (to refuse) the four living sparrows offered to it at the

new and full of each moon. Its beautiful skin, covered like the firmament with spots of gold on a dead

black surface, (to be) now yellow, flabby, wrinkled, and too large for its body; over its head was (to spread)

a downy mould; and in the corners of its eyes (to appear) little red spots that (to seem) to move.

Salammbo repeatedly (to draw) near to its silver filigree basket, and (to draw) aside the purple curtain,

the lotus leaves and bird's down—but it was continually (to coil) upon itself, stiller than a withered vine.

As a result of her intense observation she (to end) by feeling in her heart a spiral like another serpent,

which was gradually (to rise) up to her throat and (to strangle) her.

Gustave Flaubert, *Salammbo*

4. Each of the verbals in the passage below has been put in parentheses in the base form. Supply the correct form in the space above it.

I stood (transfix). (Hold) my breath and (cock) my ears I drank in the (enchant) atmosphere of the place

and the medley of odours from chocolate and (smoke) fish and earthy truffles. My fancy ran riot with

memories of fairy-stories of the paradise of children, of underground treasure-chambers where children

(be born) on Sunday might enter and fill their pockets with precious stones. It seemed like a dream;

everyday laws and dull regulations were all suspended, one might give free rein to one's desires and let

fancy rove in blissful unrestraint. I was seized with such a fever of desire on (behold) this paradise of plenty

entirely (give) over to my single person that I felt my very limbs (twitch). It took great self-control not (burst)

out in a paean of jubilation at so much richness and so much freedom. I spoke into the silence, (say):

"Good day" in quite a loud voice; I can still remember how the (strain) tones of my voice died away into

the stillness. No one answered. And the water ran into my mouth in streams at that very moment. One

quick and noiseless step and I stood beside one of the (load) tables. I made one rapturous grab into the

nearest glass urn, slipped my fistful of pralines into my coat pocket, gained the door, and by another

second was round the corner of the street.

Thomas Mann, "Felix Krull"

5. Give the relative tense of each of these verbals taken from the passage above, by stating whether the verbal happens *before*, *after*, or *at the same time as* the related whole verb in the passage. Give the whole verb.

Example: *transfixed* happens before *stood*

a. holding _____

b. cocking _____

c. enchanting _____

d. smoked _____

e. born _____

f. beholding _____

g. given _____

h. twitching _____

i. to burst _____

j. saying _____

k. strained _____

l. laden _____

6. Give the sentence function—subject, object (of verb or of preposition), complement, or modifier—of each of the verbals in the passage above.

a. transfixed: _____

b. holding: _____

c. cocking: _____

d. enchanting: _____

e. smoked: _____

f. born: _____

g. beholding: _____

h. given: _____

i. twitching: _____

j. to burst: _____

k. saying: _____

l. strained: _____

m. laden: _____

7. Write the subjunctive form of each of the following indicative conditional statements. Remember that subjunctive statements imply that the condition is *not* met.

Example:

If mother waters her begonias, they revive.

Subjunctive: If mother had watered her begonias, they would have revived.

a. If the rainfall exceeds seven inches, there are floods.

_____

b. If I have bet on the right horse, I've won.

_____

c. If you need a friend, call me.

_____

d. If Sam catches even a starfish, I'll take him out for lobster.

_____

e. If this buggy has gas in it, it runs.

_____

f. If he said that he will call, he'll call.

_____

g. If 10 equals 1 in this system, then 100 equals 10.

_____

h. If he feels a pinch, he hollers.

_____

i. If Pete has any sense, he'll be here.

_____

j. If I am a horse, I have a tail.

_____

k. If he played that number, he lost.

_____

l. If the workers who made it were conscientious, the parachute will open.

_____

8. The subjunctive forms of the indicative conditional statements above are written below. Rewrite these, putting _one_ of the clauses in the tense and voice indicated, and matching the other clause to it.

Example:

If mother had watered her begonias, they would have revived.

Perfect present, active: If mother has watered her begonias, they have revived.

a. If the rainfall had exceeded seven inches, there would have been floods.

Progressive present, active: _____

_____

b. If I had bet on the right horse, I would have won.

Perfect present, active: _____

_____

c. If you had needed a friend, you would have called me.

Simple past, active: _____

_____

d. If Sam had caught even a starfish, I would have taken him out for lobster.

Perfect present, active _____

_____

e. If this buggy had gas in it, it would run.

Perfect past, active: _____

_____

f. If he had said that he would call, he would have called.

Simple present, active: _____

_____

g. If 10 equaled 1 in this system, then 100 would have equaled 10.

Perfect past, active: _____

_____

h. If he had felt a pinch, he would have hollered.

Simple future, active: _____

_____

    i. If Pete had any sense, he would be here.

      Simple future, active: _____

      _____

    j. If I were a horse, I would have a tail.

      Perfect present, active: _____

      _____

    k. If he had played that number, he would have lost.

      Perfect future, active: _____

      _____

    l. If the workers who made it had been conscientious, the parachute would have opened.

      Perfect present, active: _____

      _____

9. Convert the following statements to indicative conditional statements, then to subjunctive statements.

   Example:

   When the bar closes, the other businesses on the street will close.

   Indicative conditional: If the bar closes, the other businesses on the street will close.

   Subjunctive: If the bar had closed, the other businesses on the street would have closed.

    a. When parents take an interest in their children's minds, children learn.

      _____

      _____

    b. The residents of this neighborhood vote; therefore they have some influence in the town.

      _____

      _____

    c. When money talks, everyone listens.

      _____

      _____

    d. When the vacuum cleaner fails, use the broom.

      _____

      _____

    e. Sam has signed the contract. He has bought himself a sinking boat.

    _____

    _____

    f. She lives in a glass house. She doesn't throw stones.

    _____

    _____

    g. Paintings look good on dark walls. We should paint the living room green.

    _____

    _____

10. Now proofread your first draft for errors in verb form and mood according to the proofreading guidelines in this chapter.

11. Proofread your first draft for sentence fragments, subject-verb agreement errors, run-on sentences, errors in parallelism, errors in punctuation, and errors in verb tense.

In-Class Writing

1. Write a passage in which you tell of something that has been promised to you, but that you have not yet received.

    a. Underline verbs twice, subjects once. Draw overlines between subject and verb.
    b. Label the tense of each verb.
    c. Check to see that the ending on each verb conforms with its auxiliary, or, if no auxiliary is present, with its subject and tense.

2. Write a passage in which you tell about something that you will fix when you have the time, and describe how you will do it. The passage should be indicative conditional: you *will do* the fixing when you *have* the time. The verbs should be indicative, present and future.

    a. Underline verbs twice, subjects once. Draw overlines between subject and verb.
    b. Label the tense of each verb.
    c. Check to see that the ending on each verb conforms with its auxiliary, or, if no auxiliary is present, with its subject and tense.

3. Write a passage telling what you would wish if the powers that be would grant you three wishes. The passage should be subjunctive conditional, with past tense verb forms to express what has not and may not happen.

    a. Underline verbs twice, subjects once. Draw overlines between subject and verb.

    b. Label the tense of each verb.

    c. Check to see that the ending on each verb conforms with its auxiliary, or, if no auxiliary is present, with its subject and tense.

4. Write a passage telling what subjects you would *not* have studied in high school if the decision had been left entirely up to you. The passage should be subjunctive contrary to fact, with past tense verbs to express the opposite meaning:

    Example: If I had had the choice, I would not have studied cooking. (meaning: I did not have the choice; I studied cooking.)

    a. Underline verbs twice, subjects once. Draw overlines between subject and verb.

    b. Label the tense of each verb.

    c. Check to see that the ending on each verb conforms with its auxiliary, or, if no auxiliary is present, with its subject and tense.

Pronoun-Antecedent Agreement

10

CAPSULE PREVIEW: In this chapter you will learn that pronouns agree with their antecedents—the words they stand for—in number and, if possible, in gender (sex). It lists the various pronoun forms and shows how they are used.

Some lapses in agreement of pronoun and antecedent have become acceptable to many people:

Everyone got *their* coats.

In this sentence, *their*, which is plural, does not agree with *everyone,* which is singular; but *their* agrees perfectly with what *everyone* means—more than one person. However, other lapses of agreement are less logical:

Someone forgot *their* coat.

Their is still plural, but *someone* is clearly *one* person. Many readers accept (and use) some singular-plural pairings between pronouns and antecedents, but you can't know who will accept what. It's better to observe what no one will question: strict agreement between pronouns and antecedents. Once you know the singular and plural forms of pronouns, it's easy to make sure they agree with their antecedents.

Proofreading Techniques

To match pronoun to antecedent, first find your pronouns and their antecedents. Then ask, ''Are they both singular, or are they both plural?'' Connecting pronouns with their antecedents quickly reveals mismatches as well as pronouns *without* antecedents:

There are certain jobs that I know I don't want. I don't want to be a teacher. They have

to stand on their feet all day and try to get students to learn even when you couldn't

care less about what they're teaching. I don't want to be an actor. Everyone thinks it's

a great career, but you could starve out there, waiting for everyone to decide that they

want you on their favorite noontime soap or on the giant, glorious, silver screen.

they—plural; doesn't match *teacher*, singular. Change *teacher* to *teachers*.
their—plural; matches *teachers*.
you—*you* should stand for *students*, but it can't. Change *you* to *they*.
they're—plural; matches *teachers*.
it's—*it* should stand for *acting*, but that word isn't in the passage. Change *it* to *acting*.
you—means *anyone*.
they—plural; doesn't match *everyone*, singular. Change *everyone* to *people*.
their—plural; matches *people*.

Your proofreading notation does the matching. You ask the questions and make the corrections. No proofreading step is simpler.

Error: Pronoun-Antecedent Agreement

Writers sometimes fail to make pronoun and antecedent agree:

                antecedent   **pronoun**
Wrong: *Somebody* sent you flowers, and *they* wrote you a note too.

                antecedent   **pronoun**
Wrong: *A poor person* can still become a millionaire today if *they*'re lucky.

RULE   **A pronoun must agree with its antecedent in number and, if possible, in gender.**

Revision

When the sex of the antecedent is not known, use a masculine pronoun:

Somebody sent you flowers, and *he* wrote you a note too.

A poor person can still become a millionaire today if *he* is lucky.

Or solve the problem of gender by making the antecedent plural:

Poor people can still become millionaires today if *they* are lucky.

Writing Assignment: First Draft

Topic: Sharing

Subject: What we all needed

Brothers and sisters share; roommates share; classmates share; neighbors share; citizens share. Try to recall something you have had to share. Describe what you shared and tell how you shared it. Then write out an idea you have about sharing. (50–100 words)

---

1. Introduction

Nouns function as subjects and objects. In a broader sense, they function as written "stand-ins" for the actual and imaginable things they name. Nouns are not themselves these things, but their function is to refer to these things. The word *marshmallow* is not itself white, sweet, spongy, or edible; it stands for the real thing in writing and speech. Nouns stand for and refer to actual or imaginable "things."

Just as words stand for things, words can also stand for words.

DEFINITION **A pronoun is a word that stands for a noun.**

2. Number

Like nouns, pronouns have singular and plural forms:

Singular

- First person, *I,* stands for the writer.
- Second person, *you,* stands for the audience or stands for anyone:

You can't escape death and taxes.

- Because *you* can mean the reader specifically or anyone at all, *you* is sometimes inaccurate:

You should spend about one quarter of your income for rent.

In the sentence above does the writer mean *you,* the reader, or *you,* anyone? Some writers tend to use *you* when they mean *I* in order to avoid an unflattering or unpleasant self-reference:

I wanted to win. I had practiced for months. But you couldn't lift that weight if you practiced for years. A guy from the Bronx won, but I don't know how he did it.

- Third person, *he or she,* stands for a person mentioned elsewhere in the passage. *He* also stands for any person mentioned in the passage when the sex of that person is not known.[1]
- Third person, *it,* stands for some thing; *it* also sometimes stands before *is, has, seems,* and a few other verbs in place of the clauses that are the subjects of those verbs:

      V   S
It is apparent *that the money has been stolen.*

Plural

- First person, *we,* stands for the writer and the audience or for several writers.
- Second person, *you,* stands for the audience.
- Third person, *they,* stands for persons mentioned elsewhere in the passage.

Exercise 1
In-class writing 1

3. Case

Subjective and Objective Pronouns

Because they stand for nouns, pronouns function as nouns do, as subjects and objects of verbs. Unlike nouns, however, some pronouns have distinctive forms, called *cases,* for these functions. Pronoun subjects are in the *subjective case;* pronoun objects are in the *objective case.*

Singular		
Subjective Case		*Objective Case*
S V O		S V O
———— loved Sam.		Sam loved ————.
I		me
You		you
He		him
She		her
It		it

---

[1] Here the system in standard English is inadequate. There are no words of double gender for reference to *any* person, male or female. Instead, *he, him,* and *his* do double duty, resulting in curiosities like this: "Sam didn't know who his pen pal was. He could have been anyone. He turned out to be Ava Gardner." *S/he,* a term invented to right this wrong, is an awkward but interesting solution.

	Plural	
Subjective Case		*Objective Case*
We		us
You		you
They		them

Pronouns have other forms and other functions as well.

Possessive Pronouns

Possessive pronouns stand for nouns and also indicate ownership:

This is *Vera's coat.* Give me *Talbot's coat.*
This is *hers.* Give me *his.*

Hers stands for *Vera's coat. His* stands for *Talbot's coat.* Possessive pronouns can be subjects or objects:

Ours stopped running a week ago.

Sam found *yours* last weekend.

Possessive adjectives on the other hand, stand only for possessive adjective *modifiers* of nouns, not for nouns at all:

     M   **M**
This is *Vera's* coat. Give me *Talbot's* coat.

    M (poss. adj.)   **M (poss. adj.)**
This is *her* coat. Give me *his* coat.

Her stands for *Vera's,* but not for *Vera's coat. His* stands for *Talbot's,* but not for *Talbot's coat.* Pronouns stand for nouns; adjectives do not. But possessive adjectives and possessive pronouns are sometimes lumped together as ''possessives.''

Reflexive Pronouns

A *reflexive pronoun* refers to a noun or pronoun already mentioned in the same clause. You can think of reflexive pronouns as ''reflecting'' a naming of the same person or thing earlier in the clause:

Claude loves *himself.*

The *children* can do the laundry by *themselves.*

We built this house *ourselves.*

No one can survive in this tundra by *himself.*

The gear should engage by *itself.*

Emelda herself said so.

Reflexive pronouns all end with the word *self* or *selves:*

> myself—possessive with *self*
> yourself—possessive with *self*
> himself—objective case with *self*
> herself—possessive with *self*
> itself—objective case with *self*
> ourselves—possessive with *selves*
> yourselves—possessive with *selves*
> themselves—objective case with *selves*

In an attempt, perhaps, to use only possessives with *self* and *selves,* speakers of some dialects use *hisself* and *theirselves,* but these forms are not standard usage.

The following chart shows how the various cases function in the sentence:

Pronoun Cases

Subjective ——— saved	Reflexive ———.	Objective Kids like ———.
I	myself	me
You	yourself	you
He	himself	him
She	herself	her
It	itself	it
We	ourselves	us
You	yourselves	you
They	themselves	them

Possessive Adjectives Here is ——— house.	Possessive Pronouns The lost and found has ———.
my	mine
your	yours
his	his
her	hers
its	its
our	ours
your	yours
their	theirs

Pronoun cases function in the following ways within sentences:

Exercises 2–7
In-class writing 2

Subject	Verb	Object	Modifier
subjective		objective	possessive adjective
possessive		possessive	
		reflexive	

4. Relative Pronouns

We have already come across another class of pronouns, called *relative pronouns,* which relate one clause to another in the same sentence. A relative pronoun replaces a noun in one clause and refers to the same noun in the preceding clause, and joins the clauses tightly together by this reference:

Alma's son ran away with the *woman who* owns the bar.

The sentence above is made up of these two clauses:

Alma's son ran away with the *woman.*

That *woman* owns the bar.

The word *who* combines them into a single sentence. *Which, that,* and *whom* function in the same way:

1. We have just passed the *rooms.*

2. Slaves built these *rooms.*

1,2. We have just passed the *rooms which* slaves built.

1. He used a *phrase.*

2. I couldn't quote the *phrase.*

1,2. He used a *phrase that* I couldn't quote.

1. The *doctor* advised surgery.

2. I consulted the *doctor.*

1,2. The *doctor whom* I consulted advised surgery.

The relative pronoun has the same function in its clause as the noun it replaced had:

S   V
The woman owns the bar.

                   S   V
Alma's son ran away with the woman *who* owns the bar.

S   V   O
Slaves built these rooms.

                O   S   V
We have just passed the rooms *which* slaves built.

S   V   O
I couldn't quote the phrase.

            O S   V
He used a phrase *that* I couldn't quote.

S   V   O
I consulted the doctor.

          O   S   V
The doctor *whom* I consulted advised surgery.

Thus, like all pronouns, relative pronouns function as subjects and objects. Notice too that *who* and *whom* show case: *who* is subjective case, *whom* objective case. In recent years this distinction has been disappearing, and *who* is now often used when it replaces an object:

          O S V
Ellen knows who I kissed.

Relative pronouns also have a possessive case form, *whose*. *Whose* replaces possessive adjectives:

1. Toni Morrison speaks at colleges everywhere.

2. Toni Morrison's *Song of Solomon* blends history and fable.

1,2. Toni Morrison *whose* *Song of Solomon* blends history and fable, speaks at colleges everywhere.

1. Every high school student in America once read Robert Frost.

2. Robert Frost's poems evoke New England.

1,2. Every high school student in America once read Robert Frost, whose poems evoke New England.

1. At this Szechuan restaurant can be found the most delicious dumplings in all Chinatown.

2. Some of this Szechuan restaurant's dishes are sublime.

1,2. At this Szechuan restaurant, some of whose dishes are sublime, can be found the most delicious dumplings in all Chinatown.

Exercise 8

Pronouns as Subordinating Conjunctions

By standing in for one noun and referring to the same noun in another clause, relative pronouns make the clause they occur in function as a *part* of the other clause. Look at this example:

Alma's son ran away with the woman *who owns the bar.*

The clause *who owns the bar* is a modifier of *woman* in the other clause:

$$\text{S} \quad \text{V} \qquad\qquad \text{O} \quad \vdash\!\!-\!\!\text{M}\!-\!\!\dashv$$
Alma's son ran away with the woman *who owns the bar.*

The following example is similar:

He used a phrase that I couldn't quote.

The clause *that I couldn't quote* is a modifier of *phrase* in the other clause:

$$\text{S} \quad \text{V} \quad \text{O} \quad \vdash\!\!-\!\!\text{M}\!-\!\!\dashv$$
He used a phrase *that I couldn't quote.*

In the following example, the clause *who I kissed* is the object of the verb *knows* in the other clause:

$$\text{S} \quad \text{V} \quad \vdash\!\!-\!\!\text{O}\!-\!\!\dashv$$
Ellen knows *who I kissed.*

Exercise 9   Clauses headed by relative pronouns are called *relative clauses*. Relative clauses usually function as modifiers or objects.

Restrictive and Nonrestrictive Relative Clauses

Consider the following two combinations:

1. The dentist, who is my cousin, will do the extraction.

2. The dentist who is my cousin will do the extraction.

Although worded alike, the two sentences have different meanings. Sentence 1 means that there is one dentist *and* he is my cousin. Sentence 2 means that there is more than one dentist involved, but the one who is my cousin will do the extraction. These sentences are in fact combinations of different clauses:

1. The dentist will do the extraction.

2. The dentist is my cousin.

1,2. The dentist, who is my cousin, will do the extraction.

1. That dentist will do the extraction.

2. He is my cousin.

1,2. The dentist who is my cousin will do the extraction.

In the second group of clauses, *that* specifies *dentist* as a particular dentist; the clause *he is my cousin* tells which one *that* dentist is. In sentence 2, then, *who is my cousin* "restricts" *dentist* to a particular dentist, the one among a number of dentists who is my cousin. In sentence 1, *the dentist* is the subject of *will do;* in sentence 2, *the dentist who is my cousin* is the subject of *will do.*

The distinction between restrictive clauses (not enclosed in commas) and nonrestrictive clauses (enclosed in commas) may seem trivial, but in fact it is not. We can see this clearly when we try to substitute *that* for *which* in a nonrestrictive clause:

Right: *Rocky,* which I saw yesterday, made me cry.

Wrong: *Rocky,* that I saw yesterday, made me cry.

That is never used in nonrestrictive clauses, but you can substitute *that* for *which* in a restrictive clause. In fact, *that* is preferred to *which* in restrictive clauses:

Less acceptable: The album which I bought has a Stevie Wonder cut on it.

Better: The album that I bought has a Stevie Wonder cut on it.

The terms *restrictive* and *nonrestrictive* refer to the two ways clauses function as modifiers: as essential information (restrictive); and as additional but not necessary information (nonrestrictive). Restrictive clauses are not separated from the nouns they modify; they are essential to the meaning of those nouns. In fact, we sometimes drop the relative pronoun itself without altering the meaning of the sentence:

The album I bought has a Stevie Wonder cut on it.

By contrast, we can't drop the relative pronoun heading a nonrestrictive clause without destroying the meaning of the sentence:

Wrong: *Rocky,* I saw yesterday, made me cry.

5. Interrogative Pronouns

The words *who, whom, which,* and *whose* are also familiar to us as the first words in questions:

Who ate my pork chop?
Whom do you want?
Which have you chosen?
Whose is it?

When these words introduce questions, they are called *interrogative pronouns.* They may begin direct questions, like those above, which are independent clauses, or indirect questions, like these:

    S   V   ┌────── O ──────────┐
    I wonder *who ate my pork chop.*

      S   V   ┌──────O──────┐
    You never know *whom you want.*

      S   V   ┌────────O──────────┐
    I always remember *which you have chosen.*

      S   V   ┌──O──┐
    Sam has forgotten *whose it is.*

Indirect questions are objects—noun clauses—so they are not independent. Indirect questions *record* questions; they are not worded like direct questions. In *direct questions,* the subject stands between the auxiliary and the rest of the verb. In indirect questions, the subject stands before the verb, just as it does in ordinary clauses. You will recall that we took a close look at direct and indirect questions in Chapter 6, "The Comma and Other Forms of Punctuation," p. 126.

6. Proofreading for Pronoun-Antecedent Agreement

The antecedent is the noun the pronoun refers to. The pronoun must agree with its antecedent in *number* and *gender*. The pronoun referring to a single male must be *he* or *him;* the pronoun referring to a single female must be *she* or *her.* Possessives must also agree with their antecedents in number and gender.

To proofread for pronoun-antecedent agreement,

1. Find each pronoun and possessive in each sentence.
2. Find and number each antecedent; then label the pronouns and possessives referring to it with the same number.
3. Check to see that pronoun and antecedent are both singular or both plural and both of the same gender. If the gender of the antecedent is unknown—"a person," "someone," "anyone," "a student,"—then *he* is the standard reference.

Only the words in the personal pronoun group (*he, him, his, she, her, hers*) are singular and have gender, and it is primarily with this group that writers have trouble. The first problem is that words like *everyone, anyone, someone, everybody, anybody,* and *somebody,* though they are *singular,* nevertheless suggest more than one person. However, only singular pronouns—*he, him, his, she, her, hers*—can refer to these words. The second problem is that these pronouns have gender: they refer to a male or a female. The words *everyone, anyone,* and so on, however, do not specify a gender. They mean *any* person, male or female, so these words don't seem to fit the singular pronouns. Writers often try to repair this bad fit by using plural pronouns:

On Friday everybody gets *their* check and leaves.

Their fits both the plural sense and the indeterminate gender of *everybody. Their* refers to more than one person, and these people can be males or females or both. This usage is gaining acceptance, but it still disturbs many people.

Relative clauses can be troublesome too. The relative pronoun, when it is a subject, must agree with the verb. If a pronoun stands for a third person singular subject of a present tense verb, then the verb must end in *-s:*

Some children who know me want to give blood.

A child who knows me wants to give blood.

Since the relative pronoun stands for and refers to the antecedent, if the antecedent is third person singular, so is the relative pronoun. To proofread for this agreement,

1. Check to see that you have drawn lines connecting all relative pronouns and their antecedents. If a relative pronoun is the subject of a verb, check to see that the verb agrees with the antecedent of the relative pronoun.

2. Finally, to be sure you know what word or words the relative pronoun stands for, in your mind try to unhitch the two clauses joined by the relative pronoun, and reproduce the two separate clauses they came from.

Here is a student passage, already proofread:

Topic: Natural rights

Subject: The right to be left alone

I can't say that everyone at all times has the right to be left alone. Someone who is up to no good does not have the right to be left alone. If a person is bothering other people or harming other people or stealing from other people, he does not have the right to be left alone. He gives up that right as soon as the evil plan hatches in his brain. And I don't believe that anyone has the right to be left alone who is about to do harm to himself. Even when someone thinks of suicide, he is still thinking of doing harm to a person. Young children don't have a complete right to be left alone, because they don't know enough to survive by themselves. But they should have some time to themselves if they want it. Sometimes they want to figure things out for themselves or sit and sulk, and they should be allowed to do both. They won't learn how to run their own lives if someone else is always standing over them. There may be others that I've overlooked who for some unusual reason should not be allowed to be alone. But for the most part, people should respect the right of others to be left alone. Most people need some time to themselves, especially as they get older. You can't let your mind wander or talk things over with yourself when other people are around. Sometimes other people are just a distraction from im-

that

↓ 9   9   ↓ 9
portant business you have with yourself. If you want to buy a car, maybe other people are

\+ ↓ 9   9   9
a help; but if you want to get married, then you need time for long talks with yourself

                                        10   ↓ ↓ 10
about things that are nobody else's business. I know that if I don't have enough time

Exercises 10–11
In-class writing
3–4

   10   11 11 10   10   ↓ 10
alone, I go into a daze. It's my way of telling myself that I want to pay a visit.

7. Using Grammar for Style

Pronouns also affect writing in a way that has nothing to do with grammar: when you write, you are writing to a pronoun audience—to *him, her, them,* or *you.* Sometimes, you may be so conscious of who some of these people are that you feel inhibited. *Him* or *her* might be your new teacher or the stranger who is suing your insurance company because you backed your car into his or hers. *Them* is a well-known enemy. *You,* however, is a friendly person, someone you're used to talking to, someone sitting in the chair under the lamp, daydreaming and only half listening.

Many writers need *you* as an audience in order to get started. They can't write to *him* or *her* or *them* or *anyone.* They need to imagine a *you* to write to.

Use you as an audience.   Talk things over with your readers; bring them into your subject with leads like

If you had been a child in Maryland in 1860 ...

You need to walk through a town that has been hit by a tornado to appreciate the power of electricity in the atmosphere ...

You may have seen the symptoms of schizophrenia among people in your community ...

and follow *you* into your subject. If your assignment calls for a more formal delivery, write your first draft with *you,* to get your content onto the page, then reword to take *you* out:

In Maryland in 1860 ...

A town that has been hit by a tornado shows the power of electricity in the atmosphere ...

The symptoms of schizophrenia are fairly common ...

You is the warm-up pronoun, something to help you relax enough to write your first draft.

Replace pronouns with nouns.   Pronouns keep us from repeating the words they stand for, but the result is not necessarily pleasing or effective, for pronouns can be repeated too often:

> For some people, headaches are a form of self-punishment. *They* get *them* when *they* go shopping, as soon as *they*'re tempted to buy *something they* don't really need. *They* get *them* when *they* finally tell off *somebody they*'ve been hating for weeks. *They* get *them* when *they* break a dish or fail a test or lose a wallet. A headache is the last thing *they* need, but *they* get *one* because *they*'re afraid that if *they* don't, *something* worse will happen. *They* think that *they* can prevent accidents by using *their* heads.

There are twenty-three pronouns in this short passage. That's too many stand-ins for a good performance. Taking our tone from the humor at the end of the passage, we can find other words for many of the pronouns:

> For some people, headaches are a form of self-punishment. These *masochists* are *stricken* when they go shopping, as soon as they're tempted to buy *perfumed room candles or earphones for the stereo. Such humble souls* get *migraines* when they finally tell off the *mooch* they've been hating for weeks. Their *heads begin to throb* when they break a dish or fail a test or lose a wallet. A headache is the last thing *migraine sufferers* need, but they *insist on suffering* because these *deluded people* are afraid that if they don't, *the sky will fall.* So they keep it up by using their heads.

This version has eleven pronouns, which is still quite a few, but it is far richer in suggestion and fact, because the words replacing the pronouns introduce ideas and images that the pronouns could not.

It isn't easy to think up words that will work where you've used pronouns, but the effort pays off. This is a controlled way to force yourself to enlarge your writing vocabulary: when you remove pronouns, you know exactly what kind of words you want, and your replacements will not alter the rest of your text very much. Yet the vocabulary you introduce to replace the pronouns polishes the entire piece of writing.

Exercises

1. This passage comes from a series of lectures on psychoanalysis that Freud delivered to an audience of students. Identify the person or persons, word or words referred to by each of the numbered pronouns and possessive adjectives in the passage.

   Every one[1] of us[2] who can look back over a fairly long experience of life would probably say that he[3] might have spared himself[4] many disappointments and painful surprises, if he[5] had had the courage and resolution to interpret as omens the little mistakes which he[6] noticed in his[7] intercourse with others,[8] and to regard them[9] as signs of tendencies still in the background. For the most part one[10] does not dare to do this; one has an impression that one would become superstitious again by a circuitous scientific path. And then, not all omens come true, and our[11] theories will show you[12] how it is that they[13] need not all come true.

   Sigmund Freud, *Introduction to Psychoanalysis*

   1. one: _____

   2. us: _____

   3. he: _____

   4. himself: _____

   5. he: _____

   6. he: _____

   7. his: _____

   8. others: _____

   9. them: _____

   10. one: _____

   11. our: _____

   12. you: _____

   13. they: _____

2. Identify the *case* of each of the numbered pronouns from the passage above.

   1. one: _____

   2. us: _____

   3. he: _____

   4. himself: _____

   5. he: _____

   6. he: _____

7. his: _____

8. others: _____

9. them: _____

10. one: _____

11. our: _____

12. you: _____

13. they: _____

3. The possessive case pronouns are *mine, yours, his, hers, its, ours, theirs*. Write five sentences using five of these as subjects.

      S   V   C
Example: *Mine* was chosen the winner.

a. _____

b. _____

c. _____

d. _____

e. _____

4. Write five sentences using possessive case pronouns as objects.

      S V O   O
Example: Annie ate *yours* and *hers.*

a. _____

b. _____

c. _____

d. _____

e. _____

5. The objective case pronouns are *me, you, him, her, it, us, you, them*. Write five sentences using objective case pronouns as objects, either of verbs or of prepositions.

       S   V O
Example: The baby swallowed *it.*

       S V prep O
The wave broke over *them.*

a. _____

b. _____

c. _____

d. _____

e. _____

6. The reflexive pronouns are *myself, yourself, himself, herself, itself, ourselves, yourselves, themselves.* Write five sentences using reflexive pronouns as objects, either of verbs or of prepositions.

                S   V   prep O   ┌—M—┐
Examples: Oscar can take care of himself in the surf.

                S   V   O
           Florence dresses herself.

a. _____

b. _____

c. _____

d. _____

e. _____

7. The possessive adjectives (not to be confused with possessive pronouns) are *my, your, his, her, its, our, your, their.* Write five sentences using possessive adjectives as modifiers of nouns.

                S   V   M ┌—O—┐
Example: Fran and Ruby ate *your* lobster tail.

a. _____

b. _____

c. _____

d. _____

e. _____

8. Divide the following sentences into two sentences. Replace the relative pronoun with the noun it stands for, and write the two clauses as separate sentences.

Example:

The chocolate pastry that you have been looking for has not arrived.

The chocolate pastry has not yet arrived.

You have been looking for the chocolate pastry.

a. The paints whose colors I prefer cost too much.

_____

_____

b. People who live in glass houses shouldn't throw stones.

_____

_____

c. But true love, which I do not claim to understand, seems to evade many nice people.

_____

_____

d. Mathematics, which I have always struggled hard to learn, is shockingly beautiful once I understand it.

_____

_____

e. Words, with which I can sometimes do wonders, failed me then.

_____

_____

f. You have been looking for a chocolate pastry that has not arrived.

_____

_____

g. I prefer the colors of the paints that cost too much.

_____

_____

h. The people who shouldn't throw stones live in glass houses.

_____

_____

i. I do not claim to understand true love, which seems to evade many nice people.

_____

_____

j. I have struggled hard to learn mathematics, which is shockingly beautiful when I understand it.

_____

_____

k. Sometimes I can do wonders with words, which failed me that time.

_____

_____

l. The fears that paralyze us are forbidden wishes in wolves' clothing.

_____

_____

m. The postal service, into whose care I entrusted the package, lost it.

_____

_____

n. Everett, around whom the scandal swirled, told a different story.

_____

_____

o. All that glitters is not gold.

_____

_____

9. Write sentences using the following nouns in the functions specified. Then combine the sentences using one of the relative pronouns: *who, whom, whose, that,* or *which.*

Example:

photographs: 1. object of preposition   2. object of verb

  1. Eulalia spilled coffee on the photographs.
  2. I was planning to sell those photographs.
  1,2. Eulalia spilled coffee on the photographs *that* I was planning to sell.

a. chocolate pastry: 1. subject   2. object of preposition

  1. _____

  2. _____

  1,2. _____

b. a man: 1. object of verb   2. subject of verb

    1. _____

    2. _____

    1,2. _____

c. the paints: 1. subject of verb   2. object of preposition

    1. _____

    2. _____

    1,2. _____

d. love: 1. object of verb   2. subject of verb

    1. _____

    2. _____

    1,2. _____

e. people: 1. subject of verb   2. subject of verb

    1. _____

    2. _____

    1,2. _____

f. mathematics: 1. subject of verb   2. object of preposition

    1. _____

    2. _____

    1,2. _____

g. elephants: 1. subject of verb   2. object of preposition

    1. _____

    2. _____

    1,2. _____

h. cheeses: 1. subject of verb   2. subject of verb

    1. _____

    2. _____

    1,2. _____

10. Now proofread your first draft according to the proofreading guidelines in this chapter for pronoun-antecedent agreement errors.

11. Proofread your first draft for sentence fragments, run-on sentences, subject-verb agreement errors, errors in parallelism, errors in punctuation, and errors in verb tense, form, and mood.

In-Class Writing

1. Write a passage telling how your parents usually treat your friends.

   a. Circle pronouns. Draw a line from each pronoun to its antecedent.
   b. Check to see that pronoun and antecedent are both singular or both plural.

2. Write a passage telling how you taught yourself to do something.

   a. Circle pronouns. Draw a line from each pronoun to its antecedent.
   b. Check to see that pronoun and antecedent are both singular or both plural.
   c. Check to see that you have not used *you* when you mean *I* or *me*.

3. Write a passage telling of the difficulties someone else might have trying to teach himself or herself how to do what you taught yourself to do.

   a. Circle pronouns. Draw a line from each pronoun to its antecedent.
   b. Check to see that pronoun and antecedent are both singular or both plural.
   c. Check to see that you have not used *you* when you mean *I* or *me*.
   d. Tell the class how you solved the problem of gender in your passage.
   e. Read your passage to the class.

4. Write a passage telling in detail how you once prepared yourself to impress someone—an interviewer, a date, an angry parent, or a youngster you were coaching, for example. Describe the result.

   a. Circle pronouns. Draw a line from each pronoun to its antecedent.
   b. Check to see that pronoun and antecedent are both singular or both plural.
   c. Check to see that you have not used *you* when you mean *I* or *me*.
   d. Read your passage to the class.

Exercises for Style

1. Write sentences that restate the ideas below without using *you:*

   You can't take it with you.

You get what you pay for.

_____

You can't tell a book by its cover.

_____

2. Write a letter to a close friend or relative on each of the two topics below. The letters should be fifty to one hundred words long. Then rewrite the letters, removing all mention of yourself and the person you wrote to so that your letters now address a general audience of strangers. Finally, write down whatever difficulty you had making the changes.

   a. your mother
   b. lending money

3. Write a short passage on the topic *blame*. First find a subject; then, write about an experience you had involving blame; finally, state your idea about it.

   a. Beneath the passage, list the number of pronouns in that draft.
   b. Reread your passage and try to cast out some of your pronouns. Replace these with other words that clearly represent the nouns the pronouns refer to.

Proofreading—Accounting and Summary

11

Now that you have studied the grammar on which the proofreading steps are based and have practiced those steps, you are ready to *account for* the forms and punctuation you use in your writing. When you can account for the structural decisions you make, you have mastered them. Follow this procedure, and measure your mastery:

1. Find each verb and underline it twice.
2. Find each subject and underline it once. Draw an overline between subject and verb.
3. Over each period, write the number of independent clauses in the sentence.
4. Account for each mark of punctuation (comma, colon, semicolon, quotation mark, and so on) within each sentence by writing the preceding word and the punctuation on a separate sheet, and then stating the reason for the punctuation.
5. Account for each coordinating conjunction by listing the words, phrases, or clauses joined by each. Be sure that coordinated words, phrases, and clauses have the *same sentence function:* all subjects, all objects, all complements, all modifiers, all verbs, or all independent clauses.
6. Account for each subordinating conjunction by listing the independent clause it is a part of.
7. Number each antecedent and label the pronouns and possessives that refer to it with the same number. Be sure that pronouns and possessives are plural if the antecedent is plural, singular if the antecedent is singular. Check to see that you do not inadvertently shift person (from *I* to *you* for example).
8. Circle each relative pronoun and draw a line to the word it refers to. Be sure that the relative pronoun and the word it refers to are written in the *same sentence*.
9. State the tense of each verb, and check to see that its ending agrees with that tense, with its auxiliaries, and with its subject.
10. Look up the spelling of each word you think you may have misspelled.

Use the sheets on pages 258–259 to record the information on punctuation (number 4) and on verbs (number 9).

Sample Punctuation Accounting Sheet

Punctuation	Reason

Sample Accounting Sheet for Subject-Verb Agreement, Tense, Voice, and Form

Subject – Verb	Tense: Present, Past, or Future	Voice: Active or Passive (active—performer is subject; passive—performer is not subject)	Reason for form (If an auxiliary is present, it determines the ending; if not, the subject and tense do.)

1. Grammatical Facts

The major sentence functions are performed by the following structures:

Subject	*Verb*	*Object/Complement*	*Modifier*
word	word	word	word
phrase	phrase	phrase	phrase
clause		clause	clause

Word classes serve in these functions:

noun	verb	noun	adjective
gerund		gerund	adverb
infinitive		infinitive	infinitive
		adjective	participle

Words, phrases, and clauses serving in these functions are identified by the signals listed in the right-hand column:

Subject and Object/Complement

word	-*s*, -*ing*, infinitive *to*
phrase	gerunds heading gerund phrases; infinitives heading infinitive phrases
clause	*that, what, whatever, whichever, whether, whoever, whomever, whose, how, which,* heading noun clauses

Verb

word·	-*s*, -*ed*, -*d*
phrase	the auxiliaries: *is, am, was, were, have, has, had, do, did, does, can, could, will, would, shall, should, might, may, must, ought to, used to*

Modifier

word	-*er*, -*ly*, -*en*, -*ed*, -*d*, -*t*, -*ing*, infinitive *to*
phrase	participles heading participial phrases; infinitives heading infinitive phrases; prepositions: *in, of, to, for, by, on, with,* and so on, heading prepositional phrases
clause	most subordinating conjunctions: *after, before, until, once, while, when, as, if, since, as if, because, unless, although, though, even if, so that, that, where, provided that,* heading adjective and adverb clauses; relative pronouns: *that, which, who, whom, whose,* heading adjective clauses

Verb Form Rules

Auxiliary	*Verb Form that Follows*
is	past participle, ending in -*ed*, -*en*, -*d*, or -*t*, or present participle, ending in -*ing*

Auxiliary	*Verb Form that Follows*
am are was were been being	past participle, ending in *-ed, -en, -d,* or *-t,* or present participle, ending in *-ing*
do did does can could shall should will would may might must ought to used to	the base form of the verb
has had have having	past participle, ending in *-ed, -en, -d,* or *-t*

2. Caution: Homonym Switches

The proofreading steps you've learned will reveal many errors, but some may still defy detection. One source of such errors is a group of words that *sound* like the words you want, but that have different meanings. Sound-alikes, *homonyms,* are all spelled differently and have very different meanings and functions. Your unconscious mind is likely to provide a homonym or near-homonym when words are coming so fast that you'll take any one that sounds right, or when you're too sleepy to care.

Here is a sampling of homonyms that are often misused. You already know what these words mean. Look for them in what you write to see that you've used them correctly.

there—introductory word: stands where the subject usually does; a place

their—belonging to them

they're—they are

which—relative pronoun

witch—noun

where—interrogative pronoun; subordinating conjunction referring to place

were—a verb

as—a subordinating conjunction

has—a verb

thing—a noun

think—a verb

why—an interrogative; a subordinating conjunction

way—a noun

even—a modifier

event—a noun

thought—a verb or a noun
through—a preposition
throughout—a preposition

when—subordinating conjunction
went—a verb

an—an article
and—a conjunction

your—a possessive adjective
you're—you are

know—a verb
no—an adjective modifier

knew—a verb
new—an adjective modifier

is—a verb
his—a possessive pronoun or adjective

the—an article
they—a pronoun
that—a subordinating conjunction; a relative pronoun

then—at that time; therefore
than—a subordinating conjunction; a preposition

hear—a verb
here—a noun
ear—a noun

or—a conjunction
are—a verb

could
should ⎫ *of* for ⎧ *could have* (could've)
would ⎭   ⎩ *should have* (should've)
                    would have (would've)

Instructions: For each writing assignment that you proofread, write in the number of errors of each kind listed in the chart below.

Error Chart

Assign-ment	Frag	R-O	S/V	/ /	Punc	Tense	VF	P/A	Errors per line
1									
2									
3									
4									
5									
6									
7									
8									
9									
10									

Frag — sentence fragment
R-O — run-on sentence
S/V — subject-verb agreement
/ / — faulty comparison or nonparallel coordinate
Punc — error in punctuation
Tense— error in verb tense
VF — error in verb form
P/A — pronoun-antecedent agreement error

The Right Word / Too Many Words / Too Few Words

12

1. Introduction

You should be able to figure out the structure of this sentence:

> Fractious pedagogues often obfuscate well-understood cultural ideologies.

Unless you know what the words mean, however, it won't tell you much. You find the words to say what you mean every day, but when you write, you have to work harder at it. You will probably not be with your readers when they read what you've written, and you want to be sure that they can understand what you mean. You must choose words carefully—not for what they mean to you, but for what they might mean to your readers.

2. The Right Word

The right word is the one that means what you want to say. The dictionary can tell you whether or not it does. The right word also fits what you've said so far, carries your idea further, and sometimes suggests other ideas. You won't know what the right word is until you've tried to draft your sentence and looked at it along with the other sentences. Oddly enough, though you may think you know what you mean to say when you start writing, you may find as you write that what you mean to say is not exactly what is hitting the page. Don't be discouraged, but don't hand in your first draft either. The *normal* writing process is to try one word, scratch it out, and try another. The techniques that follow will help.

1. Use words to engage your reader.

Vivid verbs, for example, excite the imagination. Look at this sentence:

The girl I was daydreaming about was walking toward me carrying her tray.

Was walking tells what the girl was doing, but a better verb tells how her walking felt to the writer. It gives the reader the same impression.

Revisions:

The girl I was daydreaming about materialized, carrying her tray toward me.

The girl I was daydreaming about materialized, floating toward me, carrying her tray.

Get in the habit of trying to show your reader not just how things happen, but how they *seem* as they happen—the impression you get while they are happening. This sentence tells what happened:

As she got closer, my books dropped out of my lap.

This revision tells how it *seemed*. The effect is more immediate and dramatic:

As she drew near, my books hit the floor.

The principle for choosing the right verb is the same one you use to narrow a topic to a subject: don't tell just *anything;* tell *something* specific. *Walking* is any kind of walking; *got closer* is any kind of getting closer; *dropped* is any kind of dropping. Try to find verbs that bring the action to life *and* tell how it felt.

Passive verbs blur the impression:

My lunch was forgotten as I tried to find her a chair.

Revised to active voice: I forgot my lunch as I tried to find her a chair.

Revised to more dramatic form: My cheeseburger congealed, and my soda fizzled out as I tried to find her a chair.

The right noun tells precisely what you are talking about.

Too broad: The officer behind my car wanted me.

Precise: The trooper in my rearview mirror wanted me.

Too broad: In the long run, the kind of car you have makes a difference.

Precise: After five or six years, the make and model of your car set its resale value.

Too broad: Things are getting me down.

Precise: My bills, my homework, and my family's demands are getting me down.

If you can, find a noun that gives your *impression* of what you are talking about.

As I sped down the thruway, I spotted a state-appointed *avenger* on my tail.

Standing in front of the class, pointer in hand, the *human computer* who normally sits next to me whirred out the solution.

2. When a word doesn't tell all you want it to tell, modify it.

Modifiers tell *which one, what kind of, whose, how many, when, where, why,* and *how:*

```
     ┌── which bills ──┐ ┌──── how many bills ────┐   ┌─which homework─┐          ┌─────
My telephone bills for the last four months, my math and physics homework, and my

        whose
────demands ──┐ ┌──────────────── which demands ────────────────────
family's demands that I eat with them, drive them around town, and work in the store


     ┌─────────┐
part-time are all getting me down.


what kind of trooper        ┌─which mirror─┐              ┌──────── why ────────┐
The state trooper in my rearview mirror wanted me for speeding on the thruway.
```

Modifiers, like verbs and nouns, can be selected to convey an impression:

The longer the handshake lasted, the more he felt his objection weakening, *like a lid loosening under a tight grip.*

As we passed each office, the man or woman behind the desk would look up at us, *as if peering through the bars of a cage.*

By midafternoon, the pool is alive *with bobbing heads and bodies flashing through the water.*

The *images* created by these modifiers relay an impression the writer wants the reader to associate with the facts in the piece: the weakening objection is like a tight lid gradually loosening; the people in the offices are like animals in cages; the people in the pool are like floats and fishes. These images are called *metaphors.* (For more about metaphors, see Appendix C, page 327.)

3. Keep searching for the right word.

When you've written a word you know is not the word you want, jot down more words right then and there:[1]

When the doors of the train finally opened, the people tumbled fell spilled clambered burst out onto the platform.

---

[1] Peter Elbow proposes the technique of writing nonstop in *Writing Without Teachers.*

Remembering the long lines they waited in a few years ago when news of the gas shortage came, people began to keep their tanks filled top their tanks hoard gas.

Registration always brings out reveals shows stimulates excites incites selfish low hysterical me-first outbursts in students because we know that we have to get certain classes and that classes always close, leaving somebody out in the cold out of luck out, with too few classes to fill out his program.

When setting down all the words you can think of doesn't give you the word you want, it will still give you a number of clues. Then you scan a thesaurus for synonyms until you find a word that works.

Exercises 1–4

3. Too Many Words

We deliberately wrote too many words in the last example, hoping to hit on the right one and then strike out the rest. But sometimes without realizing it, you write more words than you need. As you read the following passage, pencil out the excess words. Then compare your editing with the edited draft following the analysis.

Topic: The cost of a college education

Subject: Who should pay for college

Everybody Should Help

In my opinion, the costs that a student will have to pay when he goes to college should be paid by himself or herself and by his parents, and/or by the spouse if he or she is married. College costs too much for one person to have to pay the full amount of the price, and the benefits of a college education for the student are likely to be spread out over the whole family.

A student can't pay for his or her whole college education while he or she goes to school and expect to get good grades at the same time. A student has to have time to study, to get to and from school, and at least a little time for relaxation to refresh his or her mind and keep going. If that student has to work at the same time, then there won't be enough time to go around. He or she will have to cut corners, and that means that he or she will be late for school or work or will not get enough sleep or all of the above. If the student is married, then he or she won't have time for his or her mate, and the marriage will probably suffer.

If the student gets a loan and plans to pay it off after he or she graduates, then the student will have to spend years in debt before he or she can have an income free and clear. This debt will be a cloud over the student's head all through his or her college years. The student won't be able to plan for his or her future.

But if everyone helps to pay the tuition and the cost of books and transportation and housing, if the student needs it, then the burden will not be too heavy for anyone to bear. The parents can pinch a few pennies without denying themselves everything; the student can take out a smaller loan than the whole amount of the tuition; the student can work summers to pay his or her share of the cost; and if there is a spouse, he or she can get a full- or part-time job. This way no one suffers too much, and there will be enough time and money to go around. When he graduates, the student can get a good job, pay off his loan, and plan to help his parents when they retire.

It's important for the writer to realize that this is a first draft, not a finished piece of writing. He doesn't need every word in this draft to get his ideas across. Some of the words even get in the way; they are tiresome repetitions and expressions that can easily be cut to fewer words. When reworking a first draft, follow this rule: *take out whatever you don't need.* Here are some guidelines:

1. Weed out empty words.

in my opinion. The essay is understood to be your opinion. Your statement is always stronger without this tag.

who, which, that. Sometimes you can omit these words without changing your meaning at all: *the costs that a student will have to pay* becomes *the costs a student will have to pay* (or, better yet *the costs of a college education*); *that means that he will be late for school or work* becomes *that means he will be late for school or work.*

he or she. The effort to point out that the student in the passage might be a male or a female isn't worth the distracting use of both pronouns. Use the masculine pronoun, which convention allows to stand for a man or a woman. If you think the convention is sexist, give this student a gender: "Let's say the student is a young woman." (See footnote in Chapter 10.)

and/or. These two words tell readers to add or subtract, and that whichever they do doesn't matter. Take a stand. If the idea is worth writing, then it's worth a little reworking: "The costs should be paid by the student and his parents. If the student is married, his spouse should help too. Or the student and his spouse may be able to pay the whole cost themselves."

2. Search the passage for phrases you can shorten, replace by one word, or throw out. Each time you write you'll be dealing with different phrases, but you'll find that the hollow ones have a certain ring to them, like these:

amount of the price. Reduce this to *the price,* which means the same thing.

for the student. Take this out; of course the education is for the student.

at the same time. Drop this too; *and* will work as well.

has to have. Reduce three words to one: *needs.*

to get to and from. Reduce to *travel.*

at least a little time. Drop this phrase; it distorts a parallel series.

and keep going. Drop this; the slight additional meaning isn't worth the space.

that student. Use *he;* the antecedent is obvious.

to go around. Drop this; *enough* already carries this meaning.

or all of the above. Take this out; the bit of added precision is minimal, and this stock phrase blurs the solid words *school, work,* and *sleep.*

then. The *then* in if-then constructions is understood, especially when a comma follows the *if* clause.

to pay the tuition and the cost of books and transportation and housing. Shorten this to *pay for tuition, books, transportation, and housing.*

if the student needs it. This is understood; drop the phrase.

to bear. *Heavy* implies bearing; drop the infinitive.

whole amount of. Shorten to *total.*

to pay his or her share of the cost. This information is already implied; drop the phrase.

too much. Omit this; it weakens *suffers.*

plan to help. Shorten to *help;* this preserves the meaning and improves the series.

3. Shorten or reduce clauses to words and phrases. This condenses the meaning and gets it across quickly:

, and that means that. Use a colon, and shorten clause to the verb, *arrive.*

after he or she graduates. Shorten to *after graduation.*

before he or she can have an income free and clear. Shorten to *without a free and clear income.*

this debt will be a cloud over the student's head all through his or her college years. Shorten to *this debt clouds the college years.*

4. Take some leeway with tense. Often you can enliven a statement that is in future tense, without a change in meaning, by shifting it to present tense.

Freed of unnecessary words and brought into sharper focus by a shift to present tense, the original passage now reads:

Everyone Should Help

The costs of a college education should be paid by the student, his parents, and his spouse if he is married. College costs too much for one person to pay the full price, and the benefits of a college education are likely to be shared by the whole family.

A student can't pay for his whole college education while he goes to school and expect to get good grades. A student needs time to study, travel to school, and relax to refresh his mind. If he has to work at the same time, there isn't enough time. He has to cut corners: arrive late for school or work or not get enough sleep. If he's married, he has no time for his mate, and the marriage probably suffers.

If he gets a loan and plans to pay it off after graduation, he has to spend years without a free and clear income. This debt clouds the college years, preventing the student from planning for his future.

But if everyone helps pay for tuition, books, transportation, and housing, the burden isn't too heavy for anyone. The parents can pinch a few pennies without denying themselves everything; the student can take out a smaller loan than the total tuition, and he can work summers; if he has a wife, she can get a full- or part-time job. This way no one suffers, and there is enough time and money. When he graduates, the student can get a good job, pay off his loan, and help his parents when they retire.

4. Too Few Words

Brevity improves writing only when it sharpens meaning. It is possible to be too brief—to explain too little, to imply too much, to invite contradiction.

Generalizations

Some statements are more general than others. Look at any passage: some of the statements explain other statements; some bring detail to other statements; others provide examples. A few make the general points that the others support. These larger statements are called *generalizations*. A generalization is like a wide-angle photo: it shows the whole field, but gives few details.

Occasionally you may catch yourself writing whole passages of generalizations. Reading a passage of generalizations is like having to look at picture after picture of aerial photos. Eventually you ask, ''Aren't there any close-ups?'' Generalizations always need explaining, detailing, illustrating. You can't sustain a reader's attention if you don't get down to specifics. The following passage is too vague:

Topic: Hunger

Subject: Hunger in my neighborhood

Hunger is different from appetite. Hunger starts to hurt after a while. Appetite is a happy expectation. Hunger is a dread fear. Where I live there is a lot of hunger. Everyone struggles to make ends meet, and some don't. Food prices at the local markets are always high. Nutrition is poor. People of all ages go hungry pretty often. Even the animals are thin.

All of the statements in this passage are generalizations; there are no details. We might allow the writer the first few sentences, which take us into the subject, but after these, we want to know a great deal more about hunger in that neighborhood: *Where* is it? *What* do the hungry people look like? *How* do people struggle to make ends meet? *Why* do some of them fail? *What* is the evidence of people struggling? A brief story would help: ''Twenty-three-year-old Jane Doe, who dropped out of night school last year because she didn't have money for tuition, works ten hours a day cutting rhinestones for costume jewelry, for only a dollar an hour—hardly enough to cover her rent." *What* is the evidence of poor nutrition? We need descriptions of the undernourished people and the thin animals.

Generalizations do have a purpose. At the beginning of a passage, a generalization announces the subject and makes a statement about it. It gives you a general idea of what the writer *intends* to discuss in detail in the rest of the passage. At the end of a passage, a generalization *sums up* what the writer *has said*. It gives you a general idea that pulls together the details you've been reading; it tells the whole story in a single sentence. In effect, the writer says to the reader at the end of the passage, "In other words . . . ," and then sums up the passage.

A passage that moves from generalization to specific detail is a *deductive* development of the idea. The writer gives us the big picture first then moves in for close-ups. A passage that moves from detail to generalization is an *inductive* development of the idea: the writer begins with the close-ups and winds up with a wide-angle shot. But the point is not where the generalization comes. Whether a writer states the idea generally first and then details it, or details it and then sums it up, the point is that *a generalization needs detailing*. When you make a general statement, you have to back it up with explanations, illustrations, and facts.

Exercise 5–7

Implications

An *implication* is an idea suggested, but not written down. *This brand of laundry detergent works* implies that other brands don't. *Alice's red dress* may imply either that Alice has dresses of other colors or that she has red pants too. *The arms race* implies that there is more than one kind of race. *Smoking causes cancer* implies that cancer is not a communicable disease.

Your writing will always suggest more than what you actually write down. But since you don't want to suggest any ideas that contradict your point, you should look for implications. If you're trying to show that young people drive as well as anyone else on the road, then the statement "New cars are safer than older models" will undercut your point by implying that safety depends on the car, not the driver. You can handle that statement very well if you recognize what it implies, and take the time to show your reader how it helps to support your point: "But any good driver, young or old, knows that some vehicles are safer than others, and drives accordingly." Heading off misleading implications may add words to what you had planned to say briefly, but you will say too little if you make statements and then ignore what they imply.

Sometimes an implication makes an even stronger statement than an outright declaration. If you wrote an essay on rock music, detailing the different techniques of ten performers, telling that you have collected over three hundred popular and rare albums of rock music, and revealing that you once organized your own rock band, then you wouldn't need to say, "I love rock." The implication would be stronger than the statement.

Use to your advantage the extra meaning that implications provide. If you're writing about your first date, for the sake of humor you may want to imply, rather than state directly, that you were more frightened than your parents as the hour approached. If you suspect that the cause of hunger in your neighborhood is the scarcity of good jobs, but you can't prove it with employment statistics, you can strongly imply that it is by telling how one person who hasn't got a job keeps alive by visiting more fortunate neighbors around dinnertime; how another, who can find only odd jobs, lives on candy and day-old bread, and so on.

To make sure that you've written enough, determine what each sentence says *and* what it implies. Read through your passage asking yourself, "What does this statement mean? What does this section mean? What would a reader conclude from what I've said so far?" Do this carefully, and you'll find yourself adding explanations, clarifying your wording, putting in examples, and making other additions to avoid being misunderstood. You will also recognize those places where you don't need an explicit statement because you've managed to suggest very clearly what you mean.

The following passage can become a good argument if the writer rereads it to find out what a reader might conclude from each statement:

Topic: Prohibitions

Subject: R-rated movies

Old Enough for Dirt, Sweat, and Blood

R ratings are an absurd restriction for anyone who has a television set, who can afford to buy a magazine, or who has friends.[1] Movies get R ratings for obscene language, frontal nudity, and excessive violence.[2] But who hasn't heard dirty words?[3] Who doesn't hear them every day?[4] Who doesn't use them every day?[5] You can't be protected from what you are.[6] And one of the things that you are, every day, is nude, front and back.[7] Keeping bad language and scenes of naked bodies away from teen-agers under the age of seventeen is like trying to keep them from themselves.[8] Violence is another matter.[9] Most of us have never experienced a bloody gun battle, but eighteen-year-olds were routinely expected to when the draft was around.[10] The R rating is just a come-on.[11]

The first sentence implies that young people already have access to the kind of material seen in R-rated movies and that this material comes from sources other than teen-agers. But sentences 6, 7, and 8 say that obscenity and nudity are a part of teen-agers' lives. That's a contradiction. Sentence 7 implies that there is no difference between one's own nudity and nudity on the screen. Readers won't buy that. Up through sentence 10, the reader probably concludes that the writer resents the R rating for keeping teen-agers from seeing certain movies. Sentence 11, however, suddenly claims that the R rating is meant to attract teen-agers to these films. In this confusion, the reader can't be sure what the writer intends. Much is implied, but too little has been written to get the point across.

Exercise 8

Modifiers

An unmodified word is a lot like a generalization: it takes in a whole field of meaning. *Bird* means any variety of bird; *dancing* means any and every kind of dancing. Most of the time you don't want to make statements about all birds, any kind of dancing, all teachers, any kind of government, or all of anything. A statement like "Babies need parents" may be true, but it's too general. Sometimes you find you've written a statement that is too broad simply because you haven't modified certain key words. You haven't been specific enough. Look at this passage:

Topic: Human behavior

Subject: People who go to psychiatrists

People who go to psychiatrists tend to be self-centered. Psychiatry makes the individual ask, "Why did *I* do this?" "What do *I* want?" "What has my cousin's wedding got to do with me?" "Who is keeping *me* from getting what *I* need?" These people get so caught up in themselves that they stop functioning like normal human beings. They get into a conversation then suddenly stop talking while they try to figure out why you said *that* to them. They make a date and then cancel it and tell you they don't want to feel manipulated. They hang around and hang around while you're busy and wishing they would go away, and ask you why you keep wishing they would go away. They call you and tell you that they love you but say they can't stand your dependency. They ask you why you don't love them anymore. They set you up, and then they knock you down. Then they ask you why you keep acting so funny.

This passage isn't really about "people." It's about someone the writer knows and has in mind. At the very least, the writer should cut *people* down to *some people*. A better solution would be to modify *people* to *the person* the writer has in mind: *someone I know very well*. It is still possible, afterwards, to generalize this person's behavior to others: "This behavior is typical of people who see psychiatrists."

Modifiers don't just help you to tell the truth; they add a richness to sentences, bringing the subject to life before the reader. You can see this skillful use of modifiers in the passage below:

Topic: Food

Subject: Breakfast cereals

From the days of my early youth, I can remember a certain excitement coming as my mother and I neared the cereal aisle, the aisle of fantasy, adventure, and promise. Shelf after shelf of boxes stretched all the way to the back of the store. Cheerios, Wheaties, Trix, Kix, Captain Crunch, shredded wheat (ugh!), bran cereal (uh-uh—that always melted into a very unappealing brown mush within seconds after the milk was poured on it), Rice Krispies, Frosted Flakes, Frosted Rice—and these were only the dry ones, for spring and summertime, when your mother didn't suspect you were coming down with pneumonia. The hot cereals had less kick to them—oatmeal, Cream of Wheat, Wheatena— and were dressed in plainer packages with pictures of grown-ups on them or no pictures at all, but you could like them anyway and look forward to them because they were eaten with fancier dressing: honey, cinnamon, butter, molasses, syrup, whatever, and they did taste reassuring on gray, sleety mornings, when everything else was cold. But I didn't think of eating the cereal so much out there in the aisle. Before I made my pick I had to decide what box had the best prize or send-away offer. Did I want a glow-in-the-dark ring or a pocket compass or a super-spy magnifying glass or a set of water tattoos, which I could get instantly by pouring out all of the cereal as soon as we got home? Or did I want a baseball cap or a doll a full twelve inches high with combable hair for three proof-of-purchase seals and a dollar fifty? That was the excitement. I could never decide. When my mother couldn't stand it anymore she'd make me close my eyes and take the one I touched. If it wasn't a good one, she'd let me go and buy a box of Cracker Jacks.

Adjectives fill this passage with pictures: the cereal aisle is not a plain old aisle but *the aisle of fantasy, adventure, and promise;* the mush—though mush itself is not hard to imagine—is *a very unappealing brown* mush; we are given not just the general *spring and summertime,* but told specifically *when your mother didn't suspect you were coming down with pneumonia;* and the writer recognizes and uses the enticing adjectives of the cereal box come-ons: not a ring, but a *glow-in-the-dark* ring; not any compass, a *pocket* compass; and a doll a *full twelve inches high with combable hair.*

The rule is, once again, write about *some*thing, not about anything. Use modifiers to fix that something in your reader's mind just as you see it in yours.

Chapter 12 • The Right Word/Too Many Words/Too Few Words

Exercises

1. Add modifiers to the sentences below to make each more specific. Copy these onto a separate sheet.

   a. Some students enjoy examinations.
   b. A light snow fell slantwise.
   c. The building has a doorman.
   d. The symptom disappeared.

2. On a separate sheet, add two more sentences to each of the statements below, developing a more specific meaning or a sharper picture for each.

   a. Some students, whose zest for life yields to nothing, enjoy examinations.
   b. Down the long street, whose sloping row of brownstones was just coming clear in the first light of that winter morning, a light snow fell slantwise.
   c. The newest building in this once disintegrating neighborhood has a doorman.
   d. The symptom disappeared overnight.

3. Read this passage. On the lines below, describe the emotion the author seems to be experiencing. Underline the words and phrases in the passage that give you this impression.

   Viewed from the distance of the moon, the astonishing thing about the earth, catching the breath, is that it is alive. The photographs show the dry, pounded surface of the moon in the foreground, dead as an old bone. Aloft, floating free beneath the moist, gleaming membrane of bright blue sky, is the rising earth, the only exuberant thing in this part of the cosmos. If you could look long enough, you would see the swirling of the great drifts of white cloud, covering and uncovering the half-hidden masses of land. If you had been looking for a very long, geologic time, you could have seen the continents themselves in motion, drifting apart on their crustal plates, held afloat by the fire beneath. It has the organized, self-contained look of a live creature, full of information, marvelously skilled in handling the sun.

   Lewis Thomas, *Lives of a Cell*

   _____

   _____

   _____

4. These nouns are everyday words: *broom, door, wallet, ring*. The word *broom* means anything that can be called a broom; *door* means anything that might be called a door, and so forth. We might represent these nouns this way:

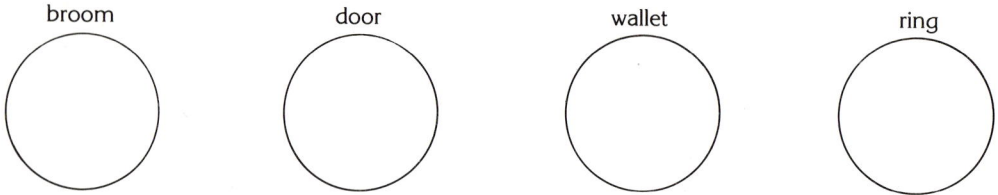

broom   door   wallet   ring

If we modify one of these, we identify a *subset* of all of the set of things that can be called by that name:

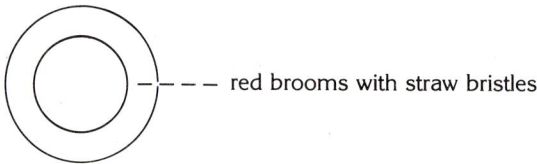

— — — red brooms with straw bristles

And we can modify a noun to designate only one particular member of the set the noun names:

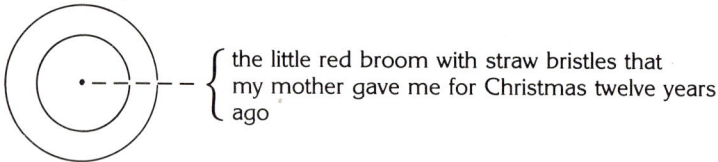

{ the little red broom with straw bristles that my mother gave me for Christmas twelve years ago

Write one sentence for each of these nouns, modifying the noun down to *one* particular member of the set named by the noun.

broom: _____

_____

door: _____

_____

wallet: _____

_____

ring: _____

_____

5. On a separate sheet, write a short story about one of the particular items in question 4.

6. Add modifiers particularizing each of the items below:

   a. military service: _____

_____

b. taxes: _____

_____

c. taking orders: _____

_____

d. leaving home: _____

_____

7. On a separate sheet, describe incidents involving each of the items you particularized above.

8. On a separate sheet, write a short story (about 300 words) in which you strongly *imply*, but do not state explicitly, how you feel about one of the items you particularized and included in an incident in 6 and 7.

Idea to Paragraph

13

1. The Paragraph

In the last chapter, you learned to examine your writing for general statements that you should develop with details. A general statement, together with its development, forms a paragraph. Paragraphs, like sentences, are units of writing. Like sentences, paragraphs have subjects, and like sentences, paragraphs usually contain modification. The subject of a paragraph is the idea expressed in the general statement. That idea is modified by whole sentences of detail that explain, illustrate, comment on, and otherwise develop the general statement or another detail.

Paragraph Structure

General statement   subject of paragraph

Development   sentences modifying the general statement by explaining, illustrating, commenting on, or otherwise detailing the general statement or another detail

2. The Idea

As we saw in the last chapter, the general statement may begin the paragraph, announcing the idea and setting the direction of the development, or it may come at the end, summing up the details and tying them together.

From general statement to detail is the direction of most paragraphs, but the writer's thoughts probably come in the opposite way—a number of details about a subject first, then a statement to sum them up. This format has been followed in the writing exercises because it seems the natural route to an idea—thoughts of corn on the cob, a mixed green salad with onions, a steak; then the idea: let's eat!

If every one of your paragraphs began with the details and wound up with the general statement, however, readers would grow uncomfortable, wondering as they read each paragraph what you were getting at. Reading general statement-to-detail paragraphs is like walking down stairs—you know where you're headed; reading detail-to-general statement paragraphs is like groping down a ladder—you are never quite sure where your foot is going to land.

In the writer's mind	*In the typical paragraph*
details	idea
↓	↓
idea	details

You don't have to take your reader on the same route you've traveled to get to your idea. You can write your first thoughts about a subject, write your idea about it, as we've been doing, and then reverse the process for the reader, putting your idea—your general statement—first. Read this passage, then try it with some of the first drafts you've done.

Topic: My roommate

Subject: My roommate's hair

It was the first thing I noticed about her, her round hair. I'd seen pictures of Afros, but I'd never known anyone who had one. It looked very fluffy, but it didn't move, no matter how she moved her head, even if the wind was blowing. When it rains, the drops just settle on it and stay drops. When she comes in, she has a cap of droplets that she just shakes out into the nearest sink. She says her scalp doesn't even get wet. When it snows, she doesn't wear a hat either. The snow just settles onto her 'fro and melts into the same little drops she gets when it rains. On great days, her hair just shines, like a new style in halos. *My roommate has all-weather hair.*

Or,

My roommate has all-weather hair. It was the first thing I noticed about her, her round hair. . . .

Exercise 1

3. Developing the Paragraph

No matter how clear your idea is to you, assume that your reader doesn't know exactly what you mean. Explain what your general statement means. Then prepare to define, describe, and tell a story. You may not have to do all of those things to make yourself clear, but you should practice all of them.

Defining

Any time you use a word that has many meanings—*love, the government, freedom,* for example—or use an unusual word, or use an ordinary word in an unusual way, explain your meaning to the reader. Don't go to your dictionary; define the word *yourself,* as you are using it. You should not have to do this often. If you write a statement that has more than one of these broad or special terms in it, you may not have the idea clearly focused in your own mind yet.

Describing

When you define a word, you establish a kind of contract with your reader that says, "This is what I mean by this word, and this is what I want you to understand by it for the rest of this piece." Description is more relaxed. Writers often describe things everybody understands—spreading butter on bread, for example—in order to recreate an experience for the reader. Descriptions entice the reader to imagine and think along with the writer.

Invite your reader to sense as well as visualize what you describe. Don't just describe what you see. Tell how it feels, how it smells, what it sounds like, what impresses you, what strikes you about this thing. Suppose it's a motorcycle. You could write a very precise visual description of the chrome, the leather, the rubber, the cylinders, the pedals, the dials, and so forth, without getting across the impression that it makes on you and that you would like to have it make on the reader. Compare these two descriptions:

Visual:

The motorcycle stood low to the ground, with wide tires, broad chrome fenders, and covered storage boxes on either side of the rear wheel. The seat was thick black leather and stretched over the rear fender. At the end of the seat there was a chrome backrest decorated with a curling chrome S, for a second passenger.

Impressionistic:

Little waves of heat were still coming from it. It gave off vapors of hot gasoline, scorched rubber, and road tar. The dust on it looked like it hadn't even settled yet. It looked like some huge insect, a giant wasp, ready to lift up all of a sudden with a loud, frightening buzz.

Impressionistic descriptions aren't substitutes for visual ones, but they are appropriate when the idea of a thing is more important than its individual characteristics.

Narrating

Definition helps you to clarify your subject for the reader. Narration, like description, helps you to illustrate your idea about the subject. A story will make your reader believe that what you're saying is true, show how you arrived at your idea, or demonstrate how your idea works. See how this story helps the writer to get her point across:

Topic: Clothes

Subject: What clothes do

Clothes don't make you what you are, but they can show what kind of person you are. In my math class last semester, there was a young woman who believed that her clothes could work miracles. She didn't know any math, but she did know how to dress. She thought that if she could catch the teacher's eye, she wouldn't have to worry about her grade. Every day she wore something to give him a special look at some part of her. One day it was tight jeans; the next day it would be a low-cut blouse; the next day it was textured stockings. On the day of the final she gave him a real treat: high heels, textured stockings, low-cut sweater, and a tight skirt with front and back slits. And I'm sure she was wearing perfume. I saw her paper when she handed it in. It was almost blank. This teacher had worked hard all semester long trying to teach us calculus. He was proud of his work. When she handed in her paper, she smiled at him a couple of times just to be sure he got the point. He didn't smile back.

Stories enliven any subject. They break up long, colorless treatments and help readers recall the ideas they illustrate. Just be careful not to lose your point in the telling.

These forms of development—defining, describing, narrating—can be used to develop any idea in any paragraph you write.

Giving Examples

You can always make good use of an example. Examples tell exactly what you're talking about and help to prove your point. Your ability to provide examples is a good indicator of the soundness and manageability of an idea. If your idea is unsound, trying to construct an example may show you what's wrong with it. Recently, a group of truckers protested that the fifty-five-mile-per-hour speed limit was inefficient, causing them to use more gas than they would use if they were allowed to drive faster. To prove their claim, they paired two trucks: one was driven at fifty-five miles per hour and the other at the speed the driver thought best for efficient use of his gas. The outcome of this demonstration proved the truckers wrong. The same thing often happens in writing. You state an idea and then give an example to prove it, only to find that the example doesn't work. The flaw in an example, however, often suggests a way of changing your idea to make it sound.

A similar thing happens when you try to find an example to support what you do not yet recognize as an unmanageable idea: ''Great art always takes time. For example. . . .'' Of course you can cite a whole string of great works that were years in the making, but you are bound to think of counterexamples too: Picasso painted fast; Stevie Wonder cuts at least one album a year. How much time do you mean when you say ''takes time''? And what do you mean by ''great art''?

Exercise 2

4. Idea to Paragraph: Putting the Parts Together

Your first try at writing a passage is not likely to produce the best version you can write. You are likely to get strings of ideas coming at once, some of which need more explaining and illustrating. The ideas may not be in the best order for readers to understand what you mean either. Here is an example of such a first draft:

Topic: Rules

Subject: Parents' rules

Before I moved out, my parents had a few rules I could not follow. I didn't move out because of these rules, but I resented them. I suppose parents have to have rules for their teen-age children, but they also have to realize these children are becoming adults. And they won't become adults if they follow every rule to the letter. They'll be shut up and cut off from their friends. Their friends will think they are stupid or afraid if they follow all their parents' rules all the time. Once I stayed out past my parents' curfew for me, and I didn't call home. I knew my mother would be worried and my father would be mad, but I didn't want to just cut the date short since I wasn't in any trouble and I was having a good time. Parents don't realize that sometimes their rules don't fit the situation and that their children begin to have some judgment of their own as they grow older. They want to know where you are, what you're doing, and who you're with, and then they set the time when you have to come home, no matter who you're with. I was at a park with my boyfriend and some of our friends. Sometimes kids have to talk, away from their parents and other people, about what they're doing and what they are going through. We were sitting in the park talking about what schools we were going to apply to and what kinds of jobs we were going to try to get over the summer, and about some other things that just concerned us. It got late, later than my curfew, but I didn't even mention that it was time for me to leave. Another rule was about who I associated with. But you can't just walk away from people and say, "My parents don't want me to be around you." I wasn't so wild about most of the kids my parents didn't want me to associate with, but I wasn't going to just jump up and leave if they came around either.

When you're at work composing, you shouldn't worry about the structure of your paragraphs. You should be trying to get your thoughts on paper. Structuring paragraphs is part of rewriting. To create your structure, keep the techniques of development in mind and find your general statements, figure out what additions you want to make to develop them, then mark off paragraphs accordingly. Follow this procedure:

1. Find each general statement and write it out on a separate sheet of paper.
2. Under each general statement, write at least one sentence explaining the statement.
3. Under each explanation, write at least one example or tell one illustrative story.
4. Add to these parts any other material from the original passage that you can use to develop the general statements.
5. Rewrite the passage, using each general statement to begin a new paragraph.

This procedure lays out a rewrite plan for you. It gives you paragraphs that develop each general statement you make in your first draft. This is how it worked on the passage you just read:

General statement for first paragraph:

Before I moved out, my parents had a few rules I could not follow.

Explanation:

My parents were afraid that I would get mixed up with the wrong crowd, that I would take drugs or become an alcoholic, or that I would get pregnant. So they had a rule that I could only go out with people I'd brought to the house and introduced them to.

Illustration:

Once I met a girl I liked. She liked to go to movies, and she wanted to see *The Deerhunter*. I had to bring her home with me before we could even make a date to go to the movie, and my parents grilled her as if each of them were Kojak and she were an escaped convict. Because they didn't happen to know her parents, they made her come to the house twice more before they let me go to the movies with her, just to make sure she wasn't some kind of drug addict or pervert.

General statement for second paragraph:

I suppose parents have to have rules for their teen-age children, but they also have to realize these children are becoming adults.

Explanation:

Kids my age (I should say *people*) do sometimes get into trouble. My parents were afraid, since they had kept me out of trouble for so long, that I wouldn't recognize trouble if it drove up to me in a fast car and waved a hypodermic needle. But I am not a mole. I read the newspapers and watch the six o'clock evening news. I know there are bad people in the world, and I know that a lot of kids my age get into trouble. I have not lived for eighteen years for nothing. I know I have to take care of myself and watch out for trouble. I don't walk out on the street expecting everyone to be a saint.

Example:

One of my friends did start to get very heavily into drugs. He knew the kids in school who sold drugs, and he considered himself very fine for knowing these kids and being able to deal in a kind of business with them. One day he borrowed his sister's car when he was high and wrecked it. He was lucky to walk away with just broken bones.

General statement:

Parents don't realize that sometimes their rules don't fit the situation and that their children begin to have some judgment of their own as they grow older.

Explanation:

This statement is the same as the one developed in the preceding paragraph. Leave it out.

General statement for third paragraph:

Sometimes kids have to talk, away from their parents and other people, about what they're doing and what they are going through.

Explanation:

Teen-agers have their own society. That's what teen-age gangs and clubs are about. When you're a teen-ager, nobody is as important as your best friend or your boyfriend or your girlfriend. Your crowd has the same problems and the same tastes as you do. They like the same music and the same food; they like to do the same things. They are excited about new ideas and people. They are not convinced that doing things one way is the best way. They want to find new ways so they are not afraid to do something different. They have a lot of energy and a lot of interests. Being with them is the most exciting part of life. You don't feel penned in; you feel you're going to make things happen.

Example:

Evelyn has been my best friend since we were freshmen in high school. We talk every day at school and at night on the phone. She knows what I feel; she knows who I like, and she can tell why I like this boy or that girl. Once we cut classes and went to a fancy restaurant. We had planned this, so we were dressed in heels and skirts like secretaries. It was exciting. Evelyn ordered quiche Lorraine, and I ordered a strawberry crepe. Nobody said anything. We did what we wanted and we got away with it. We wouldn't go out to a fancy restaurant every day; we just wanted to know if we could do it. We did, and it worked out fine.

General statement for fourth paragraph:

Another rule was about who I associated with.

Explanation:

My mother did not want me to make new friends, boys or girls. She knew my old friends, and she didn't want me to change. My mother was afraid that if I had a new friend all of a sudden, it was for some bad reason. She would always make me sit down and tell how I met this girl and why I liked her. She would make me help with dinner if I said I had a new friend and interrogate me while we set the table or did the dishes. She was obnoxious. It was almost not worth having a new friend. I knew what she was worried about, but no matter how I tried to reassure her, she would always look as if something very bad had happened and ask me what was wrong with the girls (or the boys) I had been friends with all my life. Then she would start to tell me about how long I had known so-and-so and how we used to play together in the sandbox while she talked to so-and-so's mother. My mother left no stone unturned. I felt like a traitor.

Example:

When I met my boyfriend, whom I have now been going out with for three years, she told me that after my brothers' escapades, she was almost worn out and might have failing health. I asked her why her health should fail suddenly when she had lasted through the troubles with my brothers. She said she didn't understand why I didn't like the people she knew. My boyfriend is a nice guy who wants to be a lawyer. She said she didn't know any lawyers and that I didn't know for sure that he was going to be a lawyer anyway. I told her that even if he turned out to be an unemployed cartoonist, I still liked him. She told me I was just trying to make trouble for her.

When you have sorted out the general statements and developed them, you can look them over and decide on an order for them that best expresses what you have to say. You can see, too, as you read through these developed paragraphs, what kinds of connections you need between them. These connections are called *transitions*.

Exercises 3–5

Transitions

Transitions are like road signs, telling your reader how one idea and its development are related to the next. Here is a list of common transition words, grouped under their grammatical labels:

Conjunctive Adverbs	Subordinating Conjunctions	Coordinating Conjunctions
accordingly	if	and
consequently	because	but
however	although	for
therefore	though	or
thus	provided that	nor
hence	so that	yet
moreover	in order that	so
nevertheless	unless	neither . . . nor
then	even though	either . . . or
furthermore	whereas	

Or, you may have to write sentences explaining the connections between paragraphs. The point is to make the unfolding ideas as clear to your reader as they are to you.

Exercises 6–12

5. Audience, Purpose, and Format

As you read through the development of each general statement, try to envision your audience, your readers, and decide what kind of reaction you want from them, just as you do when you talk to a friend. What do you want them to remember about what you've written? What ideas do you want them to take away with them when they finish reading? Once you are sure of your intention, you can draft an introduction and a conclusion to your essay.

An Introduction

Tell your readers what you are going to talk about. And then tell how you feel about it. This is a straightforward but undramatic opening. You may prefer to first engage your reader with a little story that illustrates your subject before you introduce it.

A Conclusion

Tell your readers how you want them to view your subject, now that they've read your discussion. And then, you may want to

1. raise questions, or
2. suggest solutions, or
3. state the implications of what you've written.

Now take a break, reread your paragraphs, and write your paper.

Exercises

1. Below are a number of *aphorisms,* which are general statements about common experience. On the lines provided for evidence, list situations and events you know of that would support the generalizations. This progression from the general (the aphorism) to the particular (the evidence) demonstrates a *deductive* process.

The squeaky wheel gets the grease.

Evidence: _____

_____

_____

As the twig is bent, so grows the tree.

Evidence: _____

_____

_____

A bird in hand is worth two in the bush.

Evidence: _____

_____

_____

You can't make an omelette without breaking some eggs.

Evidence: _____

_____

_____

A rose by any other name would smell as sweet.

Evidence: _____

_____

_____

Birds of a feather flock together.

Evidence: _____

_____

_____

2. For each of the aphorisms above, write a passage on a separate sheet explaining what the aphorism means. Then write a paragraph narrating an incident that demonstrates the truth of the aphorism.

Example: You can't tell a book by its cover.

Explanation:

In a general sense this means that things are not what they seem, but it particularly means that things may be *made* to seem different from what they are. It means that people sometimes deliberately deceive one another. It means, for example, that the buyer should beware: the foot-tall corn flakes box may contain only ten ounces of corn flakes.

Incident:

To experience the painful truth of this maxim, step into the local market and throw a few items into the shopping basket. The new longer cigarettes are also the new thinner cigarettes. The new package of raisins is just as tall as the old one, just as wide as the old one, and looks in fact exactly like the old one—except that it isn't as thick as the old one. The new cheese looks like the old cheese, unless you put on your glasses and read the wrapper: this is not cheese but "cheese food." Hmmm. It doesn't come in slices either. No, this comes in "singles," each one wrapped separately. Once we could only buy plain old slices, and they used to stick together and tear unattractively when you pulled them apart. But they used to be cheese.

3. In the sentences below, facts are listed. Write a statement for each set of facts that might account for those facts, a conclusion that might be reached, given those facts. This is the *inductive* process, moving from the particular to the general.

Example:

a. John is in Mrs. Fenster's kindergarten class.
b. Over the past two weeks, half of the children in Mrs. Fenster's class have contracted chicken pox.
c. John awoke this morning with red spots all over his body.

Conclusion: John has chicken pox.

a. A fire leveled a six-story apartment building.
b. Gasoline fumes were detected at the scene of the fire.
c. Several recently opened gasoline cans were found in the courtyard behind the building.

Conclusion: _____

d. PCB's, a manufacturing by-product, are dumped into the river by several factories along its banks.
e. PCB's have been found in the tissues of fish found dead in the river.
f. PCB's cause cancer in laboratory animals.
g. The river supplies the town's drinking water.

Conclusion: _____

h. Country X severed diplomatic ties with Country Y three years ago.
i. Country X has recently massed troops on its border with Country Y.
j. Country Y has recently acquired new aircraft and heavy artillery.

Conclusion: _____

Chapter 13 • Idea to Paragraph

4. Consider the three statements below. For each, write a short explanation and an example. Then tell which you felt most comfortable writing about, and why.

   a. American foreign policy reflects (or does not reflect) American democratic values.

   Explanation: ——

   ——

   ——

   Example: ———

   ——

   ——

   ——

   b. Dogs make good (or poor) companions.

   Explanation: ——

   ——

   ——

   Example: ———

   ——

   ——

   ——

   c. Love energizes.

   Explanation: ——

   ——

   ——

   Example: ———

   ——

   ——

   ——

   Which was the easiest topic for you to write about?

   ——

   Tell why: ——

   ——

   ——

5. On a separate sheet, write a passage in which you *explain, illustrate,* and *discuss* the following statement:

Of all cold words of tongue or pen
The worst are these: "I knew him when—"

Arthur Guiterman

6. On a separate sheet, write at least one paragraph telling *what* a student is.

7. On a separate sheet, write at least one paragraph telling *how* one becomes a student.

8. On a separate sheet, write at least one paragraph telling *when* one becomes a student.

9. On a separate sheet, write at least one paragraph telling *where* one becomes a student.

10. On a separate sheet, write at least one paragraph telling *who* becomes a student.

11. On a separate sheet, write a paragraph telling *why* people become students.

12. Now read these paragraphs and arrange them into some kind of meaningful order. Perhaps you will want all of your paragraphs to lead to the one telling *who* a student is; perhaps to the one telling *what* a student is. Decide on a direction for them, put them in that order, and write in or strike out whatever is necessary to make that direction clear.

The Essay Question—
Midterms and Finals

APPENDIX A

1. Introduction

How do you write an essay for an exam? At an exam you don't have time to write a first draft, sort out your general statements on separate sheets, develop each one with an explanation and an example, and then rewrite them. You have to think fast and write fast. Consider the following questions:

1. What is a neurosis?
2. What are the differences among mixtures, solutions, and compounds?
3. Light passes through glass but not through sand. Why?
4. Discuss the scarlet letter as a symbol.
5. Goodness is inborn. Agree or disagree.

All of these questions call for information and explanation. Let's assume for the moment that you've studied and have all the information you need. Your problem is *how* to set this information down in writing. Here are three suggestions to help you write quickly and write well.

Analyze the Question

Decide immediately what kind of information and what kind of format the question calls for:

1. Definition and illustration of *neurosis*.
2. Descriptions of mixtures, solutions, and compounds; illustrations of each; list of common features; list of differences.
3. Descriptions of glass and sand; list of their common features; explanation of the difference in question.
4. Definition of *symbol;* short narratives retelling parts of *The Scarlet Letter,* showing how the scarlet letter fits the definition of *symbol;* explanation of what the symbol means in the novel.

5. A general statement; definition of goodness; explanation of position; examples in the form of descriptions, facts, or stories.

Marshal Your Information

The time spent on analysis is worth the trouble. Even if you haven't got all the information you would like to have at hand to answer the question, once you have made your analysis, you can determine where the information you do have will fit into a development, and you can make optimum use of it by expanding that part of the development that you can handle well.

Even under the best circumstances, you may not feel that you have the right amount of information at hand. You can carpet the living room floor with the first draft of your book report, but for an essay examination, you might be able to remember only one or two facts. Either you have too much information or too little. In both situations, remembering how generalizations work can help you.

Generalizations work two ways: they pull things together, and they map things out. Pressed for time and able to think up only one or two facts in answer to a question, you can get yourself started if you can work *up to* a generalization from these few facts; if you have to tackle a whole book, you can start by boiling it *down* to a generalization.

Suppose you recall these facts concerning the question on ''goodness'':

Locke's concept of *tabula rasa*
Calvin's concept of grace
heredity vs. environment

Here is a possible generalization:

Two conflicting theories of the origin of goodness are Locke's *tabula rasa* doctrine—that what a person becomes is determined after he is born; and Calvin's doctrine of grace—that a person is born already destined to be saved or to be damned. Today the question is still raised, but it is expressed in terms of environment and heredity.

Here is a recollection of a book, boiled down to a generalization:

Gabriel Garcia Marquez's *One Hundred Years of Solitude* is a political tale of the flowering, decline, and fall of a social order and of a race, as told in the story of the Buendias family of Macondo, a village tucked away from all the world and reality itself, amid the mountains and jungles of South America.

The generalization marshals whatever information you have, whether a whole book or only a few facts. It contains the words and phrases that you must explain to develop your essay, so it provides direction for the development as well as a starting place for the essay.

Use Some Device to Unify Your Presentation

Beginnings are important. You may be tempted to begin with ''A neurosis is . . .'' just to get underway. You may even have memorized the definition for that specific purpose.

But that kind of lead doesn't promise to take you beyond your first sentence. Your yawning instructor, who is probably grading your paper along with a stack of others, may well prefer an illustration. Illustrations don't challenge the reader to follow a hair-splitting, tortuous argument made up of declarations and qualifications. Instead, illustrations invite the reader to use his imagination, and they get the point across vividly. Moreover, if you begin with an illustration, you seem to have something to say and to know what it is; you appear well organized and in control of your subject.

> Carrie stood in front of the refrigerator, as if she couldn't decide how to open it. She raised her hand but dropped it without touching the handle. She looked sad. For a moment, she seemed to be about to open the door again, but again she stopped her hand. She looked at the long white door as if it were a wall impossible to climb. At last, she turned away and went to the sink. But she pulled her hand back before it touched the faucet. She put her hand at her side, went over to the roll of paper towels hanging under the cabinet, and pulled one off. With this she turned the faucet, then washed her hands, slowly and very carefully. She discarded the towel, pulled off another to turn off the faucet, and then threw that away. She went back to the refrigerator and stood in front of it as if it was going to say something to her. Again she raised her hand—and again pulled it back. She repeated this entire sequence six times. Each time she washed her hands more meticulously; each time she carefully touched nothing but the paper towel and then threw it away. She never did bring herself to touch the refrigerator door, and she never did think to open *it* with a paper towel.
>   A neurosis is . . .

After you explain what a neurosis is, you can explain the behavior in the illustration, telling why it happens, what it represents, how long it usually lasts, and so forth. The illustration gives you something concrete to talk about. It is a reference point throughout the essay: "Like the girl at the refrigerator, neurotics do not trust their own judgment. . . ."

Exercises 2–16

Exercises

1. Tell what kind of information—definition, illustration, fact, and so on—the following directions call
   for:

   a. "Marriage is that relation between man and woman in which the independence is equal, the
      dependence mutual, and the obligation reciprocal." Louis K. Anspacher
      Discuss the statement above.

      Kind of information: _____

      _____

   b. Discuss the function of the cell membrane.

      Kind of information: _____

      _____

   c. Tell what you think ought to be done to encourage Americans to vote.

      Kind of information: _____

      _____

   d. "I tell you there is such a thing as creative hate!" Willa Cather, *The Song of the Lark*
      Agree or disagree.

      Kind of information: _____

      _____

2. For each of the questions above, write out an experience or an observation that could serve as an
   example in an essay written in answer to the question.

   Example for question a: _____

   _____

   _____

   _____

   Example for question b: _____

   _____

   _____

   _____

Example for question c: _____

_____

_____

_____

_____

Example for question d: _____

_____

_____

_____

_____

3. Read the following paragraphs. On the lines provided, tell what the subject of each passage is, and what questions the passage seems to raise.

A boy wants something very special from his father. You hear it said that fathers want their sons to be what they feel they cannot themselves be, but I tell you it also works the other way. I know that as a small boy I wanted my father to be a certain thing he was not. I wanted him to be a proud, silent, dignified father. When I was with other boys and he passed along the street, I wanted to feel a glow of pride: "There he is. That is my father."

Sherwood Anderson, "Discovery of a Father"

Subject: _____

Questions raised: _____

_____

_____

_____

A publisher in Chicago has sent us a pocket calculating machine by which we may test our writing to see whether it is intelligible. The calculator was developed by General Motors, who, not satisfied with giving the world a Cadillac, now dream of bringing perfect understanding to men. The machine (it is simply a celluloid card with a dial) is called the Reading-Ease Calculator and shows four grades of "reading ease"—Very Easy, Easy, Hard, and Very Hard. You count your words and syllables, set the dial, and an indicator lets you know whether anybody is going to understand what you have written. An instruction book came with it, and after mastering the simple rules we lost no time in running a test on the instruction book itself, to see how *that* writer was doing. The poor fellow! His leading essay, the one on the front cover, tested Very Hard.

E. B. White, "Calculating Machine"

Appendix A • The Essay Question—Midterms and Finals

Subject: _____

Questions raised: _____

_____

_____

_____

The urban villages have been marked by a special kind of family—the extended family. In its simplest form, an extended family involves the presence of any relative in the house besides a husband, wife, and their children; the patterns of housing in cities make all sorts of variations possible. In Boston, three-decker houses, with either two or three separate apartments, are common. If the owner is an older person, his or her children and even grandchildren often may be found as tenants on the other floors. In cities where single-family houses predominate in ethnic neighborhoods, relatives may not actually be in the house, but close at hand down the street. All these family arrangements can be classed as extended families because they make possible extensive family contacts day to day between related groups of parents and children. Indeed, the circle of relatives often defines the circle of friends available to individuals.

Sennett and Cobb, *The Hidden Injuries of Class*

Subject: _____

Questions raised: _____

_____

_____

4. Jot down three ideas you might use in response to the following essay topics. Then raise each set of ideas to a generalization.

Vegetarianism

a. _____

b. _____

c. _____

Generalization covering a, b, c: _____

_____

Eating Meat

a. _____

b. _____

c. _____

Generalization covering a, b, c: _____

_____

Animal Companions

a. _____

b. _____

c. _____

Generalization covering a, b, c: _____

_____

The Law of Gravity: Compliance and Defiance

a. _____

b. _____

c. _____

Generalization covering a, b, c: _____

_____

"As he brews, so shall he drink." Ben Jonson, *Every Man in His Humour*
Write an essay in which you explain, illustrate, and take a position on Jonson's generalization.

a. _____

b. _____

c. _____

Generalization covering a, b, c: _____

_____

5. Write an illustration for each of the following topics. At the end of the illustration, write the generalization you composed from your three ideas for each of these topics.

Vegetarianism: _____

_____

_____

_____

_____

_____

Appendix A • The Essay Question—Midterms and Finals

Eating Meat: _____

_____

_____

_____

_____

_____

Animal Companions: _____

_____

_____

_____

_____

_____

The Law of Gravity: Compliance and Defiance: _____

_____

_____

_____

_____

_____

"As he brews, so shall he drink": _____

_____

_____

_____

_____

_____

6. Complete an essay on one of the topics above, using your opening illustration as a focus to insure that the reader understands what you are going to talk about. References to the opening illustration can serve as transitions from one point to another in the rest of the essay.

7. Select from the list below three books that you have read. Write one generalization that might begin an essay about the book for each work.

James Baldwin, *Another Country*

Charles Dickens, *David Copperfield*

———. *A Tale of Two Cities*

E. L. Doctorow, *Ragtime*

Fyodor Dostoevsky, *Crime and Punishment*

———. *The Idiot*

• Ralph Ellison, *Invisible Man*

William Faulkner, *Absalom, Absalom*

. *Light in August*

———. *The Sound and the Fury*

Anne Frank, *The Diary of Anne Frank*

John Galsworthy, *The Forsyte Saga*

Thomas Hardy, *Jude the Obscure*

———. *The Return of the Native*

———. *Tess of the D'Urbervilles*

Nathaniel Hawthorne, *The Scarlet Letter*

Henry James, *The Turn of the Screw*

James Joyce, *A Portrait of the Artist as a Young Man*

Arthur Koestler, *Darkness at Noon*

Bernard Malamud, *The Assistant*

Thomas Mann, *The Magic Mountain*

———. *Death in Venice*

Herman Melville, *Moby Dick*

Toni Morrison, *Song of Solomon*

George Orwell, *Animal Farm*

———. *1984*

Leo Tolstoi, *War and Peace*

———. *Anna Karenina*

8. On separate sheets, write one lengthy illustration for each of the statements below.

   a. "Love is an irresistible desire to be irresistibly desired." Robert Frost
   b. Love is the wish to see someone else's wishes realized.
   c. "Political campaigns are designedly made into emotional orgies which endeavor to distract attention from the real issues involved, and they actually paralyze what slight powers of cerebration man can normally muster." James Harvey Robinson
   d. "Form ever follows function." Louis Henri Sullivan
   e. "Experience is the name everyone gives to their mistakes." Oscar Wilde
   f. "We are all in the gutter, but some of us are looking at the stars." Oscar Wilde
   g. "Public opinion is stronger than the legislature, and nearly as strong as the Ten Commandments." Charles Dudley Warner
   h. "They are slaves who fear to speak / For the fallen and the weak." James Russell Lowell
   i. "And almost everyone when age, / Disease, or sorrows strike him, / Inclines to think there is a God, / Or something very like Him." Arthur Hugh Clough
   j. "I claim not to have controlled events, but confess plainly that events have controlled me." Abraham Lincoln

9. On a separate sheet, write at least one paragraph describing a *scene* to develop the following generalization: small children need supervision.

10. On a separate sheet, write at least one paragraph describing a *situation* to develop the following hypothesis: it may be that the cause of alcoholism springs from the alcoholic's relationships with other people rather than from his or her personality.

11. On a separate sheet, write at least one paragraph describing a scene *or* a situation to develop the following proposal: all public transportation should be free.

12. On a separate sheet, write a narrative of at least one paragraph developing the following generalization: small children need supervision.

13. On a separate sheet, write a narrative of at least one paragraph developing the following hypothesis: it may be that the cause of alcoholism springs from the alcoholic's relationships with other people rather than from his or her personality.

14. On a separate sheet, write a narrative of at least one paragraph developing the following proposal: all public transportation should be free.

15. A report is a factual account whose purpose is to give detailed information about a given subject. Supply your own information and write reports of at least two paragraphs each, using description and narration, for the following headlines. Use a separate sheet for each report.

    Girl Wins Award
    A Cure Now in Sight
    New Invention Promises to Ease Energy Squeeze

16. Write an essay proposing one solution to some aspect of the energy crisis, as follows:

    a. On a separate sheet, write at least one paragraph *naming and describing* one wasteful use of energy.
    b. On a separate sheet, write at least one paragraph *narrating* an instance of this misuse.
    c. On a separate sheet, write at least one paragraph telling *why* this is a misuse of energy.
    d. On a separate sheet, write at least one paragraph telling *how* this misuse of energy can be corrected.
    e. On a separate sheet, write at least one paragraph telling *how* the energy shortage will be eased by this correction.
    f. Put these paragraphs together so that the essay ends with the proposed solution. Write in of strike out whatever you have to in order to make this solution the obvious direction of the whole essay. Note: The point here is not to invent and write down the solution to the worldwide energy crisis. Small topics drawn from your own experience are entirely appropriate: the light, the water, the gas, and so on that you have seen wasted.

Spelling and the Dictionary

APPENDIX B

1. Introduction

Mechanical conventions such as spelling and rules for punctuation are fixed forms. We observe them because consistency reduces confusion. We might easily spell the word *scholar* "skoller," "scaller," "skaller," or a number of other ways. We learn to spell it *scholar* and thereafter use that spelling to keep our readers from confusing it with other words. Similarly, we attach particular meanings to particular words, and we apply these consistently to avoid confusion. The dictionary records both conventional spellings and conventional usage of words.

2. Spelling

We cannot exhaust the list of words writers are likely to misspell, nor will we review any spelling rules here. There are a great many of them, many are complicated, and exceptions to them are plentiful. But you can spell better if you do two things: memorize words you know you misspell, and use your dictionary. Searching it will teach you much about how words are put together and will also prompt you to memorize the word you look up so you won't have to look it up again.

The words grouped below should be *memorized as lists*—the "e before i" group, the "double consonant" group, and so forth. As you write, add to these your own lists of bothersome spellings.

i before e

believe	dried	lied
besiege	field	lieu
brief	fried	mien
client	friend	nutrient
conscientious	frieze	omniscient
cried	grief	orient
died	grieve	proficient

prurient	science	tied
quiet	siege	tried
relief	sieve	view
relieve	spied	wield
reprieve	thief	yield
retrieve		
review		

e before i

conceit	freight	rein
conceive	height	seize
deceit	leisure	seizure
deceive	neigh	skein
deign	neighbor	sleigh
eight	neither	sleight
eighth	receive	vein
feign	reign	weigh

double consonants (these words follow the general rule that short vowels are followed by two consonants)

accede	hemorrhage	misstep
accelerate	illegal	occult
access	illegitimate	occupation
accomplish	illicit	occur
accord	illusion	occurring
assemble	illustrate	oppress
beggar	immature	preferred
begging	immediate	preferring
beginner	immerse	referred
command	imminent	referring
commerce	immobile	running
commission	immoral	succeed
dissemble	immortal	success
dissociate	immune	succor
dissuade	impress	succulent
effective	impression	summary
error	lessen	transferred
essay	lesson	trapped
essential	massage	unnamed
fallacy	message	unnatural
grapple	misspell	unnecessary

c or s?

| absence | curse | dispense |
| cadence | defense | evince |

expanse	juice	perverse
expense	license	practice
fierce	notice	presence
hearse	nuisance	pretense
immense	occurrence	purse
intelligence	patience	worse

-able

advisable	damnable	movable
affable	durable	notable
agreeable	estimable	parable
allowable	forceable	portable
amiable	honorable	practicable
amicable	hospitable	readable
arable	immutable	refundable
bearable	incomparable	salable
believable	inconceivable	sizable
breakable	insufferable	trainable
capable	lamentable	usable
comfortable	laughable	valuable
conceivable	lovable	variable
curable	manageable	verifiable

-ible

accessible	immersible	ostensible
crucible	inflexible	possible
discernible	invincible	reprehensible
edible	invisible	risible
fallible	irascible	sensible
feasible	irresponsible	terrible
horrible	irreversible	visible

-ance

abundance	balance	ignorance
advance	clearance	importance
alliance	dalliance	insurance
allowance	defiance	nonchalance
appearance	dissonance	nuance
appliance	endurance	penance
askance	flamboyance	pittance
assonance	governance	reliance
assurance	grievance	repentance
avoidance	happenstance	variance

-ence

abhorrence	existence	occurrence
absence	experience	pertinence
commence	flatulence	prudence
congruence	innocence	prurience
corpulence	independence	reticence
credence	influence	silence
decadence	jurisprudence	subservience
effluence	obedience	vehemence

contractions

can't	hadn't	I'd	she's	they've
couldn't	hasn't	I'm	she'd	won't
didn't	haven't	isn't	shouldn't	wouldn't
doesn't	he'd	I've	they'd	you'd
don't	he's	needn't	they're	you've

Three Spelling "Rules"

1. When you reread your first draft, put *sp* over any word you may have misspelled. Look up these words before you write your final draft.
2. List, look up, and *memorize* each word you misspell.
3. Never say, "I'm a bad speller." That just allows you to do nothing about it.

3. The Dictionary—Denotation

Dictionaries give the definitions or *denotative* meanings of words used in literature and conversation. Lexicographers, the writers of dictionaries, arrive at a word's definition by studying the word as it appears in print and as it is used and understood by people speaking to each other. A word seldom has only one meaning; dictionaries usually record several, sometimes including meanings that no longer apply. A typical entry (this one is from the *Random House Dictionary*) shows that dictionaries offer a great deal of other information as well:

> **fierce** (fērs), *adj.* fierc·er, fierc·est.   **1.** menacingly wild, savage, or hostile.   **2.** violent in force or intensity.   **3.** furiously eager or intense: *fierce competition.*   **4.** *Informal.* extremely bad or severe. [<OF<L *ferus*] — fierce′ly, *adv.* — fierce′ness, *n.* — **Syn.** **1.** barbarous, ferocious.

fierce is the word written as it is currently spelled by educated writers.

(fērs) in the entry tells how to pronounce *fierce.* The dictionary contains a pronunciation key that gives the sound values of these symbols.

adj. indicates that the word functions as an adjective. The comparative and superlative forms of this adjective, *fiercer* and *fiercest,* follow.

Next comes the definition, with each meaning numbered. One of these, called a *labeled* entry, tells us that in informal usage, that is, in conversation, *fierce* may mean extremely bad or severe.

[<*OF*<*L ferus*] the bracketed entry, tells us from what other languages, if any, the word came into English. This entry tells us that *fierce* came into English from Old French, and that it came into Old French from the Latin word *ferus.* This is a brief *etymology,* or history, of the word.

fierce'ly, adv. — *fierce'ness, n.* tells us that the word has an adverb form and a noun form that carry roughly the same meaning in other sentence functions.

Syn. introduces the *synonymy,* a list of words closely related in meaning. The synonyms share some of the meaning of *fierce,* and their shared meaning helps you to understand exactly what *fierce* means. *Barbarous* means fierce in the sense of *ungoverned; ferocious* means fierce in the sense of *wild* and *savage* and *violent,* but does not suggest intelligent intent, as *fierce* may. When you look up a word to see if it's the one you want, you may find the meaning you're looking for among the synonyms rather than in the word itself. To complete the meaning given, some entries offer *antonyms* as well, so that you can catch the sense of the word defined from words of *opposite* meaning.

Exercises 1–5

4. Other Meanings—Connotation

Synonymous words share some common meaning but differ greatly in what they suggest. These suggestions are called *connotations. Slender, thin,* and *skinny* all mean *not fat,* but *slender* is usually complimentary. *Thin* may be complimentary: "exercise keeps me thin"; or it may not: "the child is thin." *Skinny* is largely unfavorable: "he has a handsome build except for his skinny legs." The different connotations of these words are summed up in the line, "I'm slender; you're thin; he's skinny." The word *racy* has a neutral *denotation:* "having the distinctive quality of a thing in its native or genuine form; unspoiled, fresh, full-flavored; full of zest; spirited; often, piquant, pungent." But the *connotation* of *racy* changes those meanings a bit. When we say that a certain movie or a certain book is *racy,* we usually mean that it has explicit sexual content or depicts social taboos.

Suggested meanings are a bit harder to manage than literal, dictionary meanings. You must be careful not to choose words with connotations counter to your meaning, or with connotations unrelated to your meaning. For example, a recent headline, "Women on the Bottle," headed an article about female alcoholics, but the headline also suggested that the article was about women who had chosen to bottle-feed rather than breast-feed their babies—a disconcerting impression given the actual content of the article.

Connotations aren't always a worry, however; sometimes they're funny:

Outwardly, the G.E. Electric Comforter is a simple wool-and-taffeta affair which runs on the house current and automatically adjusts itself to the changing temperatures of the night. What emerges from a study of the booklet, however, is a weird complex of thermostats, transformers, and control boxes likely to frighten the putative customer out of his pants. "The heart of the Comforter," states the booklet, "is a web of 370 feet of fine flexible copper wire of low resistance arranged in a zigzag pattern." Set me down as a dusty old eccentric, but frankly, there would seem to be some more ideal haven nowadays than a skein of copper wire, no matter how fine or flexible. Nor is it any more reassuring to learn that "six rubber molded safety thermostats are placed at intervals in this web of insulated wire (you can feel these thermostats with your fingers beneath the cover of the Comforter)." It needs no vivid imagination to imagine oneself lying in the dark with eyes protruding, endlessly tallying the thermostats and expecting at any moment to be converted into roast Long Island duckling. The possibility is evidently far from academic, to judge from the question a little later on: "Can the Comforter overheat or give an electric shock?" The manufacturers shrug aside the contingency in a breezy 450-word essay, easily comprehensible to wizards like Steinmetz but unhappily just out of my reach.

"Even if the full 115 volts went through the Comforter, the body would have to be moist . . . a worn spot on the web wire inside the Comforter would have to touch the body . . . and another part of the body, as a hand or leg, would have to come in contact with a piece of metal, in order to get the sensation of an electric shock."

Given half a chance, I know I could fulfill these conditions, difficult though they seem.

S. J. Perelman, "To Sleep, Perchance to Steam"

The dreaded electric current influences the connotations throughout this passage. "The heart of the Comforter," a warm and soft expression if ever there was one, refers to "a web of 370 feet of fine flexible copper wire of low resistance arranged in a zigzag pattern." "The body" should mean a sleeping person but evokes a corpse instead, showing us that none of the manufacturer's words can be believed, because the manufacturer doesn't seem to realize that a body is a corpse. In his closing stroke, Perelman announces that he could "fulfill these conditions"—usually a positive statement, but he means that he could kill himself if he bought that comforter.

Exercises 6–15

Appendix B • Spelling and the Dictionary

Exercises

1. Find the underlined words in the passage below in a standard college dictionary and, on a separate sheet, write out the definition of each.

   Cases of <u>radical</u> withdrawal of <u>recognition</u> by society can tell us much about the social <u>character</u> of <u>identity</u>. For example, a man turned overnight from a free citizen into a convict finds himself subjected at once to a massive <u>assault</u> on his previous <u>conception</u> of himself. He may try desperately to hold on to the <u>latter</u>, but in the absence of others in his immediate environment confirming his old identity he will find it almost impossible to maintain it within his own consciousness. With frightening speed he will discover that he is acting as a convict is supposed to, and feeling all the things that a convict is expected to feel. It would be a misleading <u>perspective</u> on this process to look upon it simply as one of the <u>disintegration</u> of personality. A more accurate way of seeing the phenomenon is as a reintegration of personality, no different in its sociopsychological <u>dynamics</u> from the process in which the old identity was <u>integrated</u>. It used to be that our man was treated by all the important people around him as responsible, dignified, considerate, and <u>aesthetically</u> <u>fastidious</u>. Consequently he was able to be all these things. Now the walls of the prison separate him from those whose recognition sustained him in the <u>exhibition</u> of these <u>traits</u>. Instead he is now surrounded by people who treat him as irresponsible, <u>swinish</u> in behavior, only out for his own interests, and careless of his appearance unless forced to take care by constant supervision. The new expectations are <u>typified</u> in the convict role that responds to them just as the old ones were integrated into a different pattern of <u>conduct</u>. In both cases, identity comes with conduct and conduct occurs in response to a specific social situation.

   Peter Berger, Invitation to Sociology

2. Read the passage again several times, set it aside, and write a version of it in your own words.

3. For each word you defined above, write a sentence using the word.

   a. radical: _____

   b. recognition: _____

   c. character: _____

   d. identity: _____

   e. assault: _____

   f. conception: _____

   g. latter: _____

   h. perspective: _____

   i. disintegration: _____

   j. dynamics: _____

   k. integrated: _____

   l. aesthetically: _____

  m. fastidious: _____

   n. exhibition: _____

   o. traits: _____

   p. swinish: _____

   q. typified: _____

   r. conduct: _____

4. Write a passage in which you use ten of the words above.

5. Three full dictionary entries are given below. Write a sentence using each of the numbered meanings for each word. Then, beneath each entry, explain how each of the synonyms differs from the word defined. These entries are from *Webster's New Collegiate Dictionary*, 1981.

prize *vt* prized; priz·ing [ME *prisen,* fr. MF *prisier,* fr. LL *pretiare,* fr. L *pretium* price, value — more at PRICE] **1 :** to estimate the value of : RATE **2 :** to value highly : ESTEEM *syn* see APPRECIATE

  1. _____

  _____

  2. _____

  _____

How *appreciate* differs from *prize:*

_____

_____

sup·plant \sə-'plant\ *vt* [ME *supplanten,* fr. MF *supplanter,* fr. L *supplantare* to overthrow by tripping up, fr. *sub-* + *planta* sole of the foot — more at PLACE] **1 :** to supersede (another) esp. by force or treachery **2 a** (1) *obs:* UPROOT (2): to eradicate and supply a substitute for <efforts to ~ the vernacular> **b :** to take the place of and serve as a substitute for esp. by reason of superior excellence or power *syn* see REPLACE — **sup·plan·ta·tion** \( )sə-, plan-'tā-shən\ *n* — **sup·plant·er**\sə-'plant-ər\ *n*

  1. _____

  _____

2. _____

_____

3. _____

_____

How *replace* differs from *supplant:*

_____

_____

vin·di·cate \'vin-də-ˌkāt\ *vt* **-cat·ed; -cat·ing** [L *vindicatus,* pp. of *vindicare* to lay claim to, avenge, fr. *vindic-, vindex* claimant, avenger] **1** *obs* : to set free : DELIVER **2** : AVENGE **3 a** : EXONERATE, ABSOLVE **b** (1) : CONFIRM, SUBSTANTIATE (2) : to provide justification or defense for : JUSTIFY **c** : to protect from attack or encroachment : DEFEND **4** : to maintain a right to *syn* see MAINTAIN — **vin·di·ca·tor**\-ˌkāt-ər\ *n*

1. _____

_____

2. _____

_____

3. _____

_____

4. _____

_____

How *maintain* differs from *vindicate:*

_____

_____

_____

_____

6. For each of the underlined words in the passage below, write two sentences that are within the range of meanings possible for the word, and one sentence for each that is outside the range of possible meanings for the word. Note, as you read the passage, the unusual context it supplies to the underlined words, and try to decide what impression these words in this context leave you with.

Soups have the same <u>mission</u> as hors d'oeuvres, but a different method of approaching it. They stimulate the salivary glands and the flow of gastric juices by their heat and seasonings, and they afford to the walls of the stomach the same oily protection through the cream and butter or fat in them. That is why cold soups are as much a <u>heresy</u> as iced melon, and this is also why it is quite wrong to serve at the same meal hors d'oeuvres first and soup after. The <u>classical</u> method is hors d'oeuvres for lunch and no soup; soup for dinner and no hors d'oeuvres. With soup, which cannot be too hot, iced wine is both a gastronomical heresy and a real <u>danger</u> to <u>internal</u> <u>peace</u>. The wine served with soup should be at the temperature of the room and of fairly high alcoholic content, such as a brown sherry or an old Madeira.

Andre Simon, ''The Aesthetics of Eating''

mission: _____

_____

_____

heresy: _____

_____

_____

classical: _____

_____

_____

danger: _____

_____

_____

internal: _____

_____

_____

peace: _____

_____

_____

Briefly tell what impression these words in this context make on you: _____

_____

7. *Without* consulting your dictionary, write out what you think each of the underlined words means in the passage below.

Appendix B · Spelling and the Dictionary

But at last, in the drift of time, Hadleyburg had the ill luck to offend a passing stranger—possibly without knowing it, certainly without caring, for Hadleyburg was sufficient unto itself, and cared not a rap for strangers or their opinions. Still, it would have been well to make an exception in this one's case, for he was a bitter man and revengeful. All through his wanderings during a whole year he kept his injury in mind, and gave all his leisure-moments to trying to invent a compensating satisfaction for it. He contrived many plans, and all of them were good, but none of them was quite sweeping enough; the poorest of them would hurt a great many individuals, but what he wanted was a plan which would comprehend the entire town, and not let so much as one person escape unhurt. At last he had a fortunate idea, and when it fell into his brain it lit up his whole head with an evil joy. He began to form a plan at once, saying to himself, "That is the thing to do—I will corrupt the town."

Samuel L. Clemens, "The Man That Corrupted Hadleyburg"

In the passage, the following words mean:

drift: _____

ill: _____

bitter: _____

injury: _____

leisure: _____

contrived: _____

poorest: _____

comprehend: _____

fortunate: _____

corrupt: _____

8. Now look up each of the words above in your desk dictionary and write out the dictionary definition that seems to fit the meaning the word has in the passage.

drift: _____

ill: _____

bitter: _____

injury: _____

leisure: _____

contrived: _____

poorest: _____

comprehend: _____

fortunate: _____

corrupt: _____

On the lines below, write out any words whose denotations (dictionary definitions) do not agree with the definition you wrote in exercise 7.

_____

_____

_____

9. To observe that the meanings of words change over time, read the passage below. On the lines provided, first give the meaning each underlined word carries in this passage and, beneath that, the meaning it carries today.

Often it was past noon before he left her side; for there he was happy, say what they might. He rarely left her society, and yet he was as open-handed as ever to his knights with arms, dress, and money. There was not a tournament anywhere to which he did not send them well apparelled and equipped. Whatever the cost might be, he gave them fresh steeds for the tourney and joust. All the knights said it was a great pity and misfortune that such a valiant man as he was wont to be should no longer wish to bear arms. He was blamed so much on all sides by the knights and squires that murmurs reached Enide's ears how that her lord had turned craven about arms and deeds of chivalry, and that his manner of life was greatly changed. She grieved sorely over this, but she did not dare to show her grief; for her lord at once would take affront, if she should speak to him. So the matter remained a secret, until one morning they lay in bed where they had had sport together. There they lay in close embrace, like the true lovers they were. He was asleep, but she was awake, thinking of what many a man in the country was saying of her lord. And when she began to think it all over, she could not keep back the tears.

Chrétien de Troyes, "Erec et Enide"

society: _____

_____

apparelled (a past participle in the passage): _____

_____

steeds: _____

_____

wont: _____

_____

lord: _____

_____

craven: _____

_____

affront: _____

_____

sport: _____

_____

10. On a separate sheet, rewrite the passage above, using the English we use today.

11. Write out the connotations—the meanings suggested—of the following words. Tell whether the word carries a positive or perhaps pleasurable sense.

   Example: *distribute:* suggests an equal division and then giving of some neutral or good thing; suggests generosity of some kind.

instinct: _____

performing: _____

missteps: _____

suitable: _____

distribute: _____

ponderous: _____

neighboring: _____

marvel: _____

volume: _____

dazzles: _____

fragment: _____

embarrassment: _____

12. Read this passage. In it the words above turn out to have surprising meanings. On the lines below, write out what the words mean in the passage.

Animals seem to have an instinct for performing death alone, hidden. Even the largest, most conspicuous ones find ways to conceal themselves in time. If an elephant missteps and dies in an open place, the herd will not leave him there; the others will pick him up and carry the body from place to place, finally putting it down in some inexplicably suitable location. When elephants encounter the skeleton of an elephant out in the open, they methodically take up each of the bones and distribute them, in a ponderous ceremony, over neighboring acres.

It is a natural marvel. All of the life of the earth dies, all of the time, in the same volume as the new life that dazzles us each morning, each spring. All we see of this is the odd stump, the fly struggling on the porch floor of the summer house in October, the fragment on the highway. I have lived all my life with an embarrassment of squirrels in my backyard, they are all over the place, all year long, and I have never seen, anywhere, a dead squirrel.

Lewis Thomas, *Lives of a Cell*

instinct: _____

performing: _____

missteps: _____

suitable: _____

distribute: _____

ponderous: _____

neighboring: _____

marvel: _____

volume: _____

dazzles: _____

fragment: _____

embarrassment: _____

13. Label the words below as noun (n.), verb (v.), adjective (adj.), or adverb (adv.). Some words can function as more than one of these; show all possible functions.

interior	face	was
least	fished	then
asked	escapes	bad
deeper	fallen	hybrid
fat	glimpse	swarthy
wearing	quickening	orderly
apologetic	tongue	sometimes
senility	chaotic	emblem

Appendix B • Spelling and the Dictionary

marvel	bleating	improbably
ostensibly	honeyed	laced

14. Write a passage in which you use ten of the words above.

15. Identify the sentence function—subject, verb, object, complement, or modifier—of each of these words in your passage.

Usage

APPENDIX C

1. Introduction

Our language is alive: meanings change; writers and speakers constantly push words beyond the limits of their dictionary definitions. The English spoken today is not Shakespeare's English. He used words we don't use anymore, and many of those we still use have other meanings today.

Such changes cannot go on unchecked, however. If new words, new forms of words, and new uses for words immediately replaced the old ones, we would rapidly stop understanding each other. There must always be some fixed common ground. "Usage" is that common ground.

In its narrow sense, *usage*—the accepted practice of literate speakers and writers—settles questions of appropriateness: Is it okay to use *a lot* in an essay? Can you write *between the three* of them? If you can *finalize,* can you *prioritize?* Is *telecom* a word? In its broader sense, *usage* governs even grammar and meaning. It establishes the limits of words, the situations in which they are "right" and outside which they are "wrong."

2. Word Class Confusion

Words occur in families. A family may contain one or more nouns, verbs, adjectives, or adverbs, all sharing a common root. Sometimes the familial relation causes a writer to mistake one *word class* for another. Look at these sentences:

> Sarah didn't notice the *different.*

> That was one *satisfy* dog.

The first sentence confuses the word class of *different* (an adjective) with that of *difference* (a noun); the second confuses *satisfy* (a verb) with *satisfied* (an adjective). A word used outside the normal role of its class is instantly noticed and, unless it somehow enhances meaning, disapproved by readers.

3. Ranges of Meaning

The following sentences are noticeably odd:

Sam suddenly solved the unsuspecting equation.

This shop carries incalculable ice cream.

Sarah walked her valor to the supermarket.

All of these sentences are grammatically sound, but you can easily see that the words *unsuspecting, incalculable,* and *valor* are here used outside their normal ranges of meaning. The scope of meaning is less well defined for many words, however. Look at these:

Sam aggravated his sister so much that she finally slapped him.

The lady set herself down and wouldn't move.

We are experiencing abundant gunfire.

Sam applied his brain to the problem.

None of these sentences contains a striking irregularity. However, each of these sentences contains a word used outside the acceptable range of meaning for that word in formal writing. *Aggravate* means "to make worse," not "to annoy," and "Sam made his sister worse so much that she finally slapped him" is not the intended meaning. *Set* means "to place" but not "to place oneself"; the word needed here is *sat*. *Abundant* does mean "a great amount," but it also signifies good fortune. Heavy rain after a long drought may be *abundant;* but heavy rain flooding the countryside is not. So, even though we understand what is meant by *abundant gunfire,* this usage is outside the range of meaning for *abundant.* We can also understand what is meant in the last example, but the range of meaning for *applied* does not include this usage with *brain.* We can apply a bandage to a wound or apply grease to a joint, but we cannot apply a brain to a problem. Although an idea can apply to another idea, or a formula can apply to a problem, when a person actively applies something to something else the meaning of *apply* is strongly physical.

And there are certain words fine tuned somehow to sound right one way but not another. For example, the following usages are correct:

It is advised that you take your seat.

You are advised to take your seat.

It is suggested
  proposed
  recommended
  decided   that you take your seat.

These usages, however, are not:

You are suggested
     proposed
     recommended
     decided   to take your seat.

4. Levels of Usage

Word class and range of meaning are not the only limits on the way a word may be used. Many usages appropriate to conversation are annoying or unnecessary in formal writing. The general audience for formal writing, usually an audience outside the writer's family and friends, will not take seriously anyone who writes

The turbines of this new jet are awful big.

The management of this corporation has worked good and hard to bring out this prospectus.

The nutrients get to cross capillary membranes.

The cell had most split when the particle appeared in the nucleus.

Overweight is when the body becomes a burden to itself.

Compare the usage of *awful* in the first sentence to the usage below:

The awful risk must be taken to preserve the rights of the innocent.

In the sentence above *awful* is an adjective meaning *awesome* or *perilous.* Used as an adverb in the first sentence, *awful* simply means *very* and isn't worth its space on the page. If the turbines are big, readers want to know *how* big: as big as what? big according to whom? This use of *awful* reveals that the writer isn't working hard enough. *Good and hard* carries the same message: the writer isn't telling the reader enough. *Get to* for *are able to,* and *most* for *almost* aren't standard usages but regional ones. Phrases like *overweight is when* can be used in formal writing, but sound wrong to many readers who know perfectly well that a thing is not a time.

All of these usages are *colloquialisms,* good enough for *colloquy,* conversation, but not fit to print. You can get a feel for these two levels of usage, *formal* and *colloquial,* by comparing the writing in your textbooks to conversation. *Formal usage* is the written language of instruction, scholarship, and public address. Between these two levels there is another, *informal usage,* which is the language of magazines and newspapers, everyday writing addressed to large general audiences. A fourth category, *nonstandard usage,* includes nonstandard grammatical forms and slang.

Written Versus Oral Usage

Informal writing, aimed at a general readership, sounds more like everyday speech than formal writing does. One reason is that it uses more idioms and clichés than formal writing allows. *Idioms* are phrases whose meanings are broadly generalized versions of their word-for-word meaning. Look at this passage, for example:

> Long after they had supposedly buried the hatchet, the couple continued to air their dirty linen in public behind each other's backs because each knew that the other was thin-skinned and both still had axes to grind.

Buried the hatchet does not mean that the couple dug a hole in the ground and put a hatchet into it but that the couple had agreed to stop fighting with each other;

air their dirty linen doesn't mean that they hung soiled sheets out for all to see but that they made their secrets public;

behind each other's backs does not mean that they whispered in each other's presence but that they talked in each other's absence;

thin-skinned means sensitive or easily hurt;

and *axes to grind* has nothing to do with axes or grinding—here it means continuing resentment.

It's easy to see what kind of work idioms do and what kind they don't. Idioms are everyday usages. They label common events and situations and they point up similarities. Thus, *buried the hatchet* can mean that Egypt and Israel have signed a peace treaty just as easily as it can mean that Mrs. Muggins now speaks to her son-in-law. Idioms make the foreign seem familiar at once. But, because idioms mean that one thing is like this, that, or another, they do not carry specific information. Readers are understandably annoyed by an idiom standing where details should be.

Clichés share the shortcomings of idioms. *Clichés* are overworked or hackneyed phrases. Some are literal, some are not. Clichés are frequent in conversation, where you may not even notice them, but they have an altogether different effect on paper:

> It goes without saying that they were made for each other. He was a wolf in sheep's clothing if ever there was one, and butter wouldn't melt in her mouth. They no sooner laid eyes on each other than they were as thick as thieves. She was a hussy, born and bred, so no one had to break the ice. I hate to mention it, but in my opinion the men are few and far between who would have given her the cold shoulder. Poor Pete. His was a lost cause. He wouldn't have left her for love or money, but she dropped him like a hot potato as soon as this other one appeared on the scene. She gave Pete a graphic description of what she would do to him if he didn't beat it, but it went in one ear and out the other. For the life of me I can't understand why he ever darkened her door again, but he would have moved heaven and earth to get her back, so he went to extremes. To cut a long story short, it turned out that this newcomer couldn't deliver the goods after all, so she threw him out. And who should be standing there with open arms? You guessed it—Pete.

It is almost impossible to imagine a serious subject treated in this language. This passage is a parody, of course, but clichés in serious writing have the same effect they have here: they make meaning unclear. What does the writer mean? Clichés give the reader an unpleasant sense that the writer is not thinking.

Flabby as they are, clichés aren't always harmless. In his essay, ''Politics and the English Language,'' George Orwell demonstrated that obscure language serves the interests of those who plead groundless and evil causes: ''This mixture of vagueness and sheer incompetence is the most marked characteristic of modern English prose, and especially of any kind of political writing. As soon as certain topics are raised, the concrete melts into the abstract and no one seems able to think of turns of speech that are not hackneyed: prose consists less and less of *words* chosen for the sake of their meaning, and more and more of phrases tacked together like the sections of a prefabricated hen-house.''

Idioms and clichés come to mind for a reason. Sometimes these usages can say what you have to say just the way you want to say it, but more often they will just tell your reader that you're not making much of an effort.

Jargon

Consider the following passage:

> *Lexicography* in its narrowest sense is a subdivision of applied linguistics concerned with the techniques of gathering lexical data and of presenting them most cogently in reference works and textbooks. Conversely, the rival label *lexicology* is best reserved for such analytic inquiries as deal, in synchronic or diachronic perspective, with the total lexicon of a given language (also, on the genetic level, of a close-knit language family) or with its separate ingredients, ranging from molecules (groups of words meaningfully arranged) via atoms (individual words) to subatomic units (suffixes and other ''bound'' forms). If the attention of the investigator is focused on the origin of a word and on the initial segment of its trajectory, the resulting approach may be described as etymological.
>
> Yakov Malkiel, ''Lexicography''

Chances are, we general readers won't understand much in this passage. It is not the sort of writing we get in the mail, hear on the air, or read in the newspaper or in our Book-of-the-Month-Club selection. Because of the specialized language in this passage, it appeals exclusively to a very small sector among the students of language. The terms *applied linguistics, lexical data, synchronic, diachronic,* and probably *etymological,* though English, are not part of the vocabularies of most people. There are also terms in this passage whose usual meanings the general reader probably does know—*genetic, molecules, atoms, subatomic, bound*—but the writer has changed their meanings here. The language of this passage, made intricate by little-known words and by special usages of well-known words, is *jargon.*

The term *jargon* is used for language that purposely thwarts understanding, so that what should be clear isn't. *A jargon,* on the other hand, refers to the specialized language of a discipline or profession. It is probably inevitable that special tasks and special areas of study should generate odd words and special usages. But a writer should write intelligibly, even to an audience of specialists. The writer addressing a general audience should know that readers are not impressed by jargon. If anything, they deeply resent being written to and then mystified.

Slang

A *slang* is another sort of language made up of odd words and special usages, invented by a group and understood by few outside the group. Studies have shown that for reasons yet unknown, men create slang but women don't. Possibly for the same reasons, many slang words are sexual. One study of slang indicates that it originates among groups of prisoners, soldiers, sailors, workmen, and male groups of all kinds. Slang is always nonstandard usage, so when a slang word or term appears in formal or in informal writing, it is enclosed in quotation marks. But slang is "a gas": slang is language playing hooky and heading for the bad part of town.

One of the oldest recorded slang terms, *clink*, meaning "jail," is a word so fitting that it has thrived since 1515. More fitting still is *bones*, for *dice*, which appeared in print in 1386; and *dead as a doornail* has flourished since 1362. The same words in formal writing rarely have the humor they have as slang: *rug* for *toupee*, *vacation* for *prison sentence*, and even *fry* for *electrocute*. Slang mocks pretention: *the law* for *policeman*. It scorns delicacy: *stiff* for *corpse*. Nor does formal writing often match slang for powerful images: *cannon fodder* for *soldier*, *high* for *mild intoxication*, *stoned* for *incapacitated*, *broad* for *woman;* or for matching sound to sense: *flimflam* for *fraud*, and the common slang words for *urinate, defecate,* and *copulate*.[1]

Slang is normally regional and temporary, but plentiful. Dictionaries of slang run to thousands of pages recording current, obsolete, and revived usages. Although some slang words, like *clink*, are invented or *coined*, most are ordinary words turned to extraordinary use, like *screw* for *turnkey* or *warden* and for *copulate*. Like jargon, slang is sometimes incomprehensible to outsiders, but it is also often naughtily obvious. Even those who would rather not understand, do.

In the categories of formal, informal, and nonstandard writing, colloquialisms, idioms, clichés, jargon, and slang occur roughly as follows:

	Formal	Informal	Nonstandard
colloquialisms	rare	occasional	common
idioms	occasional	common	common
clichés	occasional	occasional	occasional
jargon	common	rare	rare
slang	only in quotation marks	usually in quotation marks	common

---

[1] Observations on slang and its origins are from J. S. Farmer and W. E. Henley, *Slang and Its Analogues*.

No single book can teach us all that is meant by the term ''good usage.'' Wide reading and good references are the best instruction. See Bergen Evans and Cornelia Evans, *A Dictionary of Contemporary Usage* (N.Y.: Random House, 1957); Henry W. Fowler, *Dictionary of Modern English Usage* (Oxford: Clarendon, 1965); and Eric Partridge, *Usage and Abusage: A Guide to Good English* (N.Y.: British Books, 1957).

5. Metaphor

In our discussion of idioms we pointed out that the idiom is not understood literally, word for word, but as a broadly generalized version of what it actually says. *Sleight of hand* is any kind of trick; *to wash one's hands of* means to absolve oneself of some kind of responsibility; *fight tooth and nail* means to struggle mightily; *to carry coals to Newcastle* refers to any futile act; *to let the cat out of the bag* refers to any premature disclosure. An idiom actually presents a picture, a likeness drawn between one situation and another— a *metaphor*. Idioms are ''stock'' metaphors, used almost like words. These successful images have survived because they make good analogies for common experiences. But as they survive, idioms lose much of their original metaphoric vigor through repetition. *To hold water* no longer discloses a likeness between a sound argument and a vessel that doesn't leak; it merely has the same force and meaning of the adjective *sound*. As a metaphor becomes an idiom, it loses most of its original reference.

Few metaphors survive to become idioms; and to most readers' tastes that is a good thing—the fresher the metaphor the better. A new metaphor has a powerful defining force: it causes the reader to see a thing or to understand an idea as never before.

> For this global war is not the old, hard, personal fight for the means of life ... which animals perpetually wage; this is a war of monsters. Not mere men but great super-personal giants, the national states, are met in combat. They do not hate and fight and wrestle as injured physical creatures do; they move heavily, inexorably, by strategy and necessity, to each other's destruction. The game of national states has come to this pass, and the desperate players ride their careening animated toys to a furious suicide.
>
> Suzanne K. Langer, ''The Prince of Creation''

The image in this passage is that of a game in which the pieces are giant robots. The players are children riding the robots, over which they have lost control. In this image, the game represents international relations, the giant robots are the lethally armed nations of the world, and the players are the national leaders. This metaphor defines the peril of impending world doom brought on by forces deliberately set in motion. Langer might have written that the nations of the world are behaving in a way that will lead to vast war in which all humankind will perish. That statement, terrible though it is, would not put before us what her image does. There is nothing in the straightforward statement to help us envision the dread automation of the world's arsenals. But the image of children riding lurching mechanical toys that they cannot stop once they have started them is close to everyday experience, chillingly familiar.

The best metaphors are fresh, improbable likenesses:

Scientists at work have the look of creatures following genetic instructions; they seem to be under the influence of a deeply placed human instinct. They are, despite their efforts at dignity, rather like young animals engaged in savage play. When they are near to an answer their hair stands on end, they sweat, they are awash in their own adrenalin. To grab the answer, and to grab it first, is for them a more powerful drive than feeding or breeding or protecting themselves against the elements.

It sometimes looks like a lonely activity, but it is as much the opposite of lonely as human behavior can be. There is nothing so social, so communal, so interdependent. An active field of science is like an immense intellectual anthill; the individual almost vanishes into the mass of minds tumbling over each other, carrying information from place to place, passing it around at the speed of light.

Lewis Thomas, Lives of a Cell

Good metaphors take work. Although surprising similarities may occur to you even before you start looking for them, comparisons that will help your reader to see what you mean may not come easily or quickly:

Like a bomb going off simultaneously in the heads of the committee members, the idea of leafleting the entire town came to everyone at once. Mrs. Campbell launched the idea first. The committee would hammer out a petition to be signed by all the members and flood the town with it.

An idea may be good, and it may come suddenly, but to say that it goes off like a bomb in the heads of committee members presents an image so grisly that readers are apt to forget what the comparison applies to. When in the next sentence they learn that the idea, which has already exploded, was also launched, they will surely wonder how that was possible. And the next *mixed metaphor,* in which the petition will be hammered out and then will flood the town, won't enlighten them at all. Unless a metaphor works, and works harmoniously, leave it out.

The temptation to ornament writing is strong. Using learned words where more common ones work as well is one form of decoration. Another is using the long form of a word whose shorter form means exactly the same thing: *competency* for *competence, orientate* for *orient, finalize* for *finish, relevancy* for *relevance*. To some writers, long forms sound more rhythmic than the short forms that mean the same thing. So do strings of fluttering modifiers:

The exceptionally delightful quality of this glowing young entertainer is his utterly untarnished enthusiasm for making his jaded but captivated audience suddenly and loudly break into gloriously uncontrollable laughter. His performances are always unfailingly, side-splittingly rewarding.

To their credit, however, these writers are at least trying to write something others will like. They do care what they put down on the page. Not all writers do:

The thing about this entertainer is that he's better than anything you've ever seen. And he doesn't seem any more aware of it than the man in the moon or the corner grocer. He's dynamite for anyone with two ears and a pair of eyes and the price of admission.

Exercises 1–2 These worn-out flourishes are *hyperboles*, impossibly overstated images, and usually ones you've heard a million times before. The rule of thumb is be specific and be spare.

Appendix C • Usage

Exercises

1. On a separate sheet, rewrite the formal passage below to make it informal. Revised into informal usage, it should sound like something you would say in conversation to a friend but convey the same information in precise language.

When a culture induces some of its members to work for its survival, what are they to do? They will need to foresee some of the difficulties the culture will encounter. These usually lie far in the future, and details are not always clear. Apocalyptic visions have had a long history, but only recently has much attention been paid to the prediction of the future. There is nothing to be done about completely unpredictable difficulties, but we may foresee some trouble by extrapolating current trends. It may be enough simply to observe a steady increase in the number of people on the earth, in the size and location of nuclear stockpiles, or in the pollution of the environment and the depletion of natural resources; we may then change practices to induce people to have fewer children, spend less on nuclear weapons, stop polluting the environment, and consume resources at a lower rate, respectively.

B. F. Skinner, Beyond Freedom and Dignity

2. Here is a list of idioms and clichés. On a separate sheet, write a passage using as many of these as you can. Then, on another sheet, write a literal, precise, specific version of your passage.

Idioms

aboveboard	think up
in the abstract	thorn in the flesh
ad nauseam	holdup
in the air	flop
apple-pie order	heart (in the sense of courage)
blue in the face	there are no flies on him
rock the boat	fluke
bosom friend	bite the dust
play it safe	dud
Pandora's box	to sow dragon's teeth
to do oneself proud	hold a candle to
pussyfoot	to know the side on which one's bread
run into the ground	is buttered
lost sheep	butter him up
spick and span	unwritten law
ups and downs	

Clichés

abject apology	as large as life
able to make head or tail of	add insult to injury
accidents will happen	all to the good
Achilles' heel	the finishing touch
acid test	last but not least

act in cold blood
ax to grind
bundle of nerves
baptism by fire
be that as it may
get down to brass tacks
to all intents and purposes
safe and sound

better left unsaid
a shattering effect
ship of state
shape of things to come
share and share alike
to say the least
far and wide
one and all

Bibliography

Bryant, Margaret M. *Current American Usage*. New York: Funk & Wagnalls, 1962.

Christensen, Bonniejean, and Francis Christensen. *A New Rhetoric*. New York: Harper & Row, 1976.

Christensen, Francis. *Notes Toward a New Rhetoric*. New York: Harper & Row, 1967.

The College Standard Dictionary of the English Language. New York: Funk & Wagnalls, 1943 ed.

Curme, George O. *English Grammar*. New York: Barnes & Noble, 1953.

D'Eloia, Sarah; Barbara Gray; Alice Trillin; Mina Shaughnessy; and Blanche Skurnick. *The English Modules*. Videotape. New York: State University of New York, 1976.

Elbow, Peter. *Writing Without Teachers*. New York: Oxford University, 1973.

Evans, Bergen, and Cornelia Evans. *A Dictionary of Contemporary Usage*. New York: Random House, 1957.

Farmer, J. S., and W. E. Henley. *Slang and Its Analogues*. Introduction by Theodore M. Bernstein. Report. New York: Arno Press, 1970.

Fowler, Henry W. *A Dictionary of Modern English Usage*. Oxford: Clarendon, 1965.

Jesperson, Otto. *Essentials of English Grammar*. Alabama Linguistic and Philological Series, no. 1. University, Ala.: University of Alabama Press, 1969.

————. *Language: Its Nature, Development, and Origin*. New York: W. W. Norton, 1964.

————. *The Philosophy of Grammar*. New York: W. W. Norton, 1965.

Joos, Martin. *The English Verb*. Madison: University of Wisconsin Press, 1968.

Keyser, Samuel Jay, and Paul Postal. *Beginning English Grammar*. New York: Harper & Row, 1976.

MLA Handbook for Writers of Research Papers, Theses, and Dissertations. New York: Modern Language Association, 1977.

Partridge, Eric. *A Dictionary of Clichés*. New York: Macmillan, 1940.

————. *Usage and Abusage: A Guide to Good English*. New York: British Books, 1957.

Shaughnessy, Mina. *Errors and Expectations: A Guide for the Teacher of Basic Writing*. New York: Oxford, 1977.

Stein, Jess, and P. Y. Su, eds. *The Random House Dictionary*. New York: Ballantine Books, 1978.

Vizetelly, Frank H., and Leander J. Debekker. *A Desk Book of Idioms and Idiomatic Phrases*. New York: Funk & Wagnalls, 1923.

Webster's New Collegiate Dictionary. Springfield, Mass.: G. & C. Merriam Co., 1953 ed.

Wentworth, H., and L. Flexner. *A Dictionary of American Slang*. New York: Crowell, 1975.